TERRITORY OF NEW GUINEA

WEST IRIAN

PAPUA

AUSTRALIA

Cape York

Markham

Ramu

Sepik

Idenburg

Wissel Lakes

Balim Valley

Star Mts.

Telefolmin

Sirfakland

Fly

Digoel

Purari

Kikori

Mt. Hagen

Goroka

Papua and Territory of New Guinea

1. Bena Bena
2. Chimbu
3. Daribi
4. Enga
5. Fore
6. Gahuku Gama
7. Gimi
8. Gururumba
9. Huli
10. Ipili
11. Kakoli
12. Kamano
13. Karam
14. Kuma
15. Kutubu
16. Kyaka
17. Manga
18. Maring
19. Melpa
20. Mendi
21. Siane
22. Tairora
23. Telefolmin

West Irian

24. Dani
25. Jalemo
26. Kapauku
27. Star Mountains

PIGS, PEARLSHELLS, AND WOMEN

Marriage In The New Guinea Highlands

A Symposium Edited by
R. M. GLASSE
AND
M. J. MEGGITT

PRENTICE-HALL, Inc. *Englewood Cliffs, N. J.*

"To the contract of marriage, besides the man and wife, there is a third party—Society."

DR. SAMUEL JOHNSON, *1776*

Current printing (last number):

10 9 8 7 6 5 4 3 2 1

PRENTICE-HALL INTERNATIONAL, INC. (*London*)
PRENTICE-HALL OF AUSTRALIA, PTY. LTD. (*Sydney*)
PRENTICE-HALL OF CANADA, LTD. (*Toronto*)
PRENTICE-HALL OF INDIA PRIVATE LIMITED (*New Delhi*)
PRENTICE-HALL OF JAPAN, INC. (*Tokyo*)

ACKNOWLEDGMENTS

In the chapter entitled "Marriage in Chimbu," Paula Brown presents certain material that has appeared in some of her earlier journal articles: "Chimbu Land and Society," *Oceania*, XXX (1959), 11; "Nonagnates among the Patrilineal Chimbu," *Journal of the Polynesian Society*, LXXI (1962), 64, 69; "Enemies and Affines," *Ethnology*, III (1964), 339, 342, 343–44; "Some Demographic Measures Applied to Chimbu Census and Field Data," *Oceania*, XXXV (1965), 176–77. We thank the Editor of *Oceania*, the Editor of *Ethnology*, and the Council of the Polynesian Society for their permission to use this material here.

R. M. G.
M. J. M.

M. J. Meggitt is Professor of Anthropology at Queens College of the City University of New York.

R. M. Glasse is Associate Professor of Anthropology at Queens College of the City University of New York.

L. L. Langness is Associate Professor of Anthropology at the University of Washington, Seattle.

Roy Wagner is Associate Professor of Anthropology at Northwestern University.

Paula Brown is Professor of Anthropology at the State University of New York at Stony Brook.

E. A. Cook is Assistant Professor of Anthropology at the University of California, Davis.

Roy A. Rappaport is Assistant Professor of Anthropology at the University of Michigan.

Andrew and Marilyn Strathern are Research Fellows in Anthropology at Australian National University.

D'Arcy Ryan is Senior Lecturer in Anthropology at the University of Western Australia.

Ruth Craig is Research Scholar in Anthropology at the University of Sidney.

Denise O'Brien is Assistant Professor of Anthropology at Temple University.

CONTENTS

PIGS, PEARLSHELLS, AND WOMEN

INTRODUCTION

M. J. Meggitt[1]

The people of the central highlands of New Guinea have lately come to assume a place of some significance in anthropological writing. There are several good reasons for this.

By the end of World War I Dutch, German, and Australian explorers had traversed the northern and southern approaches to the central cordillera of New Guinea; but it was not until the 1930's that Europeans, largely stimulated by the prospect of finding gold and aided by improved aircraft, successfully penetrated the high interior valleys lying between the Markham divide and the Wissel Lakes. There they encountered large native populations that had hitherto had little contact with the outside world (see Souter, 1963).[2] However, the war with Japan intervened, so that extensive, permanent European settlement did not begin until after 1945.

Both the Dutch and Australian colonial administrations were by then more sensitive to world opinion, and they tried with some success to regulate the activities of European missionaries, miners, planters, and traders in order to minimize or at least delay their disturbance of the indigenous highlands cultures. At the same time, professional anthropologists were on hand to exploit the situation and study these tribal societies while they remained in something like their pristine state. Their observations were significantly supplemented by those of interested and competent missionaries and patrol officers.

The ethnographic significance of the highlands peoples does not, however, depend solely on the historical accident of their recent confrontation with Europeans. More important is their potential value for comparative empirical studies of social and cultural processes. In a real

[1] Although I undertook to write this introduction alone, I circulated the penultimate draft of the paper among the contributors and invited their criticisms, which I took into account when preparing the final draft.

[2] The people of the central highlands in both West Irian and Australian New Guinea are now thought to number more than 900,000.

1

sense the highlands provide a laboratory situation in which the presence, absence, and covariation of many kinds of data may be employed to test existing hypotheses about specific social arrangements and cultural patterns, and also to suggest fresh hypotheses or models. More particularly, the feasibility of multivariate analyses of such phenomena indicates that the highlands are a fertile field for anthropologists and ecologists interested in research into systems.

At risk of putting the matter too simply—if we view the groups of the central highlands as a whole—we may perceive at least three broad divisions among them, two (perhaps all three) of which have in addition eastern and western subdivisions (see the general map, p. i). They are the region from the Markham headwaters in the east to the Strickland Gorge, the region from the Strickland Gorge west to the Star Mountains, and the region from the Baliem Valley to the Wissel Lakes in West Irian. In the central region the people appear to have more significant cultural contacts with their northern and southern neighbors than do the people of the eastern and western divisions. To some extent the people of the central region give the impression of being intruders (see, e.g., Craig, 1966, 1967). However that may be, each of these three major regions exhibits a complex of features that appear to covary without marked disjunctions. Even where eastern and western subdivisions can be seen, there remain wider continuities and regularities, whether of environment, material culture, social organization, or language.[3]

Thus, from the Markham to the Strickland and again from the Baliem Valley to the Wissel Lakes, sweet potato is the staple crop and is usually grown in relatively efficient systems of long fallow horticulture (see, e.g., Brookfield, 1964), whereas in the central Telefolmin-Star Mountains region taro is of equal or greater importance. This general dependence on nonstorable root crops clearly has significant implications for highlands economic and political organizations that deserve study. The technologies and inventories of material culture of these groups are also noticeably constant throughout each region. Everywhere pigs are prized, together with other culturally defined valuables such as shells and plumes. Moreover, the frequent public distributions or exchanges are not intended simply to contribute to the economies of the peoples concerned; they also enhance

[3] Read (1954) made the first serious attempt to discuss these patterns in Australian New Guinea; see also Barnes (1962), Paula Brown (1967: Table 1), Pouwer (1966), Watson (1964), and Wurm (1961, 1964).

the prestige of the various participants (whether individuals or local and descent groups) and hence maintain or extend their political connections. Indeed, in these societies transactions and warfare are mutually related, and both in turn may bear significantly on marriage.

In each region the systems of religious ideas and ritual action generally express the pervasive materialism of the people and at the same time offer rationalizations of the often tense relations between men and women. Furthermore, corresponding with specific differences in ecological, economic, and political military arrangements, there are usually understandable variations in local organization and social structure. But these are mostly variations on a few themes. In almost every area, as far as we now know, some emphasis falls, if only in ideological terms, on patrilineality or on patrifiliation (and sometimes on both—these concepts are not synonymous).[4] As yet, nowhere in the central highlands have fieldworkers encountered matrilineal descent systems or extensive *de facto* matrifiliation.

Anthropologists have already addressed themselves to some of the problems posed by such data, both with respect to particular New Guinea highlands societies and also in more general regional and theoretical terms. Thus, several have analyzed social systems of land use and their environmental concomitants (Brown and Brookfield, 1959, 1963; Glasse, 1968; Meggitt, 1958, 1965; Rappaport, 1968). The same writers, as well as Barnes (1962), Langness (1964), Marie de Lepervanche (1967), Marie Reay (1967), and Wagner (1967), have also been interested in a comparative way in the structure of social groups (both descent and local) in the highlands.

Highlands political and military arrangements have been an object of study, for instance, by Berndt (1964), Paula Brown (1960, 1963, 1967), Bulmer (1960), Glasse (1968), Langness (n.d.), Meggitt (1967), Read (1959), Marie Reay (1967), Sahlins (1963), Salisbury (1964b), Strathern (1966), and Watson (1967). In 1965 Lawrence and Meggitt edited a symposium on New Guinea religions that took account of several highlands societies; and a number of writers (Berndt, 1963; Glasse, 1968; Langness, 1967; Meggitt, 1964, and Newman, 1965, fol-

---

[4] Among the Kapauku of the Wissel Lakes both patriclan and bilateral kindred are recognized and functionally significant (Pospisil, 1958, 1963). This appears to be true also of the people of the Star Mountains of West Irian (Pouwer, 1964). Ruth Craig reports in this volume that the social system of the Telefolmin, near the West Irian border, is cognatic but, although there is no emphasis on patrilineal descent, villages display *de facto* viripatrilocal residence and cumulative patrifiliation.

lowing Read, 1954) have discussed the complex relations that join and separate the sexes, with reference to specific societies and to the highlands at large.

Nevertheless, despite so much industry and ingenuity, certain gaps remain in the published record, the most obvious of which are in the treatment of law (but note Pospisil, 1958), economics (but note Pospisil, 1963, and Salisbury, 1962), and marriage. Moreover, this hiatus is not confined to general or comparative studies alone. Even among the ethnographies of particular societies (some of them otherwise highly explicit) there is a surprising lack of unequivocal evidence concerning significant aspects of marriage arrangements. To date, published accounts deal with marriage in some depth among the Daribi (Wagner, 1967), Enga (Meggitt, 1958, 1965), Huli (Glasse, 1968), Kamano (Berndt, 1954–55, 1962), Kuma (Reay, 1959), and Siane (Salisbury, 1956, 1962), while less detailed treatments have appeared, for example, of the Chimbu (Brown, 1964; Nilles, 1950), Gahuku-Gama (Read, 1954), Gururumba (Newman, 1965), Ipili (Meggitt, 1957), Kapauku (Pospisil, 1958, 1963), Kutubu (Williams, 1940), Maring (Rappaport, 1968), Mbowamb (Vicedom and Tischner, 1948; Strauss and Tischner, 1962), and the Star Mountains (Pouwer, 1964).

In short, whether anthropologists are interested in constructing sophisticated models of highlands marriage arrangements, or making structural-functional comparative studies of them, or simply plotting their distribution in gross terms, there is a dearth of pertinent published material for them to use.

This book aims to meet the need by providing short but clearly focussed and comparable accounts of marriage (and divorce) for a sample of highlands societies. Originally we had hoped for more equal representation in our sample of the three major cultural divisions of the central highlands; but, given the somewhat random manner in which areas of anthropological field research are chosen, the exigencies of the field work itself, and the academic commitments of investigators out of the field, this plan proved unworkable. As it became clear that the eastern, Australian, section of the highlands could best be covered, we sought contributions that would refer to both its eastern and western subdivisions, as well as to its northern and southern fringes, and would therefore significantly augment the existing pattern of reports from this region. At the same time we made sure that the remaining two divisions of the central highlands would at least be represented. Thus, although the composition of this sample may fall short of any particular reader's ideal, the selection is not an *ad hoc* affair but rather expresses a rational scheme of the editors.

In addition to providing more ethnographic data on highlands marriage, both for the use of our anthropological colleagues and for the edification of other scholars, we wish to indicate some aspects of these social processes that would repay further investigation in the field as well as analysis in the armchair.

We have already seen that a striking characteristic of the highlands cultures is the intense interest that the people show in the circulation of valuables. Most anthropologists who have published at any length on this area have pointed to the ways in which portable objects of various kinds (some of them somewhat unlikely) are seized upon as vehicles for, and markers of, individual and group wealth and socio-political status.[5] Some of the items chosen for this purpose are, in terms of utility, durability, or multiplication, almost self-selective. Thus, everywhere in the highlands pigs are objects of such prime concern that they are set in matrices of cultural values and social transactions which, at first sight at least, are analogous to the cattle complex of east Africa demarcated years ago by Herskovits (1926). There are, of course, important differences between the two situations, some of which are summarized in one former Africanist's assertion (only half facetious) that, whereas African cattle are impressive animals intrinsically suited to reverence, the New Guinea pig is an ignoble beast. In fact New Guinea highlanders do seem to be more ready than the Africans to slaughter their livestock on public occasions to provide standardized units of meat which themselves become significant valuables before being eaten (see also Vayda, Leeds, and Smith, 1961; Vayda, n.d.).

Although the numbers of domestic pigs and the sophistication of their breeding vary from one highlands group to another (even within the same culture), it is generally the case in all that distribution of pigs or pork mark critical points in public events, either to augment the prestige of the actors or to seal and validate explicit or implicit contracts.

[5] Apart from the material provided here and elsewhere for the societies discussed in this volume, evidence of varying degrees of specificity (some of it slight indeed) has been published for the Bokondini Dani (Ploeg), Gahuku-Gama (Read), Gimi (Glick), Gururumba (Newman), Huli (Glasse), Ipili (Meggitt), Jalemo (Koch), Kakoli (Bowers), Kamano (Berndt), Kapauku (Pospisil, Dubbeldam), Karam (Bulmer), Kuma (Reay), Kuman Chimbu (Nilles), Kutubu (Williams), Kyaka (Bulmer), Mbowamb Melpa (Vicedom and Tischner), Siane (Salisbury), Star Mountains (Pouwer), and Tairora (Watson); see our bibliography for detailed references.

Marriage, particularly its initiation, is the typical situation in which this occurs. However, marriage and other public prestations do not include only objects such as pigs, pork, salt, and stone (now steel) axes which clearly have utilitarian as well as prestige value. Men also employ, depending on the locality, other less obvious but no less valuable items, such as variously treated shells (most importantly pearl and cowrie), plumes (especially of birds of paradise and cassowaries), animal teeth, and cosmetics.

Whatever the general level of wealth prevailing in the society in terms of crops, livestock, and valuables, and whatever size the marriage payments (especially the bride wealth) assume relative to other pre-scribed prestations in that society (for instance, death or homicide compensations), it seems true throughout the highlands that marriage payments are large—usually too much for an individual groom or a guardian of a bride to acquire single-handed. In all cases we observe groups of people amassing and distributing considerable amounts of valuables at various times during a marriage.[6] Frequently, in the Australian highlands, such groups are localized sets of actual or puta-tive agnates (such as the patrilineages or the subclans of the couple), aided by certain other relatives and exchange partners (who may also be military allies). However, west from Telefolmin into the mountains of West Irian, whether or not patrilineal descent groups are present in the societies, the parties to a marriage are likely to be members of small bilateral kindreds of the bride and groom (as among the Telefolmin, Star Mountains people, and Kapauku).

Such facts, are, of course, relevant to a discussion of long standing in social anthropology—namely, the bearing that marriage prestations have on the stability of marriage.[7] Although in most highlands so-cieties bride wealth is large relative to an individual's resources, rates of marital separation and divorce vary widely, not only among societies but also at different stages of married life. In some groups, such as the Telefolmin and Kamano, divorce appears to be frequent and likely to occur at any time during marriage; among others (probably the majority) divorces are common early in marriages but not later; in a few other societies, such as the Enga and, perhaps, Kapauku, divorce rates are low throughout marriage.[8]

---

[6] The Huli of Australian New Guinea are a partial exception (Glasse, 1968).

[7] See J. and Esther Goody (1967) for a recent restatement of the problem, to-gether with references to the earlier literature.

[8] I have no space here to discuss the qualifications that these broad statements might require, for instance, the need to distinguish statistically between initial annulments and early divorces, or whether divorce means the same in the presence

In the case of the Mae Enga, among whom marriage prestations are large and elaborate and bride price is substantial, I have argued (1965: chapters 5 and 6) that, while there is a significant connection or feedback between these two variables, they in turn are affected by the presence of strongly corporate, localized agnatic descent groups— a conclusion that supports the views of Gluckman (1950) and Goody (1967). Elsewhere (1968) I have extended this analysis in comparison with Aboriginal societies of central Australia in which descent groups are unilineal, divorce rates are low, but marriage payments are small and simple. The evidence suggests that, although in some societies bride wealth and divorce may covary inversely, this is a secondary phenomenon; it is more important to ascertain how marriage arrangements are set into the organization of corporate groups in a given society. Instructive in this respect is the difference between the Kamano and the Telefolmin, on the one hand, and the Enga and (maybe) the Kapauku, on the other. Among the former, for whom divorce appears to be common, the woman's group (whether family or lineage) retains a greater interest in her during marriage than is the case among the latter, for whom divorce is less frequent (cf. Goody, 1967). It may be that, although viripatrilocal residence is the norm in these as in most highlands societies, there are significant gross differences between concentrated village residence and living in scattered homesteads.

In a number of highlands societies the introduction of wage labor and cash crops by Europeans during the past decade or so has led to a growing substitution of money for traditional valuables in marriage prestations and with it a noticeable inflation of these payments. Thus it has become more difficult for a man to amass his bride price unaided, so much so that some local councils in the Australian highlands have tried, with little success, to limit the amounts demanded by relatives of marriageable women. Divorce rates, however, have by no means declined. If anything, they have risen, probably because other changing circumstances (for instance: the increased movement of people in and out of their natal or reference communities, shifts in the status of women, as well as the greater availability of "neutral" courts of law) are working to break down group control over marriage arrangements.

This returns us to the earlier characterization of the highlands as a laboratory for testing anthropologists' hypotheses such as those concerning marriage stability, bride wealth, and social systems. It would

and absence of the levirate. I can only indicate that such problems of definition exist.

be worth embarking on a series of carefully controlled comparisons of highlands societies (along the lines of the Goodys' studies [1966, 1967] of northern Ghana) in which appropriate variables are quantified and variously combined, while differing, apparently extraneous conditions are held constant from one situation to the next. An analysis-of-variance model seems relevant here.

Although it is not possible here to treat the subject of marriage rules in the complex detail that some anthropologists would demand, certain general features of highlands marriage requirements may be noted. The first concerns prohibitions. As far as we can tell from published material, whether or not marriage preferences exist in a society, there is usually a basic set of prohibitions on marriage with close relatives.[9] At the least such prohibitions concern bilateral kin of the order of first or second cousins and may be seen as statements of incest taboos; that is, such close kin may be regarded as close "siblings." Frequently the prohibition forbids marriages between "people who share one blood." In some societies, however, such as Enga, this ban may merge with broader exogamic prohibitions. Given the widespread recognition of patrilineal descent groups here, it is not surprising that these are defined as exogamous at various levels in the local hierarchies of groups.

By far the most common exogamous group in the highlands is the patriclan, which occurs, for instance, among the Bena, Chimbu, Daribi, Enga, Gahuku-Gama, Gururumba, Ipili, Kakoli, Kamano, Kuma, Kutubu, Kyaka, Manga, Maring, Melpa, Mendi, and Tairora on the Australian side and among the Kapauku and Konda Dani on the West Irian side.[10] Although these clans are the exogamous units in ideology, marriages contracted between them generally concern their constituent groups or networks such as the clan section, subclan, lineage, or sibling set. This distinction is important in understanding how marriage prohibitions and preferences, for example, for "sister" exchange, can coexist in these societies, and it helps to account for apparent contradictions between ideology and practice in some of them.[11]

[9] Notable exceptions occur in the eastern highlands. The Kamano prefer (but do not prescribe) marriage with actual MBD, FZD, and ZSD (Berndt, 1954–55, 1962). The neighboring South Fore allow marriage with MBD but not with FZD.

[10] The social entities that the various ethnographers have called patriclans are by no means identical in size or in details of genealogical structure, residential organization, or political and economic action; nevertheless, they do share significant features.

[11] It is of interest that, in most of these societies, wherever we encounter an

In other highlands societies the exogamous unit may be the moiety or the phratry of clans (Jalemo and Siane) or all known agnates (Huli), or it may be a lower order, *de facto* or putative patrilineal group such as the subclan or the lineage (Gimi, Star Mountains, South Fore, and Bokondini Dani). The obvious exception to this pattern occurs among the Telefolmin villagers who, although largely patrilocal, have no unilineal descent groups. There, marriage prohibitions refer only to bilateral kin out to and including second cousins, and village endogamy is preferred.

A common correlate of exogamous patrilineal descent groups in the highlands is the extension of marriage prohibitions to include at various levels the descent groups of certain nonagnatic relatives. This may also be phrased as a reluctance to marry people (especially of the mother's group) sharing one's own blood, but in some cases the range of prohitions is wider. Thus, the Enga forbid marriage not only with known descendants of a man's living or dead clanswomen but also with women of the subclans of wives of his own subclan and of subclans of his FM, MM, MF, MH, MZH, and WM.[12] Few highlands societies go to these lengths to disperse their marriages but some approach this distribution. The Mendi, and perhaps the Gimi, prohibit unions with any cognatically (and, for Mendi, affinally) related lineage; and the Huli exclude the agnatic parishes of the M and FZH (but not the MZH). The Maring forbid unions with clans of the M, MZH, and FZH, the Melpa with the M clan and with certain other groups (see the Stratherns' table in this volume, p. 142), the Siane with the M clan, the Bena and Kuma with the M subclan, and the Chimbu and Jalemo with the M lineage. On the other hand, despite patrilineal descent groups, there seem to be no such restrictions among the South Fore, Kamano, Manga, Kapauku, Konda Dani, and Star Mountains people.

Clearly, the concomitants of such a range of variation demand investigation. At this distance, in the light of evidence from the Enga, Mendi, Melpa, and Maring (all in the same general neighborhood), economic and political factors are probably important. There appears to be a positive correlation between dispersal of marriages and a group's need to maximize its position in the local exchanges of wealth

---

increase in the frequency of marriages within the prohibited category, this has significant substantive implications for group dynamics through processes of segmentation, fission, and the like.

[12] Throughout this paper the abbreviation of kinship terms follows the convention that F = father, M = mother, B = brother, Z = sister, H = husband, W = wife, S = son, D = daughter.

and to extend its military alliances. At the same time permanent or long-term enmity between local or descent groups, as well as their relative sizes and the distance and kind of terrain separating them, may operate as countervailing pressures to narrow marriage choices. Indeed, groups at different levels in the same hierarchy may be involved in different or even conflicting patterns of exchange and marriage. However, more data from other areas may require a revision of this view.[13]

Of particular interest is the way in which (in some of these societies) such prohibitions, which serve to spread marriages through a large number of discrete, like groups, combine with stated preferences that act, if followed consistently, to contract the range of unions so that limited sets or, sometimes, pairs of descent groups (or segments of them) intermarry intensively for long periods. Occasionally, as with intraconfederacy unions among the Dani, this gives the appearance of a pervasive dualism in the social system. Among the Manga, Maring, Melpa, Kuma, Chimbu, and Siane (again inhabitants of a limited region), despite the frequent passage of bride wealth between the negotiating parties, there is also emphasis on reciprocity or balance over time in the movement of women between groups (and, in Telefolmin, between villages) even though, as with Melpa, this balancing of accounts may be *post hoc* rather than premeditated. In this regard the people themselves may express a preference for the exchange of sisters in marriage; but as far as we can tell only in a few cases (for example, Manga) are very many actual or close classificatory sisters concerned—that is, broad categories are more important here than are specific sibling relations. In any case, these exchanges of women (however defined) are significant in the establishment and maintenance of particular economic and political ties between more or less corporate groups. Also pertinent here is the Stratherns' statement (see p. 158) that, given the politico-economic context of Melpa marriage transactions, Melpa believe that wife-taking demonstrates strength and superiority (however temporary) over wife-giving. This attitude, the reverse of that generally encountered in the ethnographic literature, may prove to be fairly common in the highlands.

In addition there are in some highlands societies certain marriage

[13] Elizabeth Crouch, in an unpublished "Agnation in the Highlands" (University of Michigan, 1966), uses evidence from Enga, Chimbu, Siane, and Kuma to argue that there is a significant connection among low divorce rates, dispersed marriages, and unitary localized clans, on the one hand, and among higher divorce rates, concentrated marriages, and fragmented clans with interdigitated territories, on the other. This line of inquiry is worth pursuing.

preferences phrased partly in kinship terms (putative or fictive) and partly in terms of group membership. Thus, the Kuma say that, although a girl should not marry into her mother's subclan, it is good (= advantageous?) for her to wed into a parallel segment of that clan, and Reay (1959) states that such marriages are frequent. Among Konda Dani marriage of men and women into the mother's clan is approved, but in fact marriage within the political confederacy takes precedence. Analogously, the Maring, despite their extensive marriage prohibitions, prefer girls to marry into their FM subclans; but in fact these unions are rare (4 per cent of the sample) and have little effect on the definition of intergroup relations.

In the situations so far mentioned we are faced with preferential marriage arrangements, in which particular kinds of unions are approved, even expected, and not with prescriptive systems, in which marriage is obligatory between specific categories or relatives and is prohibited with all other people. That is, I am here taking preferences to be simply compatible with complex marriage structures, whereas prescriptions are embedded in, or entailed by, elementary structures (cf. Lévi-Strauss, 1965). Thus, preferences tend to be structurally significant on a contingent basis, insofar as they are statistically frequent in the society, although they may of course be compatible with other ideal structures (for instance, political) in that society. This condition seems to be importantly connected with the fact that such societies are basically "open" in the sense that for each individual member there may be as many nonkin as kin to choose among and, consequently, as often as not marriage may join hitherto unrelated groups or categories of people. Acceptable choices are made on pragmatic, substantive grounds (cf. Goody, 1966: esp. 353).

Prescriptive systems, on the other hand, deny *a priori* the possibility or existence of choice at a given level so that, up to a point to be determined empirically in each society, the statistical frequency with which people do or do not adhere to the marriage rules is irrelevant. The crucial notion here is structure or system, and the marriage norms are an integral part of the definition of the social structure. Explicit examples of such elementary structures occur, for instance, among some Australian Aboriginal tribes, which in kinship terms are "closed" systems. There, marriages are enjoined with particular categories of kin, whether cross-cousins or second cousins, and with no others. Even though a majority of the men may be cohabiting with women of the wrong categories, these unions cannot be valid marriages; the system of marriage norms remains intact and contributes to the definition of the structure of the society. Of course, as we have seen in situations of social change in Australia, there are limiting cases in which sufficiently numerous and persisting deviations may destroy the normative system and, with it, the social structure at large.

In the highlands, systems of marriage that are unambiguously prescriptive are rare, if they exist at all. Thus, among the South Fore, as Glasse points out, what might at first sight appear to be a prescriptive system of matrilateral cross-cousin marriage turns out on closer inspection to be a contingent, preferential arrangement. The deceptive feature is that, in a society which emphasizes fictive kinship, in some (although not all) cases the very occurrence of marriage between groups previously unrelated in kin terms allows a *post facto* redefinition of the spouses as "cross-cousins." But this is not an enjoined change; the reformulation is not an invariant element designed to define exceptions out of existence and so give an appearance of unbroken, and unbreakable, marriage rules. Whether or not redefinition takes place depends on observable differences in actual situations, such as a desire to emphasize friendly relations existing between groups, so that statistical variations in substantive and organizational factors remain critical in the structure of the local descent group interrelations. A similar state of affairs apparently holds among the neighboring Kamano. Berndt (1954–55, 1962) notes that not only are marriages with actual or classificatory cross-cousins in a minority but also choices of previously related or unrelated spouses, within or outside the local district, vary noticeably with changing economic and political events.

There are, however, two highlands societies for which the presence of prescriptive marriage rules has been asserted—Siane and Manga. The Siane (Salisbury 1956, 1964) prohibit marriage within a man's patrilineal phratry and also with his mother's clan. His marriage must be with any of the remaining clans in the society. Because all clans are thought to have taken wives from his clan (and from all others) at various times, a man may regard all of them, except the clans of his own father and mother, as containing "FZH" (= husbands of putative female agnates?); hence all women born into these groups may be called his "FZD" (= children of putative female agnates?).

At this point Salisbury's discussion of Siane marriage is obscure. He appears to refer to it as an elementary structure in Levi-Strauss' terms; but, whereas in his earlier paper he states that "there is definitely no obligatory marriage rule in Siane" (1956: 646), only a preference for marrying a definite category of kin, later he remarks that "the marriage rule is obligatory as all men, when they marry, must be and are . . . marrying a 'father's sister's daughter.' The rule should not be called 'prescriptive,' as nothing is 'prescribed.' A young man does not have to search for a girl who falls into a specific kinship category, but when he has found an attractive girl, he sees how she fits into the category which all brides fit into" (1964: 169). It is not easy to follow these distinctions.

In the light of Salisbury's published data and of Glasse's analysis of South Fore marriage, I think that Siane marriage is instead a complex structure, one that functions on a contingent, preferential basis. It seems to me that the definition of any woman as "spouse/child of a female agnate/FZD" is not enjoined by the social structure but is significantly determined by pre-existing economic and political relations between the contracting parties (see especially Salisbury 1964). Thus, although a man (and his uterine brothers) may not marry into the clan that has already provided his mother, there appears to be no formal obstacle to other men of his lineage, subclan, or clan (whose mothers are from elsewhere) marrying into that clan at that time. Whether or not they do so is a substantive decision. For the *group* at each descent level there is then no patrilateral prescription; for each clan, because of past movements of women, every other clan is at once a potential wife-giver and wife-receiver. At most, for each man, the prohibitions on his marrying into his mother's or his own clan generate an apparent egocentric rule—"each particular person must marry into a clan that does not include either his mother or his father." [14]

Considerations of this kind might suggest that positive marriage arrangements in the highlands are always preferential and not prescriptive; nevertheless, Cook's account of Manga marriage in this volume offers a salutary check on hasty generalization. Thus, marriage arrangements among the Manga and the Maring (see Rappaport, p. 125) are in significant respects the same. Both forbid marriage within a man's own clan and with his mother's clan. Both favor sister exchange between unrelated men, although the rates of occurrence are low (*circa* 20 per cent of marriages in each society). Among both, such transactions create affinity between all the members of the two contracting

[14] The published accounts of Siane marriage have also exercised other anthropologists, for instance, Fox, 1967; Livingstone, 1964; and Schneider, 1965. Clearly my interpretation of the data differs from Livingstone's view that the Siane clans are units in a prescriptive system. The Stratherns have suggested to me that all the Siane "prescription" does is to say "we have delayed exchanges of women," so that in effect it is a *post hoc* evaluation of all marriages already made—an interpretation nicely compatible with evidence from other highlands societies.

groups so that no further exchanges of women should follow between them in that generation.

In both societies marriage of a woman into her FMB descent group (Maring subclan, Manga lineage) is approved, together with the passage of bride wealth. But, whereas Rappaport indicates that for Maring marriage with "FMBSS" is simply a stated preference rarely made (3 out of 70 cases), Cook states that for Manga such marriages, also few in fact (5 of 182 cases), express a prescriptive rule.

It is not just the *de facto* rarity of Manga marriages with "FMBSS" that poses a problem. More particularly, they concern only eldest daughters, and there is also a culturally approved way in which a man may arrange for his eldest daughter legally to marry elsewhere. That is to say, marriage with the "FMBSS" here does not seem to me to be either normatively enjoined or entailed by Manga social structure; rather it appears to be conditional on substantive factors.

On the other hand, Cook has succeeded in constructing an elegant and economical model that takes account of "FMBSS" marriage choices and preferred sister exchanges among Manga, even though it does not simultaneously treat important features such as "buying the mother" or making other licit marriages. While I doubt that the model demonstrates the existence of a "FMBSS" marriage prescription among Manga, clearly it could subsume this if it were present. In any case, Cook's material is valuable in raising again the question of the propriety of making oversharp distinctions between elementary (normative) and complex (contingent) structures (cf. Lévi-Strauss, 1965).[15]

These are only some of the aspects of marriage arrangements in the New Guinea highlands that warrant discussion. Limitations of space

[15] I am not here arguing that for practical or formal reasons patrilateral prescriptive systems cannot occur; for all I know they may be found in some dark jungle. I simply do not think that they are present among the Siane or the Manga. At this point I can only urge the reader to adjudicate on the different views. In order to resolve such potential disagreement, Cook has been kind enough to extend his comments on the Manga; they are valuable in indicating significant implications of this whole discussion. He says: "a rule can be exhaustively applicable to a range of phenomena or it can be partially selective. If the rule is exhaustive, such as applying to all first marriages, then it is systemic. The Manga have a prescriptive *rule* but they do *not* have a prescriptive marriage *system*. The model I have constructed is based upon the structure of a major preference (sister exchange) and prescriptive rule. One point of this 'bastard' model is that it is isomorphic with several aspects of the segmentary structure of the total society (and the adjoining ones). Another point is that it demonstrates the inutility of either the sole application of the descent model or of the alliance model to these data and thereby implies that when such models are promoted for New Guinea societies they will be products of the peculiarities of the New Guinea ethnographic data."

prevent my taking up in detail others of equal relevance to students of human society. Thus, for those interested in investigating the inter-relations of psychological and social phenomena there remains the question of the extent to which the highlanders' complicated attitudes towards sexual pollution, which vary greatly from one society to an-other, condition or are conditioned by their domiciliary patterns. What bearing do they have on such matters as the relative strengths of the bonds between spouses and between brothers and sisters, which in turn clearly relate to divorce frequencies in these societies? For anthro-pologists with a legal bent there is still much to be done with the whole problem of highlands jural systems and the status of marital litigation within these.

Finally, to turn to a field of anthropological inquiry rapidly growing in interest, we need more studies of the kind undertaken by Rappaport into the demographic consequences of culturally defined marriage rules and preferences and into the question of whether or not they (perhaps in conjunction with exchanges of certain commodities) dis-tribute people advantageously or adaptively through specified ecosys-tems.

In short there are good reasons why social scientists of differing persuasions should carefully consider both the variety and the impli-cations of the data now coming from studies of New Guinea highlands societies. We hope this volume will be effective in drawing some of this material to their attention and that it will perhaps encourage some of them to add to the serious research already being undertaken in this region.

Marriage in
SOUTH FORE

R. M. Glasse

INTRODUCTION

This paper describes a marriage system in the eastern highlands of
New Guinea, and is particularly concerned with ostensible marriage
"preferences" among kin. In this society, a man may marry his MBD
and certain other relatives; he is not obliged to do so, however, and
may also marry unrelated girls. He is forbidden to take his FZD as a
bride, such a match being incestuous. One might expect that these
rules would lead exogamous groups to form connubial relations
either of "wife-giver" or of "wife-receiver" (but never both) and that
from a single group brides would go to only a limited number of
receiving units. In fact, the people conceive of their lineage relations
in just this way. An observer could regard the system as one of "preferential asymmetric alliance"; yet to do so, I will argue, obscures
important facts and deflects attention from the more basic structure
of exchange based on reciprocity. From this perspective, marriage is
a single event in an elaborate chain of presentations.

I shall show that expressed marriage "preferences" really constitute
an idiom for talking about *de facto* degrees of reciprocity, achieved
before the marriage, between the families of the bride and groom.
Further, that the indigenous concept of "kinship," the code in which
preferences are expressed, is not based solely on genealogical principles,
but also includes fictive kin and age-mates of kin, all of whom provide
avenues for obtaining equally valued brides. According to this view,
"preferences" appear as a kind of window dressing. The real edifice
is the structure of reciprocal exchange.

THE PEOPLE AND THE SETTING

The Fore-speaking people, who number about 13,000, are sweet potato
cultivators living in the eastern highlands of Australian New Guinea.

Their land is in Okapa Subdistrict and ranges from 3,500 to 9,000 feet above sea level, with most gardens and settlements below 7,000 feet. At these elevations temperature varies little throughout the year. More important is the diurnal swing in temperature, which, in the settled area, is from about 45° F. at dawn to a maximum of 80° F. at midday. Frost occurs rarely and seldom damages the crops. Half the annual rainfall of roughly 100 inches comes between September and January, though few months are completely dry. As population density is low (Table 1), much of the natural vegetation, mixed-montane forest, still remains. In the last few decades Imperata grasslands have spread, probably because of repeated use of the more conveniently situated slopes.

Table 1. THE FORE POPULATION, 1962

Census Division and Dialect	Number	Area (Square miles)	Density (Persons/ square mile)
North Fore:			
Ibusa	5,600	121	46.2
South Fore:			
Atigina	4,078	100	40.1
Pamusa	3,146	175	18.0
Totals	12,824	396	

Source: 1962 Department of Native Affairs Census and Village Directory of the Territory of Papua and New Guinea.

The environmental resources available to the Fore are generally adequate to their material needs and, given their technology, they make good use of them. Gardens are productive by highland standards and, until the anthrax and swine pneumonia epidemics of the 1940's, pig herds were more extensive than they are today. Cannibalism, which spread to South Fore from the north during the last 50 years, may have become firmly established only after the pig supply declined substantially.[1] Animal protein also comes from game, such as possum, cassowary, and wild pig, but hunting does not contribute greatly to the diet or meet other material needs. More important to the economy is the collection of wild forest products, including mushrooms and

[1] For accounts of cannibalism among the Fore, see R. Berndt (1962: 269–90) and R. Glasse (1967).

herbs, medicinal plants and barks, and fibre, cane, and pandanus leaves for building, thatching, and mat-making.

Differences in elevation, topography, and soils provide a number of distinctive microenvironments in South Fore. Consequently, certain areas produce a superabundance of sweet potato or taro, others, pandanus nuts or marita palm fruit. The clans exchange crops (surplus to their requirements) following traditional patterns of reciprocity. There are no markets.

Until recently, pigs were the only domesticated animals of importance. They were not only slaughtered to provide meat but served also as a medium of exchange, along with cowrie and other shells, in transactions such as bride and mortuary payments, and war indemnities. In the last decade chickens have also begun to count in these exchanges.

Before the cessation of warfare, the South Fore went hungry from time to time despite the abundance of land, partly because fighting preoccupied the men and kept the women from the gardens and also because of rainfall fluctuations and poor planning.

Fore belongs to the East Central Family of Wurm's East New Guinea Highlands Language Phylum (1961) and includes three dialects, which the Fore call Ibusa, Atigina, and Pamusa. Ibusa is spoken in the north, Atigina in the center, and Pamusa in the south. For administrative convenience, the population has been divided into two Census Divisions (C.D.) using a prominent ridge as a boundary. This division corresponds to the dialect border between the speakers of Ibusa and Atigina. As fieldwork[2] was carried out mainly in the South Fore (in both dialect areas), this paper is primarily concerned with the marriage system there.[3]

[2] Shirley Glasse (Lindenbaum) and I carried out twenty-one months of fieldwork between June 1961 and June 1963. The first period of work (nine months) was supported by the Department of Genetics of the University of Adelaide under the terms of a Rockefeller Grant. The second period was under the auspices of the Department of Public Health of the Territory of Papua and New Guinea. We are grateful to both of these institutions for support, and to the many individuals associated with them for generous hospitality and practical help. I should particularly like to extend our thanks to Professor Robert Black of Sydney University, to the Director of Public Health, Dr. R. Scragg, and to Mr. Mert Brightwell, then officer-in-charge of Okapa Subdistrict.

[3] For an account of the traditional North Fore marriage system, circa 1950, see R. Berndt (1962: 114–30). Berndt reports a number of important differences from observations recorded here. For example, the North Fore allow marriage with the FZD and MBD, though some groups assert that only classificatory cross-cousins should wed. Certainly the South Fore recognize that a number of their customs differ from those of the North. It has seemed best in this brief report to limit discussion to the South Fore.

The Fore are well known to anthropology mostly from the work of the Berndts, who made two field trips in North Fore and studied language groups to the north between 1951 and 1953.[4] They are also known to the medical world because they and their immediate neighbors to the north and west suffer from *kuru*, a fatal neurological disorder. *Kuru* is a disease of motor coordination, which, over the span of about a year, leaves the patient completely immobilized and vulnerable to pneumonia and other infections (Gajdusek, 1963). No cure or palliative has been found and despite a decade of intensive study the cause is still unknown and the mortality rate, though declining, is still high.

Kuru is pertinent to the South Fore marriage system. Since it affects females four times as frequently as males, a shortage of women has developed. This scarcity has led to a decline in the frequency of polygyny and to an increase in the proportion of bachelors and wifeless men in the population. Women now have a greater voice about when and whom they marry. Family life has been seriously disrupted, and many men must now care for their motherless children with little hope of finding wives. Despite the suppression of warfare by the Australian administration, interclan hostility persists, for the Fore believe that sorcerers cause *kuru*, and they seek them among their enemies (Glasse [Lindenbaum], 1964).

This study is based on twenty-one months of fieldwork carried out mainly in the South Fore C.D. between June 1961 and June 1963. From about 1951, considerable quantities of European goods entered the native economy. Some of these, such as steel axes, bush knives, clothing, and newspaper (used for rolling cigarettes) were incorporated into the bride price. Cash also began to circulate and was mainly obtained by young men working as laborers on coffee and coconut plantations in other parts of the highlands or on the coast. By 1963 many South Fore men had planted coffee as a cash crop, but few trees were then bearing. While a decade of life under Australian Administration and mission influence had resulted in an increase in material goods and improved species of subsistence crops and breeds of pigs, traditional patterns of distributing payments could still be seen in 1963.

SOCIAL ORGANIZATION

The Fore-speakers cannot meaningfully be described as a "tribe." Before the arrival of the Administration they possessed no common

---

[4] See the bibliography for a list of relevant publications by the Berndts.

name, no focus of over-all unity, no political organization, and no collective rites. The situation is common in the eastern highlands; several linguistic groups often exhibit the same cultural traits (Berndt, 1962), though differences in custom may occur within the borders of one language group. Thus the Fore society is a sociological unit only in a loose sense. To treat the South Fore C.D. as an entity is of course equally arbitrary.

The Fore people are well aware of the differences in speech among the three dialect areas, as well as more minute variations in certain villages. Yet it would be an error to regard the speakers of a dialect as a corporate group. Inclusion in a dialect community does not entail any special rights or obligations, and many people are equally at home in two dialects.

The data on corporate group structure from many New Guinea highlands societies do not easily fit the unilineal models of Africanists, as Barnes (1962, 1967a) and Langness (1964, n.d.) have pointed out. This is true also of South Fore data. Nevertheless, for want of a better set of terms, I refer to their corporate groupings as "clans," "subclans," "lineages," etc. To be sure, the Fore conceive of their corporate groupings as descent hierarchies, but to use unilineal terminology suggests a greater concern with formal principles than the people manifest in their speech and behavior. Fore genealogies are short, seldom exceeding five generations; their clans bear local, not ancestral names; people rarely invoke unilineal descent to justify or to sanction social acts; they do not distinguish agnates from non-agnates in the local groups, either in terminology or by different access to clan resources; and they readily accept nonagnates as members of the clan to enhance its strength.

This absence of agnatic stress may perhaps be correlated with the presence of ample agrarian resources and low population pressure (Meggitt, 1965), relatively recent migration into the area, or, in a warlike society, the adaptive advantage of a social system in which the individual has rights of refuge and residence in several clan-territories. (Turning the argument on its head, one might equally assert that what needs to be explained in the highlands is not the absence of unilineal emphasis but the distinctive features such as patrifiliative recruitment and strong sibling bonds.)

Space does not permit detailed discussion of South Fore corporate groupings, but the following list of working definitions cover some of the main points.

In 1962, the 39 clan-parishes in South Fore C.D. ranged in size

Table 2. DEFINITION OF SOUTH FORE CORPORATE GROUPS

Unit	Definition and Characteristics
Phratry	An association of clans descended from a putative common ancestor. In fights between clans of different phratry, other members of the same phratry would sometimes assist on the basis of phratry interest; phratry membership, however, did not entail political support.
Clan	A putatively patrilineal descent group. The political and territorial group of widest span. Despite the ideology of agnation, it readily accepts nonagnates as members without concealing or stressing their foreign origin.
Clan-parish	A *de facto* corporate grouping based on the clan but not including as full members clansmen residing away from the clan-territory. Formerly it fought as a unit, and ideally settled internal quarrels without intentional killing.
Subclan	A segment of the clan. Formed either by segmentation of the clan or by attachment from another clan. It may or may not be exogamous, depending on whether it is further segmented.
Lineage	A division of the subclan, again either by segmentation or attachment; an exogamous unit whose relations with other clan segments within and without the clan are partly specified in connubial terms, e.g. "wife-giving" and "wife-receiving."
Hamlet	A named residential group, comprised of one or more clan segments or portions of clan segments, formerly surrounded by barricades. Hamlet men and older boys lived in a club house apart from the women, which has now largely been replaced by nuclear family dwellings.

from 40 to 525 members. The average size was 180, and two-thirds of the groups had membership of from 100 to 200 members. Clan segments were correspondingly small.

The suppression of warfare has undoubtedly stabilized Fore social life. The composition of the clan-parish, which formerly fluctuated with the fortunes of war, is now relatively fixed as a result of census taking; many men believe they must stay where their names have been recorded; the planting of coffee trees is an added incentive to stay put. In the past, a defeated clan often split into segments, taking refuge with cognatic kin or affines. Some families never returned home. Occasionally, a whole clan scattered, never to regroup. Segmentation within the clan took place when its members increased; alternatively, a segment might hive off from the group to settle independently on vacant land; this also resulted from intraclan fighting. No matter why a group divided, clan ties were not extinguished overnight and many South Fore still preserve ties of loyalty and allegiance to groups other than their current clan-parish of residence. The proliferation of individual interests has greatly influenced the marriage system.

THE MARRIAGE SYSTEM

The sequence of every description is arbitrary to a certain extent. Here I begin by discussing the procedures for initiating and legitimizing marriage; the emphasis is on how things are done, not the relationship among actors. Then I shall give data on marriage rates for the population as a whole, and on the cumulative marital experience of a sample of individuals. Next, the positive and negative regulations of marriage are discussed: what categories of persons are forbidden to marry, and who are "preferred" spouses. The discussion of "preference"[5] leads to an analysis of certain Fore notions of nongenealogical "kinship." This in turn brings into focus the important structure of reciprocal exchange between the families of husbands and wives.

A. Matchmaking

Establishing a legitimate match involves negotiations between representatives of the bride's and groom's families. Capturing a girl and forcing her to enter a liaison, does not result in *de jure* marriage, unless the man subsequently pays bride price to the girl's kin and thereby initiates affinal relations. Such *de facto* liaisons were never very common and no longer occur. A girl may take the first public step to launch a marriage, by presenting herself as a prospective bride at the house of her lover's mother or sister. She may also offer herself in this way to a man she has not previously known. Her brothers come to fetch her back or, if they agree to sanction the match, to discuss the terms of bride price. The great majority of first marriages were arranged by the families of the couple. In the past, the bride and groom often were not consulted.

[5] To count a system as preferential two conditions must be met: (1) The people must recognize and publicly approve of marriage between persons in stipulated categories; and (2), given the rules of exogamy that obtain, the occurrence of preferred matches must exceed the frequency that would result from random mating. If the first condition is met but not the second, "preference" is a cultural illusion. If the second is fulfilled but not the first, preference is structural, though the people are unaware of its existence.

The strong sibling bond in South Fore is revealed in the custom of infant betrothal. This is an arrangement whereby a newborn girl-child is bespoken as the future wife of her FZS, who by then should be about eight years old. The betrothal is arranged soon after the delivery, while the mother is still in the birth hut. The boy's parents bring her food to celebrate the event, and ask the girl's parents to accept their proposal. The father may choose to reject the offer; if he does refuse he justifies his decision by accusing his "sister" of not fulfilling her obligations to him. If he agrees, however, he accepts from the visitors a partly burned firebrand; his action formally and publicly establishes a contract. The girl's parents then may offer countergifts to the parents of the boy; the latter ordinarily decline the gifts saying that in due course they will take the girl herself instead.

Whatever the exact relationship between the two families concerned, betrothal is binding. If a more closely related kinsman of the mother later tries to break the contract in favor of his own son, he has scant hope of success, provided the accepted suitor's kinsmen continue to honor their relationship. The betrothal is not a solitary, isolated event but rather the first in a series of prestations and counterprestations that unite the two families before and after the formal contract. Note that infant betrothal does not occur between families without prior social ties. In *no* case of infant betrothal were the parents of the couple not "siblings" in some sense, or at least "age-mates" of a "sibling" pair. In this sense infant betrothal is "prescriptive"—it does not take place between unrelated families. Yet the use of the term is misleading. It is not that the right of betrothal is embedded in a specific jural status, but rather that an interest evolves between a man and woman who regard each other as "siblings," an interest in the marriage of their offspring. The girl's parents may reject a proposal from a family in an "approved" category, if, prior to the offer, no *de facto* relationship existed between them and the suitor's kin. In the past, the right of rejection could also be exercised by the boy's family. Nowadays competition for wives is so great that the girl's family alone makes the choice.

Many infant betrothals go awry, either because of the death of one of the pair or because some other event, such as the outbreak of war between their kin groups, seriously disrupts the relationship between the two families. When this happens the girl may be promised to someone else. Alternatively, nothing further may be done until she approaches puberty.

Parents also play a leading role in arranging the matches of

children not betrothed at birth. The mother is particularly important
in this respect, since it is among the daughters of her "brothers" and
their age-mates that a bride for her son is likely to be found. If she
neglects to act as a good "sister" and to bring them gifts of food from
time to time, they in turn may refuse to provide a bride. In the
absence of parents, the elder brother and his wife act as surrogates for
the younger children and arrange their matches.

Before the advent of the Australian Administration, young people
had little or no say in the choice of their spouses. Girls in particular
were supposed to acquiesce in their parents' wishes. A young man could
express an opinion, but most were too embarrassed by the situation
to take an active part. Since most girls married before puberty, only
a determined lass managed to veto the arrangements or to insist on
the man of her own choice. The threat of suicide was her main
weapon against her parents' wishes.

Initially the procedure is different in secondary matches. The adult
man is free to court girls he calls *nebanto*, except for actual and
classificatory FZD, and other unrelated girls. Once he has found a
girl who is willing, he then arranges the match with her family in
much the same way as a young man would. A widow usually remarries
within a year of the death of her husband; she may choose from among
her dead husband's brothers and cousins of approximately the same
age as the deceased, or from among his age-mates. The rejected
suitors customarily attack the successful candidate; this should be
mock aggression but a disappointed man may really cause harm. The
new husband is obliged to make a payment to the rejected group. By
accepting this, they relinquish further claims upon the woman.[6]

Considerable change in the procedure of matchmaking has occurred
as a result of Administration policy and mission influence. Government officers frown on the institution of "child marriage" and urge,
if not insist, that the bride's consent be obtained before the wedding.
Missionaries, too, discourage early marriage, and girls now remain with
their parents until their first menstruation.

As mentioned earlier, the payment of bride price is necessary to
legitimize the match. South Fore conceive of this payment as both an
indemnity to her family for the loss of her service and as investment

---

[6] The question arises whether this procedure should be regarded as widow inheritance or widow remarriage. I consider it to be the latter, since the parents or
older brothers of the widow attend the choosing and announce that henceforth
she will be the wife of the man she has selected. They do not receive additional
bride price, and her husband's kin group receives no payment as a group, if she
marries out of it.

in her fertility. A man who repudiates his wife cannot recover his bride price in full or in part. The only circumstance that warrants a return is the flight of his bride into the arms of another man. It is a moot point whether the payment he demands from her lover should be counted a partial return of his bride price or an indemnity for injury to his name or reputation; but a man who loses his wife has a better chance of obtaining redress from her new husband than he has from her own family.

The contributors to the bride price include the family of the groom, the groom himself, other members of his lineage and subclan, and other kin and friends from within and outside the parish. The bulk of the donations come from the groom's lineage, each member contributing according to his circumstances, the degree of his relationship with the groom, and the past history of reciprocal exchange between the groom and the contributor. The father and the elder brothers of the groom are likely to be the largest donors.

The division of the bride price among the bride's kin occasions no surprises. Suffice it to say that those persons who contributed in any way to the upbringing of the girl are entitled to share in it. Her immediate family receives both valuables and pork but cannot consume the pork themselves. To do so would be equated with eating the flesh of their own daughter or sister. This symbolic taboo on the consumption of the wedding pork has a counterpart in another realm; in this cannibal society the parents and siblings of a girl are not permitted to consume her flesh, though other close kin may do so.

As is common in the New Guinea highlands, bride price has been inflated by the influx of trade goods and money into the area. Nowadays the amount that the bride's family will accept is a subject of protracted negotiations. The amount demanded and finally paid does not appear to vary significantly with the relationship or absence of relationship between the two families; it is the same whether the couple are actual cross-cousins or unrelated persons. The rare instances of sister-exchange between unrelated families also require bride price; this may have the effect of allowing those concerned to regard each match as a more or less independent union.

B. Marriage rates

All Fore, except physical and mental misfits, expected to marry at some time during their lives, until *kuru* caused a shortage of women in the last three decades. As we have seen, parents often betrothed their daughters at birth or during early childhood, and a bride went to live with the groom's mother when she was nine or ten years old. A man, however, was not considered old enough to marry until signs of his physical maturity, such as the growth of facial and body hair, were visible. In addition, he was expected to prove his virility and courage by slaying an enemy in war. Few men acquired wives before they were twenty-three or twenty-four. Today, with the elimination of warfare and the shortage of girls, a man marries earlier, if he and his parents can find a willing bride.

By the 1960's, because of the impact of *kuru*, a man's prospects of finding a wife had become rather dim. Now fully 62 per cent of the South Fore population are male (Table 3), and for every girl who

Table 3. AGE AND SEX DISTRIBUTION IN SOUTH FORE AND THE MARITAL STATUS OF MALES IN 1962

Birth cohort	Males (by number of extant wives)					Females	Totals	Sex ratio
	0	1	2	3	All			
Pre–1900	38	21	1	1	61	27	88	2.26
1900–1904	36	19	1	1	57	29	86	1.96
1905–1909	40	21			61	12	73	5.07
1910–1914	81	64	3		148	46	194	3.21
1915–1919	141	119	7		267	83	350	3.21
1920–1924	120	161	12		293	121	414	2.42
1925–1929	136	251	15		402	158	560	2.57
1930–1934	102	146	10		258	215	473	1.20
1935–1939	193	163	3		359	194	553	1.85
1940–1944	378	80			458	163	621	2.81
1945–1949	479	4			483	266	749	1.83
1950–1954	664				664	521	1185	1.27
1955–1959	621				621	579	1200	1.07
1960–1962	354				354	324	678	1.09
Totals	3383	1049	52	2	4486	2738	7224	

reaches puberty, the minimum age of marriage imposed by the Administration, two potential husbands are available, not counting those married men who still aspire to polygyny. Thus, many Fore men may be condemned to permanent bachelorhood, a condition which Oosterwal (1959) and Bowers (1965) have reported elsewhere in New Guinea.

The majority of South Fore men are now without wives, and only

2.3 per cent have succeeded in maintaining the once coveted status of polygynist (Table 3). Of the 1,180 females over the age of fifteen in South Fore (in 1962), all but seventy-eight married. Of the unmarried, seventy-one are widows, of whom forty-five are past the age of menopause and are unlikely to wed again. Most of the younger widows are recently bereaved and will eventually remarry. Only six women in the total population have never married, of whom three are congenital defectives.

Men are not sanguine about finding wives outside South Fore territory, the high incidence area for *kuru*. Few North Fore or non-Fore are willing to expose their daughters to the risks of *kuru* sorcery. The Fore are well aware of the shortage of women and have, at public meetings, repeatedly urged all sorcerers to cease their activities. Every man who succeeds in finding a bride knows that his marriage is likely to be brief, and marriage payments most often include a mortuary settlement at the same time.

The norms of individual marital experience are illustrated in the histories of 207 living persons of all ages who have married at least once. The sample contains 137 males and 70 females. This group has contracted 315 marriages, a mean of 1.5 matches per person with no significant difference according to sex. These findings confirm the previously reported results of Glasse [Lindenbaum] (1964) based on a smaller sample. Twenty-three persons have been divorced 23 times, the women accounting for thirteen of these marital dissolutions. According to Barnes' method of computation (1949, 1967), the following divorce ratios are obtained in Table 4, which also shows the proportion of marriages ended by death of a spouse.

The figures in Table 4 indicate the impact of *kuru* on the South Fore population. Death from *kuru* overshadows divorce so greatly in terminating marriages, that the interpretation of divorce ratios is difficult and comparision with *kuru*-free societies may be meaningless. What seems clear, however, is that marriages today are fairly stable, probably because women are highly valued due to their scarcity and wives have more to say in the choice of husbands. The missions and administration support and encourage matches that have been freely made. Furthermore, a dissatisfied wife hesitates to leave her husband and risk retaliation by sorcery. If marriages were not so often terminated by *kuru*, the divorce ratio would probably be considerably higher. Thus, in part the figures in Table 4 reflect the short duration of marriage as well as the frequency of dissolution.

Table 4. SOUTH FORE MARRIAGE DISSOLUTION RATIOS, 1962

	Men	*Women*
A. Number of marriages ended in divorce expressed as a per cent of all marriages	4.7%	7.8%
B. Number of marriages ended in divorce expressed as a per cent of all marriages that have been completed by death or divorce	6.9	45.0
C. Number of marriages ended in divorce expressed as a per cent of all marriages except those ended by death	12.7	15.1
D. Number of marriages ended by death expressed as a per cent of all marriages	63.0	15.0
E. Number of marriages ended by death expressed as a per cent of all marriages that have been completed by death or divorce	93.0	55.0
F. Number of marriages ended by death expressed as a per cent of all marriages except those ended by divorce	67.0	18.0
G. Number of marriages ended by *kuru* death expressed as a per cent of all marriages	57.0	0

C. Marriage restrictions

The Fore do not allow marriage between those they regard as sharing "one blood." However, they have no precise theory about how blood is shared and with whom. When pressed to explain why FZD is classed as "one blood" but MBD is not, they fall back on the authority of the ancestors. Thus, all patrilateral cousins and matrilateral parallel cousins have the same blood and so should not wed. People who live close together, though not connected by genealogy in any way, are also ineligible as partners; behaving towards a girl as if she were a "sister" is sufficient to bar her as a spouse. The South Fore do not encourage matches with girls from enemy clans, unless the union is intended as a peacemaking gesture. Hostility between clans is not necessarily permanent, however, and most neighboring clan-parishes have at some time had affinal relations with one or another clan-segments of their current enemies.

The Fore express marriage restrictions in terms of lineage member-ship and also in kinship categories. Thus a man should not wed a girl who belongs to:

1. his own lineage or subclan, whichever is the exogamous unit;
2. a collateral lineage or subclan of the same clan regarded as a "sibling" group;
3. a lineage of subclan that traditionally receives brides from his own.

In kinship categories, the following list of relatives are forbidden partners:

a.	*nano*	M, Step-M, Fco-W, MZ, FBW
b.	*alaganto*	Z, Step-Z, half-Z, FBD, MSD
c.	*alaga*	D, Step-D, MZDD, MZSD
d.	*namamu*	FZ
e.	*nanonei*	MZD, MBDD
f.	*nokai*	WZ
g.	*aronempa*	MM, FM
h.	*nosu, nanatu*	gBW
i.	*nani*	lBW
j.	*aintai*	WM (other than MBW)

The South Fore appear to observe these restrictions fairly closely. It is difficult to estimate the actual rate of observance, for they so manipulate their kinship system that after a few years breach marriages are likely to be forgotten or simply regarded as normal matches. A person who has been assimilated into a lineage need not observe its specific prohibitions in relation to other lineages. If he becomes a member as an adult, the group may well allow him to wed one of their sisters or daughters, thereby buttressing his position in the group with affinal ties. However, if he joins the lineage as a child, the girls of the lineage itself would be forbidden to him, because they have treated him as a "brother."

One means of evading the marriage restrictions, or rather changing them, is illustrated in the following example:

Some years ago, the Luluai (administration-appointed headman) of Wanitabe clan was anxious to find a new wife after the death of his previous one. He made overtures to several lineages where he had marriageable kin, but no girls were then available. Thwarted, he decided to engineer a partition of his own subclan (an exogamous unit) to form two new lineages. First he sought and found a justification for a possible split in genealogy. The subclan founder had had two wives and without contradicting the principle of descent, the descendants of each could be regarded as independent lineages. He then had to persuade members of the subclan that segmentation was desirable. It would allow the establishment of connubial relations between the new segments, thereby reserving women for the subclan at a time when brides were becoming scarce. The members concurred with this arrangement, and the Luluai wed a girl of the new collateral lineage.

The negative regulations of marriage among the South Fore are not unusual in the New Guinea highlands. But their positive regulations, or "preferences" are uncommon and deserve a more detailed examination.

D. Marriage "preferences"

To the question "Whom do you marry?" the South Fore consistently respond in roughly the following terms:

> We marry our *nebantos*, the daughters of our *anagus;* we send them food and they give us their daughters in return. If we cannot find an *anagu* who will give up his daughter, then we wed *togina* (unrelated women).

To interpret this statement, first it is necessary to make clear how the Fore use *nebanto* and *anagu*, and then to explain the extent of their preferential interest in *nebanto*. For convenience, the discussion will center on male Ego.

The Fore refer to MB as *anagu* and to MBD and FZD as *nebanto*. As mentioned earlier, FZD is not marriageable in South Fore, and hence this reference of the term is not relevant in this context. *Anagu* also applies to classificatory MB, and *nebanto* to real and classificatory FMBD and MBSD. The latter kin types may be regarded as extensions of MBD, up and down one generation respectively. In other words, Ego calls his father's female cross-cousin and his own male cross-cousin's daughter on the matrilateral side *nebanto*. Also he uses this term for certain fictive (*kagisa*) kin and for the daughter of his MB's age-mates (*nagaiya*). Both of these categories require further discussion.

A literal meaning for *kagisa* was difficult to discover, for Fore often use it in a metaphorical sense, particularly in the context of kinship. The best translation seems to be "time when the sun is directly overhead," meaning the hot, bright midday period or early afternoon. In the kinship realm *kagisa* denotes a category of genealogically unrelated people who are treated as if they were consanguines. To distinguish them from genealogical kin, they may be called fictive kin. They differ from adopted kin; the Fore do adopt orphans and sometimes conceal from the children the fact that they are not true offspring. No such subterfuge is necessary for *kagisa* kin; *kagisa* relationships are valid in their own right. Clearly it would be a mistake here to identify Fore kinship exclusively with genealogical relatedness. It is better to view kinship as a broader spectrum of relatedness in which genealogical connection, actual or putative, is one important element. Then *kagisa* relations would have a place under this wider rubric of relations of solidarity and reciprocity. For the Fore, of course, there is nothing "fictional" about *kagisa* relationships, they are just as real as those based on genealogical ties. That *kagisa* kin refer to one another by kin terms is a matter of convenience for the Fore. Since the behavior of fictive kin closely resembles that of genealogical kin there is no need for a separate nomenclature.

From this standpoint, the symbolism of *kagisa* may be interpreted. The "time when the sun is overhead" is the time when people gather to prepare communal meals. Kinship in the broader sense suggested here implies commensality and reciprocity. Consequently, the term may refer to the origin of the relationship, a common meal at which the relationship is founded. Two examples will indicate some of the ways that fictive kin are recruited:

1. A boy, Kisopa, lived far from the clan-territory of his MB; because of the length of the journey, the MB was an infrequent visitor to the territory of his ZS and hence could not fulfil his avuncular role towards the boy. To make up for this, the MB asked a friend who lived near Kisopa to take over his obligations to the boy. The friend agreed to do so, and later became a fictive MB to the boy by sharing a common meal with his family.

2. Following the defeat of his clan, a man and his son took refuge with a friendly clan. Neither of the refugees was genealogically connected with the host clan, but, as they decided to stay for some time, their hosts gave them the right to use a portion of clan land. The sister of the host gave the pair a gift of food and agreed to become a *kagisa* "sister" to the man. Later the younger sisters of this woman followed suit and also became fictive kin.

Fictive kinship is of great importance in Fore society, though a full discussion is beyond the scope of this paper. The important point here is that everyone in South Fore has a number of fictive kin, both male and female, and that these relationships are just as important to the people as those founded on genealogical connection.

Age-mates (*nagaiya*) too may be included under the broader rubric of kinship mentioned above. Two or more people are age-mates if they were born on the same day or, by extension, within several days of each other. Alternatively, men initiated during the same time period are also *nagaiya*. They may at the same time be genealogical or fictive kin. The crucial point about age-mates in the present context is that Ego has a "preference" to wed not only the daughters of his MB's but also of his MB's age-mates. Thus, both fictive kin and age-mate relations are avenues for the recruitment of wives in South Fore. Obviously it makes little sense to classify a system with options such as these as a "matrilateral cross-cousin marriage."

How frequently do "preferential" matches occur in comparison with other matches? At present only a crude answer can be given, for further analysis is needed. Rough tabulations suggest, however, that the rate of "preferential" marriage varies from place to place and from time to time. The broad trends are indicated in Table 5, which includes marriages during the past fifty years in both dialect areas of South Fore.

Table 5. THE INCIDENCE OF "PREFERRED" MARRIAGE IN SOUTH FORE

Marriage type	Number	Per Cent
"Preferred":		
Man with His "True" MBD	159	24.8%
Man with His "Classificatory" MBD	124	19.3
Man with His "True" and "Classificatory" FMBD	37	5.8
All "Preferred"	320	49.9
Other Marriages (i.e., Non-Kin)	321	50.1
Totals	621	100

Half of all marriages in this sample were with girls listed as "preferred" spouses, and within this category matches with "kin" described as "true" MBD represent about fifty per cent of the total. To interpret these figures, a description of how they were collected is necessary. One of the major aims of fieldwork was to record unusually large numbers of genealogies for use in the genetical analysis of *kuru*. As there was little hope of learning Fore in the nine months initially available for research, pidgin-speaking South Fore interpreters were employed and were impressed with the importance of distinguishing between actual and classificatory kin and of determining the precise relationships between husbands and wives. The Fore do not ordinarily find it necessary to distinguish in their conversations between actual and classificatory kin. Nevertheless the interpreters had little diffi-

culty in eliciting this information, and checks several months later
revealed fairly consistent results. Of course reliable data are not
necessarily accurate. When the genealogies were assembled, it became
apparent that classificatory and *kagisa* kin were often listed as "true"
MBD, both by informants and interpreters. Even the daughters of
MB's age-mates were sometimes counted this way. Frequently, informants could not trace their connection to classificatory kin, yet
clearly considered the relationships to be important. Given these
ambiguities, what significance, if any, can be attached to the figures
in Table 5?

The consistency of their responses suggests that the South Fore do
have categories in mind when they respond to questions about the
nature of the kin ties with their spouses. They do distinguish between
"true" and "tenuous" relationships, but their distinction refers to the
importance and solidarity of the bond and not necessarily to its
genealogical closeness. In the nature of things, "true" relationships
often turn out to be those with close genealogical kin but they are
not restricted to that category, and not all close kin are counted as
"true" relatives. Sometimes *kagisa* kin are more important to a person
than are genealogical kin, and so with good reason a man may refer
to his *kagisa anagu* as his "true" MB. That the South Fore express
their norms of solidarity and potential affinity in the idiom of kin
terms, is confusing only if kinship is equated with genealogical relatedness. Like most New Guinea highlanders, the South Fore are
pragmatists. *Anagu* does not simply mean "mother's brother," though
it includes this connotation; it means rather "person to whom I give
and who reciprocates." The "true" *anagu* is the most reliable of all
anagus. The "small" *anagu* is less dependable and less committed as a
potential wife-giver, even if he is nearer kin. When a man weds the
daughter of an unrelated man (*togina*), the reciprocity and solidarity
in the relationship come after and not before the wedding.

The figures in Table 5 now appear in a new light. What they suggest is that a quarter of all marriages take place between families that
have well-established reciprocal exchange relations before the match
is made. In the past many of these unions were based on infant betrothal. Many no doubt involve actual matrilateral cross-cousins. This
of course is expected in a society where sibling ties are exceptionally
strong. But this category also may include *kagisa* and classificatory
kin, as well as families linked through an age-mate relationship between the brothers-in-law. In the same vein, classificatory MBD and

FMBD in Table 6 really represent unions based on a tenuous exchange relationship before the marriage. Matches with non-kin are those in which no exchange relationship preceded the wedding.

Regional and temporal fluctuations in marriage "preference" rates assume new importance when seen from this perspective. There are good grounds for suspecting, for instance, that ecological factors, such as regional differences in food production, may encourage or inhibit the development of inter-family reciprocity upon which "preferred" marriages depend. One might also predict that factors such as differential population density, or residence in a central, as opposed to a fringe area, play an important role in creating differences in the incidence.

MARRIAGE AND RECIPROCITY

The argument so far has partly followed a negative course. It has been suggested:

1. that the ostensible norms of marital preference in South Fore in fact obscure the channel of affinity that runs beneath them; and

2. that kin term usage hides the fact that finding a wife depends ultimately on reciprocal exchange between the families involved.

The ideological basis for reciprocity stems from the sentimental and jural bonds between a brother and a sister. The converse is also true: persons of opposite sex who make gifts to one another come to regard each other as "siblings," thereby justifying their relationship to the world at large. A "sister" ought to provide food for her "brother" and he in return should supply her with material goods, such as salt, arm bands, and other adornments. Nowadays, he also gives her a spade, clothing, soap, tinned meat, and tradestore beads. As mentioned earlier, men create *kagisa* or fictive relationships where they lack genealogical kin, and such relationships may in the course of time equal or surpass in importance those based upon consanguinity. We have seen how a "brother" and a "sister" may betroth their children. If the marriage is to take place, however, the two families concerned must continue to exchange gifts until the wedding. Generally, food passes from the boy's family to the girl's, and this is reciprocated with material goods, such as cowrie shells, and salt, and sometimes pork. The exchanges take place in the context of general reciprocity, though certain prestations require a formal response. For example, when a boy is initiated (at the age of about eight or nine), his father makes a large payment of pigs and other gifts to the boy's MB. This is called *yona,* and the recipient should reply with a gift of cowrie shell and other material goods to the father of the boy (*kota-potei*). Failure to send *yona* to the MB weakens the relationship, and for this reason the MB may refuse to give his daughter to the boy.

Though it legitimitizes marriage, bride price should be regarded as only one link in the chain of reciprocity. In the past, the wedding usually took place before the girl's first menstruation and the match was not immediately consummated. This called for a special meal given by the groom's family to that of the bride (*ti ena*), which the latter reciprocated with cowrie shell or other goods. Later when the bride became pregnant, her husband and his brothers hunted for wild game which they sent to the bride's family. This again was recipro-cated with cowrie shell or other valuables. The birth of a child called for yet another exchange, first by the husband and his family, and then by the wife's group. In addition, small prestations were given whenever affines visited one another. When a woman died, her husband formerly made a large mortuary payment to her kin group. This practice is declining, for so many brides die from *kuru* within a few years of marriage that the groom's family now secure an agree-ment to dispense with this payment when the bride price is nego-tiated. The death of a wife does not stop the flow of prestations, for the husband still has an interest in preserving the relationship to ensure his son a future bride. When a man dies, his MB, who is also in many instances his WF, is entitled to both a large mortuary pay-ment and to the body of the dead man, for possible cannibal consump-tion. Thus the chain of reciprocity that first unites "brother" and "sister" later extends to their children of opposite sex who may eventually marry, thereby linking their families in continuous ex-changes. Much the same process occurs when a couple are not *nebanto* before the wedding; reciprocity commences with the payment of bride price and continues with the bride's first menstruation, the delivery of her child, and her or her husband's death.

CONCLUSION

This paper has not been concerned with the specific pattern of alliance created by marriage in South Fore, but rather with the concepts and perspective necessary to elucidate that pattern. In this sense it is a preliminary study which I intend to continue elsewhere. Though the marriage pattern has not been considered in detail, I should like to raise three issues that relate to the anthropologist's conception of that pattern. These may be relevant to other societies too.

1. An ethnographer versed in the controversy over the causes of "matrilateral cross-cousin marriage" might be tempted to conclude after studying the South Fore data that the system should be classed as one of "preferential asymmetrical alliance." I myself once saw the system from this standpoint, but the more one examines genealogies and marital histories the more it becomes clear that marriages do not often take place between male Ego and his actual MBD. As we have seen, the exact rate is difficult to calculate, for the South Fore also count as "true" cross-cousins persons the anthropologist describes as classificatory and fictive kin. I hope to show elsewhere that, as in other parts of the highlands, marriages are not confined to a small number of wife-receiving lineages but are dispersed among many scattered exogamous groups. Despite the fact that the Fore speak of interlineage relations as unidirectional avenues for the recruitment of wives, the actual data do not support this view. "Mother's brothers" can be found in many lineages, and where they do not exist there are processes for "creating" them. From this standpoint it is difficult to attach significance to the concept of marriage "preference." I suggest that the so-called "preference" is no more than the expectation of marriage arising in a reciprocal relationship entailing long-term property exchanges in both directions. In this respect it is noteworthy that there is little, if any, difference in the character of affinal relations whether or not the couple regarded each other as "preferred kin" before the union.

2. We have seen that "preferential" marriage does not entail any diminution of the bride price in comparison with other unions. Is it not a paradox that there is no encouragement by society to conform to the "ideal"? The paradox vanishes when we view "preferential" matches simply as unions that take place within the context of an enduring exchange relationship. However a bride may be acquired, she is equally valuable to her husband, and it makes sense to recognize this when negotiating bride price. The man in an exchange relationship has a greater assurance of marrying the daughter of his partner (i.e., his *anagu*) than one who is not, but the wife he acquires is no more valuable than a spouse obtained without such a preexisting relationship. In any event, as we have seen, his affinal connections will be of much the same character.

3. Finally, I believe the discussion sheds some light on the relation

between kinship and reciprocity in New Guinea. In Melanesia, generally, I believe it can be shown that kinship ultimately rests on the principle of reciprocity, a conclusion valid in many parts of the world. In New Guinea, those who behave towards one another in a positive, reciprocal manner regard each other as kin, whether or not they are known or believed to be genealogically connected. By the same token, in New Guinea distinctions of status based upon descent are of limited relevance to group recruitment. Once a man demonstrates his loyalty to a group by appropriate acts and participation in corporate affairs he belongs to the group in a full sense. The other members care little whether he is an agnate, a cognate, or even an unrelated man. They take pains neither to conceal his "foreign" origin or to discriminate against him because of it. This may be one reason why unilineal models have limited usefulness in explaining New Guinea highlands data.

Marriage in
BENA BENA[1]

L. L. Langness

SOCIAL ORGANIZATION

The Bena Bena-speaking peoples, of whom there are approximately 14,000, live to the east of the town of Goroka in the eastern highlands of New Guinea. There are some sixty-five named "tribes," formerly autonomous but now united by the Bena Council (Langness, 1963). Each tribe comprises two to five exogamous patrilineal clans which occupy adjacent ridge tops within well-defined territories. Clans of the same tribe formerly aided one another in warfare, sometimes initiated their youths together, and cooperated in pig exchanges with other tribes; otherwise, clans are autonomous and are the most significant permanent units of Bena Bena social structure. The members of each named clan claim descent from a common, named ancestor, although precise genealogical connections are unknown. Tribesmen have no belief in a common ancestor, the constituent clans residing together, they say, "because our ancestors did."

Bena Bena clans include subclans and lineages. Members of a subclan assert descent from a named son of the clan founder, although again with no genealogical precision. Each subclan comprises several small lineages in which genealogical knowledge is precise. Both subclans and lineages are referred to by the name of the eldest surviving male member. Members of subclans and lineages tend to aid one another but there are exceptions. Subclans function most importantly with respect to marriage, funerals, and certain religious activities; lineages deal mainly with domestic tasks.[2]

[1] The field work upon which this paper is based was conducted during the period January 1, 1961–May 15, 1962, at which time I held a Predoctoral Fellowship and Supplemental Research Grant (No. M-4377) from the National Institute of Mental Health, United States Public Health Service. Their generosity is gratefully acknowledged.
[2] I use the idiom of lineage and clan advisedly and for want of a better language. The units of social structure outlined here bear only superficial resemblance to lineages and clans as they are usually described (Langness, 1964).

Korofeigu, the tribe with which I worked, consists of four clans occupying adjacent territories. Nupasafa clan, the second largest, has 232 members in five subclans which have from three to six lineages each. The Nupasafans today reside in three villages although formerly they lived in one stockaded village. Each village has one men's house and a separate house for each married woman where she, her children, and the pigs sleep. Generally, men of one subclan occupy the same house, and women's houses tend to cluster by subclan affiliations; but there are exceptions.

My discussion of marriage is based upon data from Nupasafa clan, supplemented by observations of some other clans. Although it cannot be generalized to all Bena Bena, it is valid for those who inhabit grasslands rather than "bush."

The Nupasafans are horticulturalists and pig raisers. Unlike many groups farther to the west, they have never fought over land. New gardens are cut in uncultivated clan grasslands, and tilling establishes individual ownership. People may graze pigs freely on uncultivated ground. Gardens are extensive; men do the fencing, while women, also working in groups, till the ground. Women plant sweet potatoes (the staple), tapioc, corn, and a variety of greens; men plant only sugar cane, yams, and bananas. Garden preparation intensifies just prior to the summer wet season. Hunting is unimportant.

Associated with the residential separation of the sexes are many beliefs about the polluting nature of women and sanctions designed to reduce contact between males and females. These mainly concern menstruation and childbirth.[3] Male superiority is a theme continually stressed as children mature. Boys, although continuing to sleep in the women's houses, withdraw from women and girls and spend most of their time with age-mates. At approximately five years of age they undergo the first of the male initiation rites; they have their ears pierced and are feasted with pork. About three years later their septums are pierced. More and more they imitate their fathers and brothers in the male tasks they will later perform; and they clearly perceive the inferior status of females. During the final initiation period, when the youths are from fourteen to eighteen years of age, they are secluded for at least one month. Their food is prepared exclusively by males, and they are ritually cleansed of the pollution of female contact by letting blood from the urethra, tongue, and nostrils and by vomiting. No male who has recently copulated can take part in the initiation ceremony.

[3] See Langness (1965, 1967) for more detailed accounts.

The sacred bamboo flutes from the men's house are played in pairs during the proceedings. They represent not only the ancestors and ancestral power but also the voice of *nama,* a mythical bird-like demon who is believed to be controlled by, and to reside with, the men at this time. The emphasis is clearly upon male superiority and solidarity, and the youths are impressed with the importance of the age-mate bonds that are formed for life by the initiation. Although women may not participate in the ceremonies, at least once during the period they attack the men and youths with sticks and stones. This is not merely mock attack; and, if a man is injured, his age-mates shoot an arrow into the thigh of the offending woman. This ritual expresses both the antagonism existing between males and females and the significance of the age-mate bond and male solidarity. There is, however, a contradiction in male initiation. Although the youths are continually told of male superiority and the uncleanliness of women, they are also taught love magic and learn that the greatest good is to be married and have many children.

After initiation, the youths, handsomely dressed for the first time as adults, dramatically return to the village for a feast. They are still not considered adult, however; this comes only after marriage, having children, and entering into pig exchanges. For a time the youths roam at will, courting, trying to entice women, stealing pigs and, formerly, raiding. During this time their fathers begin to purchase brides for them.[4]

MARRIAGE ARRANGEMENTS

A man decides, in consultation with others, that it is time to find a bride for his son and that they have enough pigs and money for the core of the bride price. He then announces his intentions so that other members of the clan may contribute. Marriage is fundamentally a subclan responsibility; but, even if a subclan could by itself buy a bride, it would be improper to do so. Raising a bride price should be a clan-wide enterprise. Once this bride price is collected and the quest for a bride begun, the father of another age-mate follows suit. He need not wait until the first man is successful. If the father of a youth is

---

[4] I use the term "purchase" deliberately as the acquisition of wives is essentially a commercial transaction and is regarded by the Bena themselves as such. Pigs, shells, and other valuables are exchanged for brides, in addition to the exchange of pork that accompanies a wedding, and with no expectation that the wealth will be returned in kind or in total at any later date.

not prepared to act, another man may substitute for him. Of forty-three cases known to me, thirty-five brides were chosen by either the "true" father of the youth, the father's brother, or another man of his subclan; in six cases brides were acquired for youths by other clansmen and in two by men of other clans who helped to rear the boys in question.

Table 1. Affiliations of Korofeigu Contributors to Bride Price (*Number of Contributors*)

	Money			Pigs			Shells			
	Sub-clan	Clan	Other	Sub-clan	Clan	Other	Sub-clan	Clan	Other	Total[a]
Example A	2	8	1	4	4	—	2	7	2	26
Example B	4	21	15	4	9	2	3	7	10	65

[a] These totals do not square with the figures across the columns because in some cases an individual contributed in more than one category. Likewise, the figures do not represent numbers of pigs or shells given; one contributor might contribute more than one item of the same kind.

The examples in Table 1 represent two extremes of the cases I witnessed. In example A, a man acquired a bride for his eldest brother's son because his eldest brother had bought *his* bride and he was thus repaying an obligation. The subclan, represented by only two brothers, furnished 86 per cent of the money (50 of 58 Australian pounds); the remainder came from 8 other clan members and one from a different clan. The subclan also gave 80 per cent of the pigs (17 out of 21) and 18 per cent of the shell (2 items out of 11). In fact this subclan could easily have provided everything but deliberately did not do so lest it make an unfavorable impression.

Example B is more complex. A man desired a bride for his son. He had a dual affiliation in that his second wife resided with another Korofeigu clan and he divided his time between the two places. His subclan did not possess enough money to make up the bride price easily but finally offered 60 per cent (twenty-five out of forty-two pounds); the remainder came from small contributions by other members of Nupasafa and of the clan where his second wife resided. Friendly members of the other two clans of Korofeigu made minor gifts. The subclan put up 52 per cent of the pigs (twelve of twenty-three) and approximately 15 per cent of the shell (three of twenty items).

It should be made clear that not all of the pigs listed were given as bride price. Bride price is paid in live pigs. In example A, ten pigs were given for this purpose, four were killed and presented to the bride's clan, and seven were killed and distributed among the groom's clan for the help given. In example B, thirteen pigs were given as bride price, five were killed and presented to those who had contributed money and shell, and five were exchanged with the bride's clan. The pork given to the bride's clan demands exact repayment at the wedding ceremony.

A girl's father is not in charge of negotiations for her marriage. The people explain this custom by saying, "it is wrong for a man to take pay for his own semen." Thus, every Bena Bena girl is adopted in infancy by a man who becomes responsible for her initiation ceremonies and, finally, her marriage. For this he receives most of her bride price; the rest goes mainly to her brothers. The adoptive fathers give their charges pork and shell from time to time and, in general, act in a benevolent manner. Of fifty-six girls I inquired about, twenty-one were adopted by members of their own subclan, twenty-nine by members of their clan, and six by men outside the clan.

Girls have less liberty than boys and must work much harder. Small girls follow their mothers and learn to cultivate sweet potatoes, to care for pigs, to make net bags, and all the other female tasks. There are no formal age grades for girls. Not until after a girl's first menstruation, with its ritual and month-long seclusion, does she enjoy any great leisure. Then she joins with other adolescent girls, traveling to clans nearby for courting parties and doing virtually no work at all.

COURTING AND PRELIMINARIES TO MARRIAGE

Bena Bena courting is relatively uninhibited. Formal courting parties, held in the men's houses, occur about once a month, when unmarried girls and both married and unmarried young men from one clan visit another clan. The girls of each clan lie down along opposite sides of the house and call out for partners from the young men. There are always more men than girls. The men chosen lie alongside the girls and all begin to sing. The fire eventually dies and the courting becomes more ardent. Although girls are warned not to engage in intercourse, everyone is aware that it happens; however, nobody believes that one act of intercourse can result in pregnancy. Surprisingly few girls get pregnant; and, if they do, it constitutes only a temporary frustration for their legal guardians. A pregnancy simply postpones plans for marriage. The bastard is raised by the girl's parents as her sibling and she later marries as if nothing had happened. Indeed, the proof of her fertility can make her more desirable, although this fact is seldom brought up in the negotiations for marriage.

Courting has little direct bearing on marriage, for neither boys nor girls are consulted about their marriages. When the bride price is displayed in front of the house of the guardian's wife, there is much speculation as to whether or not he will ultimately accept it. A bride price is never accepted the first time it is offered, and the girl's relatives have standardized ways of indicating interest or disinterest. If they are totally uninterested, they simply ignore the waiting men, who quickly leave. If, on the other hand, the hosts are somewhat interested, they bring fire to warm the men while they discuss what to do. An offer of tobacco is a more encouraging sign, whereas a gift of food is virtually an indication of eventual acceptance. If there are positive signs the bride price is displayed again and again. Indeed, it may be put out serially in several promising places until accepted. For example, a bride price first offered on August 7, 1961 was put out thirteen times at ten different places until acceptance on October 10, 1961. When one bride price was accepted within one month, people remarked how quickly it had been accepted and attributed this to the fact that a powerful and prestigious subclan was concerned. Also involved, however, were a very generous bride price and the promise of a specific girl in return.

Brides are rarely promised in exchange; when they are, the promise is not always kept. The original marriage may not endure, the two groups may be enemies when the promised girl reaches marriageable age, or, if the debtor clansmen are strong enough, they may simply refuse to keep their word. Nevertheless, a marriage always involves some expectations that the groom's clan will later consider a request for a bride.

Obviously, Bena Bena have no strong marriage preferences and avoidances. Moreover, marriages are widely dispersed. Thus, a sample of sixty wives of Nupa men represent twenty-four different tribal groups and thirty-five clans. There are no more than five wives from any one tribe except in the case of the other three clans of Korofeigu itself (from which there are fourteen wives: six from Nagamitobo, five from Benimeto and three from Wai'atagusa). Likewise, of twenty-four

Nupa women married out, there are no more than three in any place (tribe or clan) except in the other three Korofeigu clans, in which there are nine (three in each), and the marriages are spread out in ten tribal groups and fourteen different clans.

The rules for marriage specify only that one cannot marry into his own clan or into the subclan of his mother. In practice this is more complicated because residence is important. Thus an adopted child cannot marry into the family, lineage, subclan, or clan in which he or she is adopted; anyone who has been incorporated into a clan as a refugee, and who expresses his intention of remaining permanently, cannot marry into that clan; and people who were reared in one clan and who later reside in another, cannot marry into either. Furthermore, there are two clans with which the Nupa will not marry at all, because some members of the Nupa resided with them for a time and now regard them as siblings.

When a bride is found, preparations are made for the wedding. A day is agreed upon, pork in the specified amount is cooked, and a path of flowers is laid the length of the groom's village. The bride's clan arrive *en masse* at one end of the village, with the bride hidden in their midst. A man, usually the bride's guardian, makes a speech emphasizing the ties that are being formed, the fact that now the two clans should not fight, that the bride will work and bear children. The groom's father or a close agnate replies and then walks the path of flowers to receive the bride. The bride's clan suddenly opens ranks to reveal her. She is covered with pig fat, has her face painted, and wears a headdress and a new skirt. Suspended from her shoulders and waist are pieces of pork. The groom's spokesman carries her along the path and places her in front of pork specially cooked for her, her mother, and anyone else mourning her departure. The women of the groom's clan rush forward, untie the pork suspended from her and seat her among the men. Men of both clans now exchange pork, sweet potatoes are distributed to be eaten on the spot, and the two clans sit at opposite ends of the village. The bride, assisted by her brothers, walks among the women of the groom's clan and hands each one a piece of pork. The bride's clan soon depart with their pork, leaving behind the bride and her mother or her guardian to stay with her until she has settled down and is unlikely to run away.

Neither the groom nor any of his age-mates attends the ceremony for they should not see the bride. Bride and groom can have no contact until all the youths of that age grade have married. Thus a series of ceremonies of the kind described takes place and then, when all have secured brides, another ceremony is held in which the grooms take food from the hands of their respective brides and are then properly wed.

MARRIAGE

Brides who were purchased earliest have a considerable wait until they can live with their husbands; the avoidance period may last from one or two months to as long as two or three years. During this time brides are not permitted any sexual relations and cannot attend courting ceremonies. Their husbands, however, continue courting. Given the period of premarital liberty that girls enjoy and the fact that they do not want to marry against their will and leave their natal groups, it is not surprising that many brides attempt to abscond. I estimate that between 35 to 50 per cent of them attempt to escape at least once. A runaway bride does not return to her own group because if her people had wanted her to stay, they would not have accepted the bride price. She usually goes to some young man she has met at a courting party and asks him to marry her. The groom's father and kinsmen bring her back, sometimes forcibly but, if the girl is strong-willed, she continues to run away until the men are forced to concede. They recover the original bride price and new arrangements are made. The young man whom a girl runs to encourages her whether he wants her as wife or not, for this brings him prestige. He may even marry the girl, usually for a reduced bride price, and everyone has to make the best of things.

Sometimes a bride engages in sexual relations with a father, brother, or other clansmen of the groom. Four such cases are known within the Nupasafa clan and three cases are reported for other clans nearby. In these situations the girl is blamed and the bride price is recovered. Although this kind of adultery is morally condemned, it causes little overt hostility between clansmen or between fathers and sons. Men must act as though women are unimportant.

A bride is well treated during her first few weeks in the village and is expected to do no work "until her new skirt is dirty." On the morning following her wedding she receives presents and meets the members of her husband's clan. Her father-in-law and sometimes other men give her sows to raise for her husband. Others give her bean seed, tubes of pig fat, tobacco, knives, and pots. She also receives a new name, for the name given her by her own clansmen is taboo to her husband's clan. During this time she resides with her mother-in-law and accompanies the women to their gardens, where she performs minor tasks such as fetching water.

At this time the groom's father calls on his clansmen to help prepare a "marriage garden" that will belong to his son and will be tended by the bride. Marriage gardens are larger than others and have a special name, but like all gardens are a communal enterprise. By the time the garden is fenced, tilled, and planted, almost everyone in the clan has helped in some way. When the garden bears, plots are assigned to all who contributed to the bride price or helped in the gardening. The recipients may dig the mature sweet potatoes once; then the plot is replanted and belongs exclusively to the new husband and wife. As a garden may be planted for three or four years in succession, the gift of a marriage garden gets the young couple off to a good start.

During this time the young husbands do not help in any way. They spend their time courting, hunting, playing cards, and wandering around. Formerly they also went raiding. After the final wedding ceremony older people urge the young married men to settle down into adult activities. They are told to build houses for their wives and to begin gardening and raising pigs, for they now have to help others buy brides and to enter into pig exchanges with relatives and with other groups—activities which bring prestige, indicate adult status, and, if diligently pursued, give a man a "name." Some men accept these responsibilities easily, but many resist and neglect their wives, their gardens, and their pigs. Some find that they dislike their wives and attempt to get new ones. In effect, sociological adulthood comes late for men, usually after they have one or two children, at the point when they cease to attract girls during courting, and after a great deal of nagging by the older men (Langness, 1965).

There are deviations from the typical marriage pattern. Some brides are purchased before their first menstruation, occasionally when only eight or ten years of age. Roughly 15 per cent of Nupa marriages involve prepubertal girls (11 out of 73 known cases). The child is purchased without ceremony and brought to live with her affines. Usually such brides are acquired for the remaining youths in the age grade. Interestingly, although Korofeigans purchase young brides, they do not offer their own preadolescent girls for marriage and they disparage people who do so. This follows, I believe, from the greater wealth in pigs of the Korofeigans. Young brides come from "bush" villages where pigs are scarce.

If a man is wealthy enough to provide most of the bride price, he purchases his second and subsequent wives in the way described above. Few men, however, can afford a spinster as second wife. Instead, to reduce or eliminate bride prices, the man persuades a married woman to run away. Formerly wives were sometimes captured. A man might also acquire a second wife through leviratic inheritance or even by stealing a fellow clansman's wife (this happened three times in two years within the Nupasafa).

Eventually everyone, except some mentally or physically handicapped individuals, settles down more or less permanently. To be an adult is to be married and have children. A man, in order to be a man, needs gardens and pigs to fulfil his social obligations and to have these he must have a wife to help him. Likewise, a woman must have a husband if she is to be a social person with a garden and pigs. She might survive physically without a husband's aid but it would be a marginal existence, living on handouts from brothers, left out or last when pork is distributed, having no one to fence her gardens or to plant crops that only men can plant, and lacking a protector. In short, for men and women to fulfil the normal cultural expectations of the Bena Bena there must be mutual dependence and cooperation between them. Thus, despite the ethos of male superiority and the absence of romantic love, strong bonds of affection can develop between husbands and wives, built up over the years out of respect for one another's labor and skills, shared experiences, and common endeavors. Husband and wife constitute a team, and both gain in status and prestige.

Women settled in marriage involve themselves in the clans of their husbands by adopting "brothers." These are always chosen from within the clan but outside the husband's subclan; and they behave as true brothers. The Bena say that, because the women come from afar and no longer see their own brothers, they need fictive brothers to support them in case of trouble with their husbands or when they need other help. Of sixty-five Bena wives inquired about, thirty-nine have such "brothers"; of the remaining twenty-six, four were so old it seemed not to matter, four were newly arrived brides, and three cases were unknown. The remaining fifteen wives maintained ties with their true brothers; eleven of these were from Korofeigu itself and the other four were from the three nearest tribes.

This is not to deny that those who do settle down have marital problems. Much of the discord can be traced to polygyny. In Nupasafa between 25 and 30 per cent of married men have more than one wife at a time. This high incidence of polygyny is related to wealth in pigs.[6] Cowives are jealous of attention, and fights are frequent, disruptive, and violent. If a man fails to come for the food a wife has cooked, if he fails to repair her fence or house, or if he favors one wife in any way, disputes follow. There is much suspicion between cowives who believe that one will work sorcery against another to gain the husband's favor.[7] There is little sexual jealousy *per se* so long as a man treats his wives equally but it becomes intense when he neglects one. Whatever the immediate cause of a wife's anger, she invariably asserts that her husband no longer copulates with her.

Normally, spouses copulate about once a week in the woman's house, and a man with more than one wife goes to them every other week. But, from the time a woman is pregnant until her child cuts its second tooth, she is forbidden intercourse, whereas her husband can have sexual experiences elsewhere. The woman knows this and is resentful. She becomes angry with her cowife, or fears her husband is looking for another wife.

DIVORCE

Divorces occur, although their exact frequency is difficult to determine. There is no formal ceremony associated with divorce. The typical pattern is either for a woman to run away to another man, or for a man to neglect his wife until she takes some action. A woman treated in this way eventually turns to others for help and insists that her husband state whether he is divorcing her. This is a public issue, not only because a woman is fundamentally clan property, but also because in this position she becomes an object of controversy. Other men become interested in her, not only as a mistress but also as a wife. They press her husband either to divorce her or take care of her. The woman has trouble performing her daily tasks because men attempt to seduce or rape her if they find her alone. Because a wife is the property of the subclan and clan, both the man responsible for buying her and his clansmen do not wish her to leave; if her husband refuses to look after her properly, they want her to take a new husband in that clan. The father of the husband will usually

---

[6] The greater number of pigs, although I cannot discuss it here, appears to be related to grassland as opposed to "bush" dwelling.

[7] On the other hand, Bena men do not believe their wives would use sorcery on them. They assume that once a woman settles down her loyalty is to her husband's clan.

urge him to keep her and serious friction can occur between them.

If divorce means the dissolution of marriage either by the return of bride price or, after children are born and bride price need not be returned, by the permanent separation of the partners for any reason other than death, then almost every middle-aged Bena has had one or more divorces. If the definition is restricted by assuming that divorce can only occur after the final marriage ceremony, the incidence is still high. Of forty-one Nupa men who had gone through the final ceremony and actually lived with wives, twenty-five are known to me to have been "divorced" from one or more women. The data are not satisfactory, however, for a man may take a second and third wife simply by enticing her from another place for a time. Only in some of these "marriages" is bride price actually paid so that it becomes difficult to define "marriage" adequately or to speak of "divorce." Moreover, the twenty-five cases mentioned are only those I am sure occurred. Clearly, this figure is extremely conservative, and divorce is frequent.

There are recognized grounds for divorce by men, such as barrenness, adultery, and failure to cook food or to perform other domestic tasks. This is a highly individual matter, however. Thus, a man who gets along with his wife would probably not divorce her for barrenness; or a man may choose merely to beat an adulterous wife. Failure to perform domestic tasks is more likely to result in divorce. In every case of divorce I knew the reason offered was simply that a man didn't like his wife because she nagged, did not work, or did not obey. Women generally divorce men by running away with other men. Only an older woman or one who has borne several children would return to her natal clan. The reasons why women leave husbands, I suspect, are many, but most separations seem to follow either neglect or beatings.[8] In any case, it is evident that there are stable and happy marriages which endure in addition to those which break up or are unsatisfactory. Individual personalities must be taken into account as well as the cultural expectations and pressures.

CONCLUSION

The Korofeigans, unlike some other New Guinea Highlanders, do not say "we marry those we fight" (Elkin, 1953; Meggitt, 1958, 1965;

---

[8] Not all men beat their wives, even though it is considered quite proper to do so in certain circumstances. Four informants agreed that of thirty men I named, eighteen were known to beat their wives often and twelve were said to have never beaten their wives.

Salisbury, 1962). Indeed, they have fought everyone within reach at one time or another and are well known for this. There is, therefore, little direct relationship between marital ties and warfare.[9]

Similarly, Bena marriage seems to have few political functions. Brides are treated as chattels, just as among Kuma (Reay, 1959). They are bought and sold; there is no question of groups making an equivalent exchange. Enduring ties between groups are not necessarily established by marriage. Moreover, marriages are widely dispersed and brides may come from distant places. Many Bena wives never see their families of orientation again; for those who do, visits are infrequent and of little significance for group activities. This is related to the custom of wives adopting "brothers" within their husband's clans. Here we touch upon an exceedingly complex situation in which one must distinguish between ideals and realities. Men normally would like to establish lasting ties through marriage. This can be seen in their speeches at weddings and also in their actual attempts to find brides. For instance, a man would prefer a bride from a strong clan rather than from a weak one. He would prefer a bride from a nearby clan rather than from a distant one. He would also prefer a woman to a child. But, given the complex procedures involved in obtaining a bride, the distances involved, the need to acquire a number of brides in a finite time, and the patterns of current hostilities, men cannot always achieve their ideals. One can say that the probability of enduring ties existing between a man and his affines is roughly proportional to the physical distance between them. Also important is the age of the bride, for if she was purchased before her first menstruation there is little likelihood of ties being formed. The matter is complicated by other variables: the nature of the man's other commitments (he has only limited wealth he can exchange and he must exchange for a variety of reasons), his own success in producing wealth, the nature of the terrain through which he must pass (that of enemy, friend, or neutral), and the relationship between his group and his wife's group (for this fluctuates from time to time). A man's loyalty is always to his clan. In the event of hostilities with other groups, affinal connections can only be second best.

Because of these interacting factors, the ideal marriage is seldom

[9] The relations of affines in warfare are not clear, however. Although some Bena informants say they would spare affines in battle, many report that they were not spared Likewise, although Berndt (1962) reports that affines were spared among neighboring Kamano, Fortune, writing earlier about the same area (1947), reports otherwise.

achieved. Insofar as the people themselves are aware that they must take brides when and where they can, I do not believe the motive for particular marriages invariably lies in the wish to establish permanent ties with other groups; nor, as is obvious, do marriages always serve that function. More important is the desire to marry and have children, ensuring a stronger clan and greater security in an hostile environment. Thus, the fact that marriages are dispersed does not imply that they are "deliberately dispersed" for political reasons (Barnes, 1962). The high divorce rate itself indicates the brittle ties existing between groups, and the marriage patterns described illustrate that marriage creates as many problems as it solves. The fact that there are relatively few marriages between Nupa and the other Korofeigu clans demonstrates that whatever holds those groups together, it is not significantly determined by affinal ties. That marriages are made within the tribe probably reflects the desire to marry daughters as close to home as possible rather than to place them in politically advantageous situations. People say, "we are sorry when our daughters must marry and go away. It is not good for them to go far away." Similarly, when a marriage is being arranged, an important consideration is whether or not a Nupa woman is already there so the new bride will have a friend (this also reduces the chance that she will run away). Obviously this is not consistent with the notion that once a marriage has been accomplished it is a bar to further marriages between those groups (Barnes, 1962).

Although I have expressed this in lineage and clan idiom, when permanent ties are formed by marriage they are ties between individuals rather than between groups (Langness, n.d.). Bena marriage customs tend to maximize the number of people involved in marriages but at the same time minimize relations between groups as corporate entities. Consider all the people involved in a marriage: the bride, her guardian and his close relatives, her parents and close relatives, other members of her clan who may have received some of her bride price, the groom's parents and close relatives, other individuals who contributed substantially to the bride price, plus the "brother" she eventually adopts from her husband's clan and his close relatives. In addition, when she has a child, a ritual is performed for the child and its "mother's brother"—but this cannot be the woman's true brother. It must be a classificatory mother's brother, further extending the network of individuals with whom the child has connections. The true mother's brother, if accessible, is by no means ignored by the child but cannot be the recipient of formal gifts. The explanation for this is basically the same as for the guardianship of girls, "it is wrong to take pay (gifts) for your own child."

It must be emphasized that these are primarily ties between individuals, not between groups *qua* groups. It is not simply a matter of lineages acting *vis-a-vis* similar lineages, or of subclans *vis-a-vis* subclans. The people involved in any specific exchange are not recruited strictly on the basis of lineage or subclan membership. Indeed, a man is apt to get as much or more help from an age-mate as from a brother, or even from another clansman who is a friend or debtor. Sometimes one or more of a man's own brothers may have nothing to do with the marriage of his son or ward. Furthermore, the group that makes a gift to a mother's brother is not necessarily the same as that which originally bought the bride but simply comprises those who wish to contribute and who have something available at that moment. The relationship is established by the men in charge and is extended to others because of their participation; but the actual depth and permanence of these relationships depend on how much reinforcement follows. This is true of the principal as well as his assistants. A man does not always elect to maintain ties with affines, particularly if they are a distant or a weak group. Thus, considering that substitutes for agnates and affines are easily made on the basis of proximity and residence, the number and kinds of individual ties that can be formed are almost infinite. If a bride is from close by, and if satisfactory ties can be maintained with various members of her natal group, so much the better; but, if not, some substitute can readily be found.

In short, substitution and flexibility seem to be at the heart of the Bena system of marriage. When a bride obtained by capture, for example, has a child, its "mother's brother" will most likely be an adopted brother within the clan. When a child is born and the mother's clan is either too distant, or currently hostile, or has been destroyed, a similar substitution is made. If there is a classificatory brother of the mother living nearby but not in her natal clan, he might be singled out simply because of his proximity. Thus, from the point of view of any individual, many ties with other individuals are possible, only some of which he will choose to maintain. But, from the point of view of formal structural principles, the specific ties cannot be predicted. Most men recognize a "mother's brother," but one cannot predict just who it will be; indeed, because of the presence of nonagnates in local groups, one cannot be sure that this man will reside with the mother's natal group. Likewise, one can predict that a woman will have a brother who protects and helps her, but not whether he will be her true brother or an adopted one. In this case, however, one can predict with greater accuracy if one knows from what distance she came, what her age was at marriage, and what the present relationship is between her group and her husband's group. One could almost say that except for the rule of exogamy a clan is completely autonomous and self-sufficient. This is true not only for production and defense but also in the sense that within the clan itself individuals can be found with whom to interact and fulfil the normal social obligations contingent upon marriage. The Bena system is geared to clan solidarity and independence in the face of unpredictable events and insures that necessary activities can be carried on even in adverse circumstances.

This same flexibility can be seen in the custom of guardianship itself. First of all it means that no man need have all children of the same sex, thus insuring all men of "sons-in-law" as well as "daughters-in-law." Secondly, it enables men greater flexibility in arranging marriages as the wards can be traded. Thus a man with sufficient resources to enter into a marriage, but who has no ward of the proper age at the proper moment, can exchange a younger girl with a clansman who has an older one. This, in fact, happens; and it not only allows a man to extend his interpersonal relations to his advantage but also to maximize his resources.

At the same time one sees the utility of the fiction of patrilineal descent and of male solidarity. Relationships, when they are established, are created between men and they persist independently of the acts of women. Divorce, for example, carries no stigma and does not necessarily affect established relationships. Children belong to men. One cannot predict a man's ties from the identity of his current spouse. If a man has a child by a former wife and has established a relationship for that child with its mother's brother, the latter is not relieved of his obligations simply because of the divorce—such obligations are the affairs of men and should not be disrupted by the movements of women. There has to be some basis for continuing interaction, a permanence that would be most difficult to maintain if men did not act independently of women; the Bena establish it by the concepts of patrilineal descent and male solidarity. So, from the standpoint of an individual man, what one finds is a series of egocentric networks resulting, not from the operation of well defined structural principles, but from the personal histories of specific individuals. A man's ties afford him and his family refuge in time of trouble, they give him access to sweet potatoes in time of drought, and they allow him to receive help in other ways; but they do not insure similar privileges for his lineage, subclan, or clan. More importantly they give him political power and legal backing when necessary (Langness, n.d.). Before the Australian Administration prohibited warfare, clans were often forced to flee, and they typically broke up into families, a fact doubtless associated with the loose application of agnatic principles (Langness, 1964). This is not to say that a lineage or subclan never took refuge as a group; but, if it did, this depended upon the size of the groups involved, the availability of resources, and the number and quality of the individual ties involved. It was not simply a matter of the obligations of one descent group to another.

The significant units of Bena Bena society are individuals and clans. Because of adoptions, residence, guardianships, age-mate bonds, the exigencies of pig-raising and of warfare, and personal inclinations and loyalties, lineage and subclan bonds are relatively unimportant. On the one hand, they are made subservient to the needs of individuals and, on the other, to the needs of the clan. Although marriages are ostensibly arranged between subclans and clans they result not in relations between the groups as such but in the extension and proliferation of interpersonal ties. Marriages do not preclude warring between groups nor do they invariably result in enduring relationships between groups or even individuals.

The Bena clan, having large numbers of nonagnates present, cannot be said to be held together by bonds of common ancestry, although such a fiction is maintained. It is held together by a complex network of individual relationships established in large part by the necessity for survival in an hostile environment. As clans as such cannot easily take refuge, the ramification of personal ties established by clan members not only ensures refuge for the largest number of people but also militates against their eventual regrouping. Thus, nonagnates are present in local groups and, in fact, are at times actively recruited. It is to a man's advantage to extend his ties to as many other individuals and to as many other groups as possible, to guarantee him help when he needs it and a choice of alternatives. He can do this through marriage, even though such marriages break up, and also by trading and through personal friendships. He also may have ties by virtue of having been raised in a place other than his natal territory, or because his father was raised elsewhere. He may have ties with a mother's brother, who may or may not be residing in his natal group, and so on. But, when a clan is together, clan loyalty must come first, whether at the expense of subgroups within it or of group relations outside. Bena marriage patterns are consistent with this obligation. They allow people to find brides where and when they can, to maintain ties with affines if possible, but to put others in their place if necessary. They allow men to discontinue such relationships if the interests of the clan are threatened. Women who remain with their husbands' clan after marriage and thus indicate they are willing to be members, are members;[10] any loyalties they may have to their natal group are overridden. A woman's only security is with her husband, for her agnates cannot or will not keep her. It is for this reason that formerly women sometimes committed suicide when their husbands died rather than return to their natal groups or take a new husband (Langness, 1967). As a woman's husband and his group flourish, so she flourishes.

[10] Although it is widely reported for the New Guinea highlands that women retain rights in their natal groups after marriage (I have reported this myself [1964]) it has never been made clear just what this means. There is not space to pursue this here but I would suggest that such statements are often misleading in the extreme, they imply a significance to descent group membership which does not in some cases exist, and they give an erroneous impression as to the position of female agnates. In the Bena case, everything considered, a much stronger case could be made for asserting that women at marriage become members of their husband's group than for any other conclusion.

Marriage Among the
DARIBI

Roy Wagner

ENVIRONMENT AND SUBSISTENCE

The Migaru Page Daribi[1] ("Karimui-base-Daribi") are a distinct social and linguistic subgroup within a range of Daribi speakers extending from Karimui and Bomai Patrol Posts southwest into Papua. The southern limits of the language are still unknown.[2] The term "Mikaru," based on the Daribi name for Mt. Karimui, has been retained as a label for the Daribi language by Wurm (1964) and the Summer Institute of Linguistics.

Approximately 3,000 Daribi live on the volcanic plateau north of Mt. Karimui and in the adjacent limestone country to the west; they have intermarried extensively with a pocket of 1,000 Tudawe (S. I. L. "Pawaia") speakers living northeast of the mountain. The society is isolated from other Daribi speakers by a great westward loop of the Tua River, which becomes the Purari just south of Mt. Karimui. The Karimui area is bisected by the Papua-New Guinea frontier, and lies between 144°30' and 144°50'E, and 7°20' and 7°30'S, south of the Wahgi Valley.

Although encountered in 1930 by Leahy and Dwyer, and in 1936 by Champion, the Daribi were first officially contacted around 1953, and the patrol post was built in 1960–61.

One of a series of extinct, eroded Pleistocene volcanoes marking

[1] I spent sixteen months among the Daribi, from October 1963 to February 1965, studying religion and social structure on a research grant from the New Guinea Native Religions Project of the University of Washington, sponsored by the Bollingen Foundation. Dr. Robert Glasse had visited Karimui in September, 1962, investigating native conceptualization of leprosy.

[2] Wurm (1964) lists Mikaru as distantly related to his East New Guinea Highlands Phylum. I have noted quite distinct series of cognates linking the language to that of Lake Kutubu (as reported by Williams) and to the Metlpa language of Mount Hagen, though in each case the number of cognates is unimpressive. Orthography is given here in a standard Latin format, with the apostrophe (') indicating a high tone.

the southern approaches to the highlands, Mt. Karimui is about 8,700 feet high, while its sloping plateau averages around 3,000 feet above sea level. Southwest of the mountain a series of low, parallel limestone ridges, running southeast-northwest, extends about 100 miles west to the Lake Kutubu area.

The whole region is overgrown with virgin rain forest, except where there has been cultivation. The character of the forest changes with altitude and soil-type, with immense stands on the plateau. The vegetation is more lush than that of the central highlands, and extremes of altitude permit both coastal and highland floral and faunal varieties.

The total area used by the Daribi at Karimui equals about 160 square miles, giving a density of approximately nineteen persons per square mile. A clan shifts its gardens periodically within a territory of two to three square miles; the remaining land is used for hunting and the gathering of bush resources. Land is not scarce, and the frequently changing residence pattern among clans, as they combine to form communities, varies with the political situation.

When it moves to a new location, a clan first builds a *sigibe'*, a two-story longhouse, then builds gardens in wedge-shaped segments surrounding it; when these gardens are exhausted, in two or three years, individual men or groups of brothers build separate gardens and single-story *kerobe'* in peripheral areas. When these gardens are exhausted, the cycle may begin again elsewhere. Houses disintegrate after two years.

Land is cleared by cutting or ringbarking trees; brush is piled at the bases of the larger trees and burned. The plot is fenced, and sweet potato vines planted in the unprepared soil. These quickly cover tree trunks and debris left lying about the garden. In addition to this staple, sago is cultivated in deep ravines and low limestone valleys, often in artificial swamps. Bananas, taro, yams, beans, sugar cane, edible *pitpit,* and various native greens are also grown, as are the introduced maize, manioc, and cucumbers. Breadfruit seeds and oil-bearing pandanus fruit supplement the diet considerably. Domestic pigs, said to be recently introduced, are scarcer than in the central highlands.

SOCIAL STRUCTURE

The Daribi at Karimui are subdivided into about forty clans, *hane* or *bidihane,* and include from fifty to eighty persons each. Two to four allied clans often live together in what I call a community, a consequence of the concentration of alliance-ties among a few units to form a kind of superclan, an assemblage of distinct yet closely associated units. This has sometimes given the erroneous impression that Daribi marry within their own clans, and that these are fewer and larger than they actually are.

Daribi define clan membership in terms of exchange symbolism;[3] members of a clan are those who "share wealth" or "share meat" together, nonclan members are those with whom one exchanges wealth or meat. The membership of every person in a clan should be validated from time to time through such exchanges; in the case of a man or a child, payments must be made to his mother's brothers or *pagebidi,* his "owners." In the case of a woman, marriage amounts to "recruitment" to the clan of her husband, and payments are made continually to her *pagebidi,* in this case her brothers. Collateral for these payments may be solicited from all adult male clan members, whose wealth can be seen as a "pool" used in this way to define clan membership. Wealth received by members in the form of recruitment payments given to them for their own sisters and sisters' children is thus available to their clanmates.

The Daribi trace consanguineal relationship equally through the maternal and the paternal lines, or through both in series. Consanguineal ties, and the consequent obligations, may be "closer" or "more distant" according to the genealogical relationship of the persons concerned. A distinction is drawn between paternal substance (*kawa,* semen), transmitted by males and forming the outer envelope of an embryo, and maternal substance (*pagekamine,* mother's blood), transmitted by females and making up its blood, bones, and internal organs. This distinction corresponds to what I call the *normative system,* which prescribes the mode, or norms of interaction between the principles of consanguinity and exchange.

Insofar as consanguineal relationship is traced through bodily substance and becomes more "distant" with genealogical separation, it follows that the closest relationship is shared among a group of full siblings, who embody the same paternal and maternal substances. Such a unit is called a *zibi;* its members share responsibility for each other's protection and support. Male *zibi* members share primary rights to

[3] A complete account of Daribi social structure, as well as an extended discussion of the theoretical implications of the model outlined here, is presented in Roy Wagner, *The Curse of Souw: Principles of Daribi Clan Definition and Alliance,* University of Chicago Press, 1967.

bridewealth brought in by a sister's marriage; this forms the basis for the claims they make to inherit each other's wives under the levirate, for the wife of each *zibi* member has been obtained to some extent with "common" funds. As rights and obligations within the *zibi* are organized in terms of seniority, the levirate becomes a junior levirate, and *zibi* members are subject to the authority of the *gominaibidi,* the eldest male of the group. A clan comprises several such *zibi,* and the *gominaibidi* of one of these (ideally the latest in a series of "eldest sons of eldest sons") functions as a hortatory leader of the clan as a whole.

It is a norm of Daribi society that a father recruit his children to his own clan. To do this, he must make recruitment payments on their behalf to their mother's brother(s), their *awa,* or *pagebidi.* The latter is regarded as the "owner" of the child (as the owner of a pig or an ax is its *pagebidi*), his "cause" or "origin," and may freely take any property belonging to the child, to whom he refers as "his." If his claims are not satisfied, a *pagebidi* may either claim his sister's child or curse him with sickness, infertility, or death. The father, nevertheless, retains the option to keep the child provided he makes the requisite payments. If these payments are not made, the father loses his option, and the child is recruited into his *awa*'s clan, in whose exchange activities he henceforth participates as a member.

Corresponding to this norm of recruitment for children is one of virilocal residence, relating to the "recruitment" of a woman to the clan of her husband. Here too a man has the option of giving payments to his wife's *pagebidi,* her brothers, as compensation for her, but he may forgo this and live with his wife at her clan, whereupon he becomes a fully participating member.

The word "norm" is not used here in a statistical sense, but refers rather to culturally prescribed rules for behavior, which are expressed in the kinship system. I distinguish such norms from the *principles* of Daribi social structure, exchange, and consanguinity, which remain in operation regardless of whether the norms are obeyed. A child may be recruited to its mother's brother's clan, a man may live with his wife's clan, yet the consanguineal relationships of each remain unchanged, for these are given by birth, and each will henceforth still share wealth with the members of one clan and exchange wealth with those of others. Put in the simplest terms, the normative system correlates the transmission of paternal substance with the sharing of wealth, and the transmission of maternal substance with the exchange of wealth. A clan, in other words, should normally "redeem" the offspring of its male members, and accept compensation for the offspring of its out-marrying females. Because of this norm, a clan will come to be identified with a particular "core" patriline and trace the consanguineal relationships of all of its members through that line to an ancestral point of convergence of several such patrilines, the common ancestor of its phratry. Because clans are defined through exchange activities, member clans of a phratry may intermarry; indeed, I have not been able to ascertain any specific function which is carried on at the phratry level. I have used the term "normative patriliny" to denote this identification of a clan with a particular patriline.[4]

MARRIAGE RULES AND NORMS

There are two aspects of the Daribi marriage rule, corresponding to the two basic principles of Daribi social structure—exchange and consanguinity. These aspects are, accordingly, expressible in terms of the native symbolism relating to bodily substance and the sharing and exchange of wealth. Members of a clan share among themselves the wealth used in recruitment and marriage exchanges, and the clan is therefore exogamous by definition. Those who share wealth may not intermarry. Individuals may be more or less closely related through bodily substance in proportion to the genealogical distance between them, irrespective of the particular "kinds" of substance through which the links are traced. Marriage between persons separated by five or fewer degrees of kinship (i.e., those related as "second cousins" or closer, in our terminology) is regarded as incestuous.[5]

The regulations concerning exogamy and incest, taken together, constitute the Daribi marriage rule. Whereas cases of incest are sometimes encountered, instances involving marriage "within the clan" generally turn out, on closer inspection, to mark the final stages of segmentation, for it is in this way that the separation is formalized.

Although permissible in itself when it involves neither incest nor a breach of exogamy, sister-exchange is frowned upon by the Daribi in

---

[4] I use this term purely in a descriptive sense, and I am anxious that it not be mistaken for a classificatory label or part of a typology. The current concern with the "problem" of unilineal descent units is to a large extent a result of the unquestioning assumption of classificatory "descent" labels in situations where a more holistic approach might prove more rewarding.

[5] Punishment in cases of incest varies widely according to the political situation; it may amount to a severe beating administered to the couple, or may not occur at all. I have heard the belief expressed that the child conceived of an incestuous union will die in the womb.

that each party is compensated by a woman, and a woman, unlike pigs or pearlshells, cannot be divided among several brothers. Participants in sister-exchange must either be men without brothers, or be able to compensate those brothers of their wives who are not parties to the exchange. Even so, sister-exchange tends to isolate those who take part in it from the general cycle of exchange and dependence in the society by building a "closed system" of interdependence. This opposition to sister-exchange can be stated in general terms as a norm: *no one zibi should stand in the relationship of wife-giver and that of wife-taker to any other.* On the other hand, once a woman has passed from one *zibi* to another in marriage, the further giving of women in the same direction is enjoined by the kinship system.

As an alternative to sister-exchange, Daribi sometimes resort to a sister-daughter exchange, whereby a man gives his daughter by one wife in marriage to the brother of another of his wives. This has the advantage of splitting the wife-giving and wife-taking relationships generationally, so that the *zibi* which originally gave its sister remains a "wife-giver" to her husband, while it stands in the relationship of "wife-taker" to his sons. While it thus overcomes some of the difficulties of sister-exchange, sister-daughter exchange still interferes with an important feature of the Daribi kinship system; the expectation that a *zibi* which stands in the relationship of wife-taker to another will stand in the same relationship to the *zibi* of its children, with whom the reciprocal *yage* is used, and to those of its grandchildren, with whom the reciprocal *yame* is used. As in sister-exchange, this kind of on-going relationship through several generations is precluded by the fact that the lines have exchanged women in both directions.

Both sister-exchange and sister-daughter exchange involve the giving of a woman in direct exchange for another, and represent means of "short circuiting" the standard procedure in which marriages are eventually reciprocated by others in a cycle of delayed reciprocity. Although the series of payments given for a woman is sufficient compensation, it is felt that every marriage should be reciprocated by another in the opposite direction. Since the strongest interests in a woman are those of her *zibi*-mates, who "give" her in marriage, it is the *zibi* which functions as the unit of relationship in marriage reciprocity. We can express the functions of a *zibi* in terms of marriage reciprocity as a norm: *each woman given to a zibi by an external clan should be reciprocated by the giving of a woman in return to that clan; each woman given by a zibi to an external clan should be reciprocated by the giving of a woman in return by that clan to the zibi.*

Taking this norm together with the one given above to the effect that no *zibi* should stand in the relationship both of wife-giver and of wife-taker to another, we can generate a model for Daribi marriage reciprocity. Each *zibi* of a clan should divide its functions with regard to wife-giving and wife-taking among the *zibi* of the clan with which marriages are contracted, so that it achieves a balance with respect to the clan as a whole, while relating to each of the component sub-units either as wife-giver or wife-taker.[6] As a consequence, a cycle of four individual marriages is necessary to bring the reciprocity between two clans and their component *zibi* to a state of equilibrium. This is schematized in Figure 1. *Zibi* a of clan A gives a wife to *zibi* 1 of clan

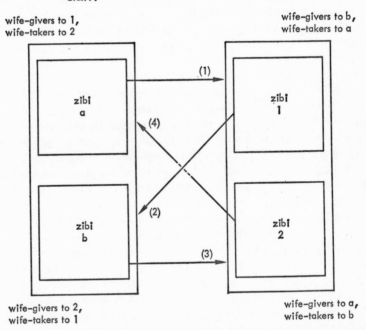

Figure 1. IDEAL MARRIAGE RECIPROCITY CYCLE AMONG THE DARIBI

I (1); since 1 cannot reciprocate by giving a wife directly to a, it discharges its obligation by giving a wife to *zibi* b of clan A (2). *Zibi* b, as wife-taker to 1, must discharge the obligation incurred by this mar-

---

[6] This structural aspect of reciprocity is well known to the Daribi, and forms part of their "conscious model."

riage by giving a wife to *zibi* 2 of clan I (3). *Zibi* 2, in turn, as it is wife-taker to b, can only reciprocate by giving a wife to *zibi* a (4), which satisfies the expectation created when the latter contracted the marriage which began the cycle.

Each *zibi* in this cycle can of course take further wives from the *zibi* composed of the children and grandchildren of its wife-givers in this cycle, barring prior sister-daughter exchanges, and each can of course continue to take as wives the sisters of those women it has already married.

The idealized cycle of marriage reciprocity presented here is not always completed; *zibi* may feel obliged to reciprocate certain marriages, but often other factors intervene. The cycle merely represents part of a model, the result of a series of culturally sanctioned expectations.

THE DARIBI ALLIANCE BOND

Because the Daribi clan defines itself in terms of exchange symbolism as a group of people who "share wealth," whereas wealth is "exchanged" with members of other clans, and the Daribi trace consanguineal relationship bilaterally, it follows that Daribi clans are superimposed on a society-wide network of interlinked consanguineal ties. A Daribi, as a result of clan exogamy, always has close consanguineal kinsmen both within and outside the clan of which he is a member. Because of what I call "normative patriliny," it is a person's matrilateral kinsmen, and also his sisters and father's sisters, who will belong to other clans. Yet, as we have seen, a person's mother's brother, normally a member of another clan, is regarded as his "owner," against whose claims he must redeem his own clan membership, while he in turn is regarded as the "owner" of his sister's children. The blood bonds which connect members of different clans represent strong claims; each member of a clan is "claimed" by someone of another clan, *and it is against precisely these claims that the exchanges which define the clan are made.* A clan, in order to exist, must define itself against its blood kin; payments are made, in marriage and recruitment, to *oppose* blood ties. It follows logically therefore that exchange in this kind of system merely draws boundaries; it is consanguinity which "relates" people. How then is alliance effected?

We have seen how unit definition stems from the interaction of the principles of exchange and consanguinity, wherein the exchange of wealth imposes boundaries on a network of consanguineal relation-

ships. The other side of the coin is that relationship between individuals, given at conception, can only arise as the result of marriage
between (necessarily) exogamous clans. Each child relates the clans of
its parents by embodying in its person the substances of their respective clans, opposing the boundaries of exchange by consanguinity.

Just as exchange provides the criterion by which clans exist as discrete units, so consanguinity provides the idiom by which clan
boundaries are transcended, and the two, working in opposition,
generate the social system. In marriage, the bond of consanguinity between a woman and her natal clan is opposed by the series of payments
given to her *pagebidi* (close blood kin), beginning with betrothal.
While the payments settle for the time being the issue of her clan
membership, the consanguineal relationship, whose claims they oppose,
remains in effect all her life. The same opposition is encountered in
the recruitment of children.

A person's consanguineal connection with his mother's brother is
therefore never abrogated; it is merely the latter's claims that are
opposed. As we have seen, a man is regarded as the "owner" of his
sister's children, but he also plays the role of "father," which he must
validate by payments, to his own children. He is, in fact, a kind of consanguineal "parent" to each set of children. It is because of this
that Daribi say cross-cousins are "the same as brothers," for, like
brothers, they share a "parent." Because cross-cousins (*hai'*) are the
same as brothers, they are entitled to the privileges of brotherhood,
which amount to a sharing of common interest in each other's sisters.
This common interest is formally expressed in (a) the sharing of wealth
given in exchange for the sisters, and (b) the junior levirate, ultimately
based on such sharing. Because *hai'* normally belong to different clans,
the shared privileges are transmuted into discrete payments of wealth,
which are nevertheless distinct from those associated with clan definition.[7] When his female *hai'* marries, ego receives a share of the bride-
price. A direct levirate between *hai'* would, however, effectively transfer
the inherited wife from her clan of marriage without compensating
her former husband's clanmates, so *hai'* are obliged to pay each other
for levirate privileges. Such payments are refunded if the widow passes
to the brother of the deceased.

The extension of privileges of "brotherhood" to *hai'* constitutes the
formal expression of the Daribi alliance bond, based as it is on con-

[7] *Hai'* also participate in the *pagebidi* relationship; the mother's brother's son
is ego's *hai' pagebidi,* and ego must give him payments on this account, but such
payments are kept separate from those associated with sharing between *hai'*.

sanguineal ties extending between clans. Such bonds are automatically generated by the social system, for a clan cannot define itself except against consanguineal ties, and it cannot reproduce itself without creating such ties. Although alliance in the Daribi system differs from that found in societies where alliance is based on affinity, the two kinds of system are similar in that the distribution of alliance-ties in each case corresponds to the distribution of marriages. In one, marriages themselves express or activate alliances; in the other, they effect alliance through the conception of children.

PATTERN OF EXOGAMY

Although the presence of alliance bonds is given by the social system, their distribution is not. Because exchange acts to define the unit in Daribi society, the opposition created is "centrifugal," opposing the clan to all others for exchange functions, rather than "diametric," as in a society based on "dual organization." Thus my informants, perhaps to distinguish themselves from the Gumine highlanders to the north, told me that Daribi can "marry all over, and not just in one place." Respecting the incest rule, and the norms for marriage reciprocity, a clan can make as many or as few marriages with another as preferable. As each marriage can be regarded as a contract for the conception of children, the number of marriages made between clans is a rough measure of the degree to which they will be related by blood in the following generation.

It can be seen that if enough marriages occur between two clans, perhaps along the lines of the norms for marriage reciprocity, in the following generation all the *zibi* of each will stand in the relationship of *hai'* to those of the other, so that *although clan boundaries are maintained, obligations of "sharing" with hai' will obtain generally between the two clans, giving rise to a kind of "superclan," bound in alliance by blood ties, yet subdivided by exchange boundaries.* What I have called a "community" is the result of two or more clans, linked in this way, taking up residence together. Often clans undergoing segmentation will intermarry extensively in the process, thus perpetuating their association as a community, and in fact segmentation and alliance can be viewed as distinct aspects of a single process.[8]

Whether or not a community is formed thereby, the concentration of marriages, and therefore of alliances, is an optative element in

[8] This process is described and analyzed in Chapter 7 of *The Curse of Souw.*

Daribi social structure, subject to conscious manipulation, as is warfare. The technique of concentrating alliance ties by making many marriages in one place is a tactic within the system of "multiple and distributive opposition" (cf. Salisbury, 1964: 169) obtaining among clans.

Apart from those involving marriage reciprocity, no system of norms or principles governs marriage distribution. In approaching this aspect of Daribi marriage we pass from the realm of the mechanical model to that of statistics, for we are dealing with the political *use* of structure, the way in which structural "givens" are manipulated to accommodate the realities of clan interaction.

Table 1 shows the distribution of marriages for two clans living in community at Noru, Karimui. Pobori and Wazo clans were formed from a single ancestral unit by segmentation, but have since intermarried heavily. The figures presented here were taken from genealogies with an effective depth of four generations, and are cumulative over that span, for the effects of an alliance are felt in the generations after its contraction. I have counted both the giving and the taking of wives as "marriages," as both types of exchange result in bonds between units.

Table 1 also shows cumulative figures for the community; marriages made within the community are necessarily counted twice here, as each utilizes two bonds, one of "giving" and one of "taking," which the community could otherwise distribute elsewhere.

The distribution of marriages involving the Noru community is plotted schematically on a contour map of the area in Figure 2, the width of the arrows indicating relative frequencies. Most marriages fall within a three mile radius of Noru, with the highest concentration (54.2 per cent) in the enclosed valley within which Noru is located.

In Figure 3, no. 1, the percentage of marriages with each of a number of external clans, ranked in order of concentration, is plotted for four Daribi clans. Although the *possibilities* for marriage distribution given by the social structure might lead us to expect anything from an even distribution among many clans to a total concentration among a few, in fact marriage distribution in all four clans follows a consistent pattern, and this is represented on the "average" curve of Figure 3, no. 2. The pattern indicates a scattering of marriages (one or two each) with most of the clans involved, and a significant concentration with a group of four to six clans. The isolated marriages probably reflect betrothals arranged for random personal reasons; the high concentration seems to indicate concerted policy. (As Figure 2

Table 1. MARRIAGE CONCENTRATION AT NORU, KARIMUI

Clan	Marriages	Per Cent
Pobori Clan		
Wazo	20	26%
Hagani	11	14
Sora'	8	10
Dobu	8	10
Denege	5	6
Tiligi'	3	4
Bobe	3	4
Di'be'	3	4
8 Clans	61	78
13 Clans	17	22
21	78	98
Wazo Clan		
Pobori	21	26
Hagani	13	16
Di'be'	8	10
Hobe	7	9
Sora'	4	5
Masi	4	5
6 Clans	57	71
17 Clans	23	28
23	80	99
Total Community		
Within Community	41	26.0
Hagani	24	15.0
Sora'	12	7.5
Di'be'	11	6.9
Dobu	10	6.3
Hobe	9	5.7
Masi	6	3.8
Denege	5	3.2
Tiligi'	5	3.2
Bobe	3	1.9
Weriai	3	1.9
Mabere	3	1.9
13 Clans	132	83.3
20 clans	26	16.5
33	158	99.8

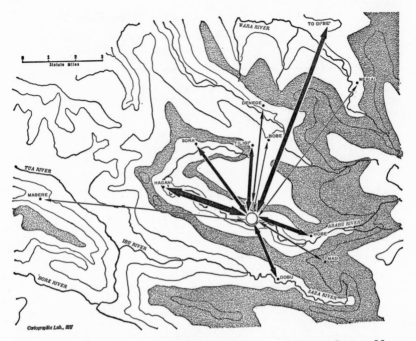

Figure 2. MARRIAGE DISTRIBUTION OF POBORI AND WAZO CLANS, NORU
PHRATRY, KARIMUI

indicates, proximity may well affect this, but Daribi clans tend to
move together following an alliance, and in any case it is good policy
to cover one's approaches.)

Because Pobori and Wazo clans have cemented their alliance by
many intermarriages since segmentation, whereas the marriages which
are to effect the segmentation of Kurube' and Noruai are still in the
planning and betrothal stage, their respective distribution curves in
Figure 3 show considerable variation.

INDIVIDUAL MARRIAGE

Unlike many highland societies, Daribi betroth virtually all girls at an
early age, often in infancy, and thereby forgo the pleasantries of group
courting found further north, or what Pospisil (1963) terms "dating"
among the Kapauku. A girl is marked (*noma' sabo,* "taking the soul")
by mutual consent of her parents to someone whom they have chosen,

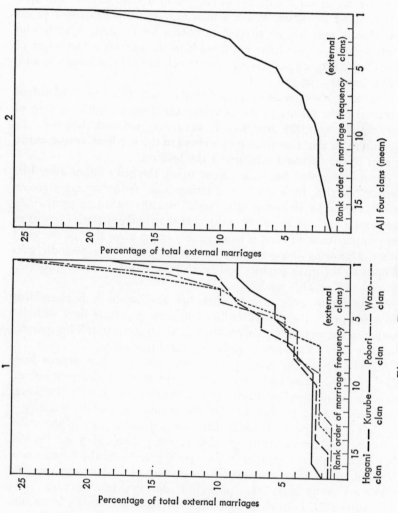

Figure 3. DARIBI PATTERNS OF EXOGAMY

perhaps because he is wealthy, well known, or has proven a good son-in-law to them in the past; also he may be someone who belongs to a clan to which a wife is "owed," or to a clan with which their own is allied by policy. When a man is selected, a messenger of his own clan is sent by the parents to obtain his consent. A man who wants to mark a particular child sends to the parents a messenger of their clan to inquire politely whether the child has been bespoken and, if not, to relay the proposal.

Because it favors wealthy or influential men, this system of infant betrothal often results in the marriage of adolescent girls to men of late middle age; the inequity is somewhat reduced, however, by provisions for the transmission of widows to the brothers, cross-cousins, or sons of the deceased man under the levirate.

When a betrothal has been agreed upon, the girl's father assembles "female" wealth, bark cloaks and string bags; the prospective groom readies the major betrothal gift, "male" wealth, including pearlshells, axes, and a pig, and these are exchanged shortly thereafter. The gift of the prospective son-in-law is considerably larger than that of the girl's father. Following this payment, the groom must make periodic gifts of meat to the girl's parents and brothers, and these are reciprocated by gifts of "female" wealth.

At the age of eight or ten, when her husband-to-be is assembling the bride price, the girl visits his clan, staying several days with his mother in the women's quarters (aribe'). She returns to tell her parents that her future husband is gathering the bride price.

A girl is given in marriage at about the time her breasts have filled out; if she marries before her first menstruation, she must remain with her mother-in-law until after it occurs; meanwhile the latter continues to cook for her son. On the evening before the wedding a songfest is held for the bride by her clan and community in the aribe' of her former house. Although men of the groom's clan are invited, they usually elect to remain in the men's quarters of the hosts, where they indulge in long conversations regarding exchanges and the like.

The ceremony itself takes place next day shortly after noon. The bride price is laid out on the ground in front of the bride's house; the groom and about four of his clansmen, their bodies covered with soot, wearing white shell ornaments and cassowary plumes, stand in single file before the front door. Each holds a bow and arrows in his left hand, and pearlshells from the bride price in his right. The bride, highly decorated, emerges from the house and passes down the file of men, collecting the shells from each, and then presenting them to her father. The groom and his party return to their house; afterward the bride follows in the charge of the groom's mother, with whom she remains for about five days. Bride and groom then go on a six day trip into the bush, during which an animal is killed, steamed, and dried over the fire. The couple return to the groom's house for one night, then take the meat to the bride's father. Only after this, upon returning to the groom's house, may the marriage be consummated, provided of course that the bride has passed her menarche.

A man must continue payments to the father and brothers of his wife for the duration of the marriage; these are presented intermittently during casual visits. Complete avoidance is enjoined between a man and his mother-in-law (*au*); if this fails, an exchange between them is necessary, exactly as at Kutubu (Williams, 1940: 61).[9] A man maintains a somewhat less guarded relationship with his father-in-law (*wai*) and an easier one with his *baze*, brother-in-law.

The bride price of "male" goods is divided into two categories; *were oromawai* ("given without return for the wife"), and *we pona siare* ("wife-pay finished"), the amount covered by the dowry of "female" goods given with the bride. The latter averages slightly less than half the total bride price. About one fifth of the *were oromawai* is given to the bride's *pagebidi*.

Divorce may be effected by either the husband or the wife. A woman need only return with good cause to her father or brothers and they will refund the bride price. A man sometimes "gives" his wife to a relative or friend, perhaps asking for payment then or later; an elder brother, who should find a wife for his younger brother, frequently gives the latter one of his own wives in this way. When a married man dies, his wives should return to their clans of origin before being "inherited" through the levirate. The prospective husband comes smeared with mourning clay to her clan, and her clanmates ask if she wishes to follow him. If she does, they are considered married, and he assumes the obligation of paying for her. In all cases I recorded, however, this procedure was not followed; the widow went directly to the brother or son (by another wife) of her late husband, or "shopped

[9] Interestingly enough, like Williams, I recorded a case of mother-in-law rape at Karimui; it set off open warfare between the clans involved. An informant conjectured that the culprit raped the woman because "he thought her vagina would be large, like her daughter's." "Man who copulates with his mother-in-law" is a common pejorative at Karimui.

around," attempting to seduce potential mates. Members of the deceased man's clan often present candidates to such a woman outright, asking her if she wishes to marry them.

RATES OF POLYGYNY AND MARRIAGE

In my earlier discussion of the principles and norms governing Daribi marriage, I touched upon certain conditions which might be expressed in the rates of marriage and polygyny. Let me attempt to discover such expressions with the aid of a mathematical model.

Since Daribi accumulate wives one by one, we can express the rate of any particular degree of polygyny in terms of conditional probability: given that a man has already married x wives, the probability that he will have one more $(x + 1)$ is $P[(x + 1)/x]$. Thus an expression of the relative number of men having $x + n$ wives is proportional to:

$$P(x) \cdot P[(x + 1)/x] \cdot P[(x + 2)/(x + 1)] \cdots P[(x + n)/(x + n - 1)]$$

A Daribi man must make payments for his wife from the time of her betrothal onwards to validate her "membership" within his clan. A clan, however, is a group of men who "share wealth," and a man's demands on the "pooled" wealth of his clan and $zibi$ increase in direct proportion to the number of wives for which he must pay. We can assume that a man's liabilities in this respect are a direct measure of the number of his wives; consequently the likelihood of his obtaining another wife varies inversely with the number of wives for which he will then have to pay. Let us postulate that this likelihood, the factor of conditional probability for n, is equal to $1/n$.

Given this assumption, that $P[(x + 1)/x]$ is in each case equal to $1/(x + 1)$, the rate of n degree of polygyny (R_n) is proportional to

$$P(x) \cdot \left(\frac{1}{x + 1}\right) \cdot \left(\frac{1}{x + 2}\right) \cdots \left(\frac{1}{n}\right)$$

We can simplify our equation so that $R_n \sim x/n!$. Thus the rate of n degree of polygyny, or the relative number of men with n wives each, is inversely proportional to n factorial.

It can be shown that if we take $x = 1$, the lowest number of wives in my sample, and arbitrarily take $n = 7$ (the highest number in my sample) as an upper limit, the value of R_x in our equation, expressed in terms of percentage, is 58.2 per cent. We can therefore compute expected percentages for each degree of polygyny, and also compute numerical expectations on the basis of the sample (Table 2).

Table 2. DARIBI POLYGYNY

Present Adult and First Ascending Generations (194 Men)							
n	1	2	3	4	5	6	7
Per Cent Expectation	58.2%	29.1	9.7	2.4	.49	.08	.01
Per Cent of Sample	57.2	28.3	10.3	2.5	1.0	.00	.5
Numerical Expectation	112.9	56.5	18.8	4.7	.95	.16	.02
Number in Sample	111.0	55.0	20.0	5.0	2.0	.00	1.0

Present Adult Generation Only (120 Men)							
Per Cent Expectation	58.2%	29.1	9.7	2.4	.49	.08	.01
Per Cent of Sample	59.2	30.0	10.0	.8	.00	.00	.00
Numerical Expectation	69.8	34.9	11.6	2.8	.58	.09	.01
Number in Sample	71.0	36.0	12.0	1.0	.00	.00	.00

Secondary Marriages

	Number	Expected	Rate
Total Marriages	318	306.5	—
Total Secondary Marriages	124	112.5	$\frac{124}{318}$: 39.0%
Total Known Sororal Marriages	15	—	$\frac{15}{124}$: 12.1
Additional Wives from Same Clan	44	—	$\frac{44}{124}$: 35.3

The sample is based on genealogies of eight Daribi clan units; Hagani and Kurube' clans, four components of the Dobu community, and two Noru units. In the interests of accuracy I have limited the sample to the present adult and first ascending generations, and have also recorded figures for only the present adult generation. Because the samples are small, individual clans vary widely with respect to our expectations, but with increasing sample size the correspondence becomes close (Table 2). Note that for higher values of n the variation between the expected and manifest results increases; this reflects an area of ambiguity, contingent upon the activities of "big men" in their manipulation of the exchange system.

Assuming that the equation holds, at least for the lower values of n, we can in each case multiply the expected percentage of men having a certain number of wives by n, the number of wives, and compute an expected ratio of married women to married men, which is 1.58. This compares with a ratio of 1.64 for our first sample, and 1.53 for our

second. We can also compute expectations for total marriages, which
are recorded in Table 2, together with results from our first sample
for secondary marriages as well as for rates of secondary marriage
involving a clan from which wives were previously taken by the same
man, and for known cases of sororal polygyny.

Table 3 is based on household censuses of Kurube' and Hagani clans

Table 3. DARIBI MARRIAGE RATES

	Men		Women		Total	
	Number	*Per Cent*	*Number*	*Per Cent*	*Number*	*Per Cent*
Kurube'						
Married	15	62.5%	26	86.7%	41	75.9%
Unmarried	9	37.5	4	13.3	13	24.0
Total	24	100.0	30	100.0	54	99.9
Hagani						
Married	12	66.6%	16	88.8%	28	77.7%
Unmarried	6	33.3	2	11.2	8	22.2
Total	18	99.9	18	100.0	36	99.9
Totals						
Married	27	64.3%	42	87.5%	69	76.6%
Unmarried	15	35.7	6	12.5	21	23.3
Total	42	100.0	48	100.0	90	99.9

and lists all persons of marriageable age: a total sample of 90 persons.
Included are three widows, three divorced single women, one widower
and one permanent bachelor (a cripple), as well as thirteen young
men who have not yet married. Males make up 46.7% of the sample,
females 53.3%.

A COMPARATIVE NOTE

Some features of the Daribi system are no doubt common to many or
perhaps all New Guinea societies, but others seem to have a more
limited distribution. Specifically, Williams' account of the natives of

the Lake Kutubu region suggests the operation of analogous structural principles in an area far to the west of Mt. Karimui.[10]

The Kutubu are grouped into dispersed totemic clans, *amindoba,* membership in which is determined by patrilineal descent (Williams, 1940: 45). The exogamic prohibition for any individual includes both his own and his mother's clans, and the argument against marriage within the clan is based on exchange considerations:

> That a clan should at once be liable for and entitled to payment in respect of the same girl is regarded as absurd and undesirable, because it would lead to dissatisfaction and disputes about the bride price. It is as if the bride price had become the matter of major importance (52).

The extension of the marriage prohibition to the mother's *amindoba* is also understandable in these terms, for

> On the one side the bride-price (*búnuka*) is got together by both paternal and maternal clans of the groom: they are the donors. On the other side, it is divided (in exactly equal proportions) between the paternal and maternal clans of the bride: they are the recipients (52).

It is clear then that at least as regards marriage, the exogamic unit tends to be defined in terms of exchange. It is also clear, however, that this unit does not correspond to an entire *dispersed amindoba,* for "it is not to be supposed that the bride price . . . is divided among all the members of the girl's *amindoba,* wherever they are living; it is, on the contrary, given to the local or tribal representatives of the clan, who form a group of patrilineal kinsmen" (51). In fact, there is evidence to suggest that it is the village (*aa,* men's house) which functions in this way; Williams speaks of ". . . the bride-price which the whole village gets together" (44), and at Herebu, where two clans share such an *aa,* there is no marriage between them because ". . . a union between Kwidobo and Kibidobo would tend once more to be a mere shuffling of possessions in the Herebu men's house" (53).

Whether we speak of local lineages or "village" groups, the criterion

---

[10] There is reason to believe that a continuum of more or less closely related cultures, similar in their interrelationship to those of the highland areas to the north, but smaller in extent and population and different in content, exists in the limestone ridge country south of the Erave River between Mount Karimui and Lake Kutubu. Apart from Williams' Kutubu monograph, no ethnographic studies have been attempted in this area prior to the 1960's. At present Edward L. Schieffelin of the University of Chicago is doing fieldwork at Mt. Bosavi, and Charles Langlas of the University of Hawaii has been working at Lake Kutubu.

for exogamy seems to be that of exchange. What of the alliance of such units? Both the maternal and paternal *amindoba* of a girl receive portions of the bride price, and the corresponding clans of her husband contribute to this. What this means, in effect, is that an individual forms a link between the *amindoba* (or equivalent units) of his parents; each has an interest in him. A suggestion that this link may be one of consanguinity, that is of the joining of substances of the respective clans in one individual, is given by the Kutubu conception theory, according to which flesh and the soft parts of the body are formed of maternal blood, whereas hard, "white" parts are formed of paternal semen (145). Assuming this to be the case, we should expect to find some kind of adjustment which mediates between the conflicting consanguineal claims in order to effect recruitment, as in the case of the Daribi *pagebidi*.

Williams does not identify the payments given by a Kutubuan to his *abia*, or mother's brother, as recruitment payments, yet the details presented in his monograph certainly accommodate such an interpretation. The payments must be given continually, and we find here, also as at Karimui, sanctions against their neglect (in the form of an attack upon the nephew by ancestral ghosts of the *abia*). These gifts, at Kutubu, are typically gifts of meat (63).

Thus there is evidence that at Kutubu, as at Karimui, membership in the segmental unit is validated by exchange, "recruitment" being effected for a woman by the bride price, for a child or man by the *abia* payment, whereas alliance is brought about through the mingling of substances at conception.

Of course there are differences between the social structures in the two areas and the data are subject to several interpretations, but it is significant that Kutubu resembles Karimui in precisely those points which play a crucial role in the social structure. Perhaps further research at Kutubu will yield more positive evidence.

Marriage in
CHIMBU

Paula Brown

The Chimbu are centrally located in the highlands of Australian New Guinea, inhabiting the eastern end of the Wahgi valley and the valleys of two large tributaries, the Chimbu and the Koronigl. Closely related people are found east, south, and west of them. The valleys are at about 5,000 feet and the mountains rise to 15,000 feet. In the very densely settled Chimbu valley, foodstuffs are cultivated at altitudes up to and over 8,000 feet. The dietary staple is sweet potatoes, and a large variety of other foods is grown. The diet is poor in animal protein and fats, as pork, nowadays supplemented by chicken, beef, and horsemeat, is eaten only on special occasions. The main sources of fat and protein are vegetables, which now include peanuts and other introduced foods. Forest products have always been used in house building and for tools and clothing.

Chimbu has had a government station at Kundiawa since 1934, when it put a stop to tribal warfare. Today cotton clothing, blankets, axes, knives, shovels, utensils, and some foods are purchased in local trade stores. The main money income is from the sale of coffee as berries or as dried beans, mostly through the Chimbu Cooperative established in 1964. Coffee groves and processing stations have been established throughout the area, under government guidance, but the dense native settlement precludes European plantations in the area. Since 1950 most young men have spent several years in employment, either as agreement labor on coastal plantations or in casual labor in the highlands. Most have some years of schooling, but literacy, even in Pidgin English, is rare. Some sort of medical service has been available for many years, but local health stations, infant welfare inspections, etc., are little used. Catholic and Lutheran missions were established in the 1930's. All these conditions are rapidly changing and they affect infant mortality, family size, the incidence of polygyny, husband-wife relations, marriage payments, feasts, and contact with other Chimbu tribes and with outsiders.

My first visit to the Mintima area of Chimbu was in 1958, my last in 1965.[1] The information in this paper derives from these visits; the tables were made up at different times in this period, and the cases vary somewhat as new marriages were added or data superseded. The population for most of the figures is about 1,000 people, but cases from previous generations are included in some calculations.

The Chimbu, more densely settled but otherwise much like the other highlanders around them, especially those to the west of them, have a scattered pattern of settlement. Men's houses, located on high lookout points, contain up to twenty or thirty men and boys. A recent trend has been to a greater number of small independent men's house groups and to family house clusters.[2] The men's houses are concentrated in the center of the group territory. Women, living in separate houses with their daughters and young sons, are more scattered. Women's houses adjoin the fence which separates them from garden land and pig-grazing areas. It is the woman's job to feed the pigs daily, and she sometimes shares the pig house, although most women have more than one house. Houses are usually located on the land of the male head of the household.

The land holdings of an elementary family are scattered over an area that usually exceeds a square mile. Each family has more than one garden under cultivation at any time, and there is frequent daily travel to and from the gardens. The collective territory of the individual members of a clan segment is found in several parcels; clan land is often in one large block but may have outliers; subtribes and tribes are territorial units.

The Chimbu are unlike most other highland societies in having what are called phratries which are quite distinct from the large territorial tribes. A phratry is composed of a number of exogamous clans. It is thought of as an agnatic group with the founder's sons as clan founders. Tribes (population 1,000–4,000) are the effective political units. While they may rarely act as fighting forces and have never fully succeeded in keeping internal peace, they have a collective interest in the tribe's welfare, territory, and reputation. Some large vegetable displays and distributions (*mogenambiri*) are given by

[1] All field work was supported by the Australian National University, where I was a member of the Department of Anthropology and Sociology from 1956 to 1966. Some of the material is taken from previous publications, and further data will be found in Brown, 1960, 1961, 1962, 1963, 1966, 1967a, and 1967b; in Brown and Brookfield, 1959 and 1967; in Brookfield and Brown, 1963; and in Brown and Winefield, 1965.

[2] Brown and Brookfield, 1967.

tribes and the pig feast (*buga gende*) is a tribal affair held simultaneously on a number of ceremonial grounds. Such feasts require joint planning and collaboration among the leading members of all subgroups. Each tribe's reputation and local status rest upon its success in maintaining or expanding territory and on its ceremonial showing in personal decoration and the amount of food distributed.

Within the tribe clans are the most important named groups. The clans of a phratry are often grouped in one or more local clusters separated by other clans. Traditions often state that such phratries were once territorially united but migrations of segments brought about the present dispersal. Further, the once exogamous units are often said to have subsequently divided into two or more intermarrying groups which now form subtribes. The tribe, then, is often an alliance of two clusters of clans; each cluster is on the one hand a subtribe that is a closely integrated territorial unit and on the other a subphratry conceived as having divided from one clan to several.

I call the exogamous group a clan and usually it is a named group with internal segments which have a tradition of former connection with other groups. In the material on Naregu tribe to follow, it will be seen that Numambugu and Pentagu clans have intermarried more often in the present generation than in the past; these two groups were a single exogamous unit—the first marriage between them occurred within living memory. Such traditions of recent segmentation are common and support other evidence of population increase. Nonetheless, the size of clans varies greatly throughout the Chimbu from less than 200 to more than 1,500 people. The factors leading to fission into two clans include population growth, separation of territories, and disputes in which the participants took separate action at time of crisis. Alliances between adjacent clans or sections of clans occur but I have never heard of these giving rise to new exogamous groups as appears to be the case among the Mendi (Ryan, 1959). On the contrary, an important unifying force between adjacent clans is the great number of ties of kinship and affinity between the members. Nearly everyone has close kinsmen and affines in all the neighboring clans and they are more important helpers and contributors to payments than distant fellow clansmen.

Relations established by marriage are of great importance—not only in mutual assistance, but in social, economic, political, and ceremonial activities. Affines and nonagnatic kinsmen become exchange partners, donors, and recipients of valuables; they are the audience, and the lenders and helpers, both publicly and privately, in all phases of the

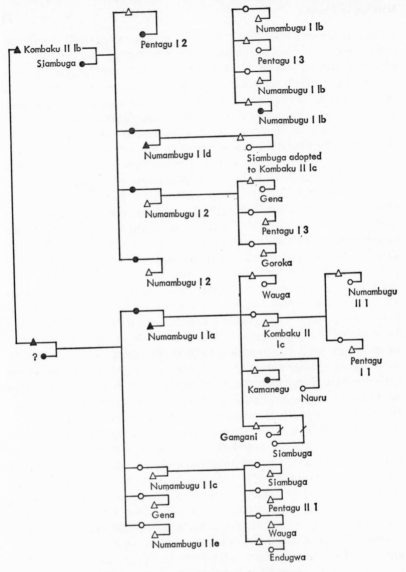

Diagram 1. A CHIMBU GENEALOGY

A genealogy showing extensive intermarriage between neighbors. Persons are shown by their group membership. Segments of three clans of Naregu tribe: Pentagu, Kombaku, and Numambugu are distinguished with clan sections in Roman numerals, subclans in Arabic numerals, and subclan sections in lower case letters. Only the names of other tribes are given. Deceased persons are shown in solid circles or triangles. Diagonal lines indicate broken marriages.

exchange economy. While subsistence activities are carried out mostly by families, the families are often assisted by others in the local segment in a portion of the food production, and in most special crops (sugar cane, banana); and all pigs are communally raised for distribution on special occasions. Marriages and funerals which involve kinsmen and affines are also occasions for the distribution of goods and food. The whole ceremonial and distributional economy (which uses shells, feathers, axes, and money) centers about affinal and, in the next generation, nonagnatic kinship relations. Each marriage initiates new interpersonal and exchange relations, not only for the marrying pair, but for their close kinsmen and the offspring that may be born.

Marriage prohibitions are few—no one in the clan is a permitted partner for the clan is defined most clearly as the exogamic group. My sole case of intraclan marriage is an aberrant case in which both parties were living with kin elsewhere at the time of marriage.

The Chimbu do not express concern about incest: although boys sleep in the men's house from about the age of seven, there is no avoidance of sisters or restraint with clanswomen. Visiting married sisters are well treated and are welcome to remain with their agnates. A young orphaned brother often lives with a married sister and her husband, sleeping in the men's house and helping in their domestic activities.

The prohibitions against marriage with kin are more difficult to define and tend to shift somewhat. The rule can perhaps be put best as a prohibition of marriage into the mother's subclan section. What I call the subclan section is generally termed in Chimbu *boromai suara* (blood one).[3] It is an agnatic group, sometimes a patrilineage centered upon a founding ancestor or group of ancestors, but it is as often a recognized segment of a subclan whose male members may be associated with one men's house. The *boromai suara* hold some of their land in adjoining plots, and make up the core of the group assembling a marriage or death payment; they also cooperate in exchange relations, in which one of the older members serves as leader.

This group is not formally constituted and only a few are identifiable by the name of a locality or a founder. It has no exclusive activities and is not marked out by the Chimbu in any distinctive way. But its members feel especially close whether or not a genealogy is known to interrelate them. They may collectively own a pair of flutes and the tunes used at pig feasts; they are reliable supporters in time of need. However, when marriages are being planned, no great attention is

[3] Brown, 1967a.

paid them as units of matrilateral exogamy. It is often said that one should not marry into the mother's subclan but in fact marriage into other segments of the mother's subclan is common, and only the mother's "one blood" group is fairly often avoided.

The agnatic exogamic rules are not quite clear-cut either—long separated and spatially distant phratry sections may rarely or never marry. Sometimes it is claimed that this is prohibited but in fact the members rarely meet and there is little opportunity to arrange marriage between the groups. Marriage is arranged with persons known to both parties— the frequency of marriage between neighboring clans clearly reflects their social interconnections. When boys live with other relatives or affines, such as a sister and her husband, they should not court or attempt to marry girls in the host subclan. But the difficulty concerning payment, since the host is a main contributor to a young male guest's bride wealth, is probably more important than considerations of propriety.

Marriage between groups is sometimes discussed as if it were a delayed exchange of women. That is, after a woman marries, her natal group expects to get a bride from her husband's group in the future. Occasionally the woman's own daughter marries into her subclan but in a different section; more often it is the woman's subclan section that obtains a bride from the woman's husband's subclan section. But a return bride from subclan to subclan or clan section is also suitable, or even from clan to clan, at a distance. The speeches made at a marriage always mention the state of the exchange between groups: it may be noted that several girls from one group have married into the other without any return or that this is a return after two or three in the other direction, or that the last married pair have long been dead. But the marriage is always by payment, never by direct woman exchange; and, as every subclan has affinal ties with most others in the area, whenever a marriage is proposed the state of the exchange relationship can be discussed. It does not determine the choice but may be a point of negotiation. When the young people have not selected their partners, the elders make the choice for them, not by consideration for social position but mainly by the acceptability of the payment offered and the agreement of all parties.

I define Chimbu marriage by the formal payment ceremony. A wide range of clansmen, kin, and affines participate and witness the event. This prevents a breach of exogamic rules, and young women who leave home and live in the household of unsuitable mates are taken home by their kinsmen. A girl's visit to a man's home is not recognized as marriage, even though men may speak of the girl's coming to them as though it were.

In the Chimbu area both married and unmarried men (aged 17–30) visit unmarried girls (aged 14–19). Adolescence is a period of pleasure for girls; they do little work and spend their days lolling and walking about, inviting men to visit them at night, to sing and caress them. Young men seek favors from the girls, who sometimes as a group invite young men from a nearby clan or tribe to a large courting party. Young people of both sexes visit their kin, meet other young people, and attend courting parties. Distant visits are rare, and only the bravest young men go into enemy territory. Large ceremonial visits at which the girls are accompanied by their older male clansmen are made infrequently.

Individual attachments occur at this period. A young woman sometimes spends a few days with the female kin of a young man to whom she is attracted, but these visits are not always followed by marriage; more often the girl is decorated (with grease, paint, and feathers) by the man's agnates and returns to her parents. Some men are reluctant to marry, or claim they are too young. Sometimes the young woman decides that she does not wish to stay. The kin of either may discourage the match.

The visit does not usually involve sexual relations or cohabitation. The Chimbu believe that conception results from successive acts of copulation. If pregnancy follows a single act or a few acts, the woman is suspected by her mate of having relations with other men, and the offspring is said to be that of many men. Sometimes a girl remains with the young man's relatives for some months while negotiations are pending, and pregnancy, for which the young man may or may not accept full responsibility, may then precede marriage. If the attachment develops into marriage, the girl returns to her home for the wedding; I know of no case in which a girl remained at a man's home without marrying him.

Marriage is a formal transaction which includes the transfer of valuable goods. In the majority of cases, the young people do not choose one another. When a youth is considered ready for marriage—at the age of about 20 to 22—his elders collect feathers, shells, axes, and now, money, and invite the relatives of an eligible girl (aged 17 to 19) to examine the goods. The groom's close male agnates and the leading men of his subclan undertake the negotiations, often with some participation by his close nonagnatic kin. The bride is often related to a friend, kinsman, or affine of one of the groom's party. When an agreement is reached about the payment and the pigs are to be exchanged, a date is set for the wedding and a series of exchanges follows. The wishes of the couple to be married are not wholly disregarded; either may refuse and stop the proceedings, but in most cases they accept passively the spouse chosen for them, although they may never have met.[4]

Each marriage is a separate arrangement, negotiated between the groups of the bride and groom. Furthermore, separation is so common that the first marriage arranged for a person is rarely the one which lasts to bind together the two bodies of kin. Table 1 shows the distribution of affinal ties which results from Chimbu mariages. It includes ties which have been broken or modified by divorce and death. Those of previous generations are now matrilateral ties.

Marriage payments are large—more than any individual or small group of agnates can provide unaided. They are regarded as the price of "upfostering" (cf. Radcliffe–Brown, 1950:44). Contributions are necessary, and this involves support from many men. The sets of contributors and recipients do not correspond to the exogamous groups. In Chimbu the largest contributors are the close agnates of the groom, often assisted by their own exchange partners; one or more items are contributed by most members of the groom's subclan section as well as by many members of other sections of his subclan. Members of the groom's clan who are especially friendly with his close agnates also contribute as individuals, as do the groom's kinsmen outside his clan and his affines. Contributors are not strictly determined by nearness to the groom; some close relatives may have used their valuables for other obligations, but they participate in the proceedings nonetheless. The bride's party provides a smaller return gift, with contributions from the same categories of relationship to her but from a narrower range of participants. The groom's payment and the meat are widely shared, being allocated by the bride's father and the men who have contributed pigs to the return gift.

Contributions to the groom's marriage payment are often assembled before a bride has been found, and the payment may be rejected by one or more sets of girls' relatives before the collection of valuables is handed over to a bride's group. Thus the contributors do not choose the marriage partner; they merely support the groom in providing a

[4] Brown, 1964: 339.

payment. Similarly, the contributors to the bride's prestation support her father and the leaders of her group. Even at the wedding, members of the party making the payment may not know the names of subclan membership of the principal recipients.

The marriage is a public event at which the wide sharing of goods and pork is essential for recognition. Once agreement has been reached between the parties of the bride and groom, larger supporting groups become active. The pigs of each group are killed and cooked by the donors and helpers from their subclan section, their kin, and their affines. On the night before the marriage the subclansmen of the groom, with their wives and children and some of his other relatives, go to the house of the bride's father and exchange some of the wedding pork. Men of the bride's subclan lecture her about her marital responsibilities, and women who have married into her subclan sing, wash her with oil, and counsel her about her future duties. Her instructions stress hard work and the providing of food to members of the groom's group. She is told to work for his group and not to visit home too often to help her parents nor to hang about the government station.[5]

On the next day the groom's party makes a ceremonial entrance. The group is made up of most members of the groom's subclan section, many of his subclansmen, his close kin, and affines outside the clan. They carry a display board (*minge-ende,* shell-wood) to which shells and several kinds of bird-of-paradise, parrot, and hawk feathers are attached. Cooked pigs are brought and often also one or two live pigs to begin a family herd. The composition of the marriage payment has been changing: pieces of kangaroo fur, stone axes, and dog's teeth were eliminated before 1956 and cowrie shell headbands and strands dropped from use after 1959. Money has become the most important item—reaching about £A200 (about $450) by 1965, despite a local Government Council regulation restricting the asking price by the girl's kin to £A25.

During the period 1958–65 I attended the preparations and ceremonies of many marriages, but it was never possible to obtain a complete record of the contributions to the groom's and bride's prestations, goods exchanged, objects used to decorate the bride and attendants, and the distribution of things received by the bride's and groom's groups. The list below is a general indication of the amounts and types of goods presented by the groom's group. Sometimes between

[5] Brown, 1964: 343–44.

Table 1. MARRIAGES OF SOME MEN IN NAREGU TRIBE

Group of Wife	Previous Generations				Present Generation						Totals	
	Numambugu		Kombaku		Numambugu		Kombaku		Pentagu		Totals	
	Number	Per Cent	Number	Per Cent	Number	Per Cent	Number	Per Cent	Number	Per Cent	Number	Per Cent
Pentagu	1	0.8%	27	20.6%	20	14.4%	25	17.7%	0	—%		
Kombaku	31	25.0	0	—	40	28.8	1	0.7	29	24.0		
Numambugu	0	—	26	19.8	0	—	46	32.6	14	11.6		
Gamgani	17	13.7	0	—	7	5.0	5	3.5	0	—		
Intratribal Total	49	39.5	53	40.5	67	48.2	77	54.6	43	35.6	289	44.1%
Kamanegu	7	5.6	15	11.5	10	7.2	20	14.2	14	11.6		
Endugwa	13	10.5	15	11.5	13	9.4	7	5.0	13	10.7		
Nauru	0	—	0	—	2	1.4	1	0.7	0	—		
Siambuga	22	17.7	10	7.7	11	7.9	8	5.6	8	6.6		
Wauga	10	8.1	5	3.8	7	5.0	0	—	2	1.7		
Gena	13	10.5	14	10.7	17	12.2	17	12.1	25	20.6		
Kombuku	1	0.8	2	1.5	1	0.7	1	0.7	0	—		

	66	53.2	61	46.6	61	43.9	54	38.3	62	51.2	304	46.3
Near Tribe Total												
Yonggamugl	4	3.2	9	6.9	4	2.9	1	0.7	11	9.1		
Upper Chimbu	1	0.8	4	3.1	3	2.2	1	0.7	1	0.8		
Kerowagi	0	—	0	—	0	—	4	2.8	1	0.8		
Other Chimbu Total	5	4.0	13	9.9	7	5.0	6	4.3	13	10.7	44	6.7
West and Southwest	4	3.2	1	0.8	2	1.4	1	0.7	1	0.8		
Southeast	0	—	3	2.3	1	0.7	1	0.7	2	1.7		
North	0	—	0	—	1	0.7	0	—	0	—		
Far Distant	0	—	0	—	0	—	2	1.4	0	—		
Other Groups Total	4	3.2	4	3.1	4	2.9	4	2.8	3	2.5	19	2.9
Total	124		131		139		141		121		656	

Source: Brown 1964: 342.

one-quarter and one-half of this amount was given by the bride's group as a countergift, but the number of pigs was usually equal or nearly so.

Shells:	20 goldlip mother-of-pearl shells (increased to 30 later) 3 bailer shells. 15 headbands decorated with cowrie shells (given until about 1960, then omitted).
Feathers:	15 pairs red bird-of-paradise feathers (*Paradisaea apoda salvadorii*). 3 pairs yellow bird-of-paradise feathers (*P. minor finschi*). 10 pairs black plumes (*Astrapia stephaniae*). 1 superb bird-of-paradise feather (*Lophorina superba femina*). 12 Pesquetts parrot (*Psittrichus fulgidus*) headdresses. 10 other feathered headdresses, including hawk. Occasionally other plumes.
Metal goods:	20 steel axes. 2 knives (rare in later years).
Pigs:	6 (often one or two given live).
Money:	Australian pound notes and rolls of 100 shillings, increasing from £15 in 1958 to £200 in 1965.

The variations in quantity and proportions of the various items are very great, but the only consistent trend was the increase in money. The circumstances of the marriage influence the quantities and the form of ceremony. Some marriages were held while the groom was away at work; in these the bride and her attendants carried out the ceremony without him, but these marriages seem to involve lesser payments and were more often terminated without cohabitation. Marriages celebrated after long cohabitation also involved less payment. Sometimes the marriage of a sister is held just before that of her brother; except for the pigs, most of the payment is used for her brother's marriage and not distributed by the bride's group. Widows and divorcées are married with a smaller payment, of which some may be given to the bride's agnates, some to her former husband's group —the circumstances of the termination of marriage, time before remarriage, presence of children, etc., affect this greatly. Some marriages are combined with other festivities in which food, especially pork, is distributed; in these the marriage pork is distributed with the other food, and the marriage feast becomes larger and more widely celebrated than for a simple marriage.

It is common, but not essential, that at the same time as the marriage with its gift and countergift, some goods are presented by both parties for exchange. Then the shells, feathers, or whatever are closely matched and exchanged, thus initiating or continuing the exchange relationship between the parties that marriage makes possible.

The bride is decorated by her agnates in feathers and shells, which become her property. A member of the groom's subclan is also decorated by the bride's agnates. This man has a close affinal or kinship relation with the bride's group and is chosen as her helper, mediator, and supporter after marriage. He is also given a payment by the husband's subclan when the wife dies.

Speeches proclaim that the two groups should in the future be friendly and exchange visits and food. The bride and groom share a single piece of pork provided by her kin. The bride departs with the groom's party. Sometimes members of the bride's party follow them in a mock pursuit with leaves and branches of a stinging tree.[6]

The increased interest in money and imported goods was accompanied by a declining interest in ornaments, although their quantity did not change much during the eight years. By 1964 there was little occasion for wearing ornaments and almost none for the full headdresses which were worn during the dancing before the large pig feast, no longer celebrated. Brides and their attendants were decorated and occasionally girls at large Catholic festivals wore bird-of-paradise plumes, but men hardly ever did. After a marriage payment has been received, the shells and feathers are distributed among the bride's party and, nowadays, put aside until the next marriage. The less valuable parrot and hawk headdresses are often offered to, and refused by, the young men, who do not wear them to courting parties as their elders did.

After the bride is taken to her husband's group, her agnates divide the payment among themselves and her mother's agnates. A few days later there is another gathering of the two parties, this time at the groom's home. The bride's party brings a large quantity of vegetable food to exchange with the groom's party, and the women married into the groom's group present the new bride with a quantity of household goods and personal articles.[7]

This completes the marriage transactions, but the newly married pair does not immediately establish a separate household, nor is the marriage

---

[6] Brown, 1964: 344.
[7] Brown, 1962: 64.

consummated for some time. In the next few months, gardens are prepared for the bride. She lives at first with an older woman in the groom's group; then a house is built for her, and the husband visits her there. Brides do not always accept easily the separation from their kin and the hard work of marriage, and some effort is made, especially by other women, to fit them into group activities.[8]

Chimbu marriage is viewed as bringing groups together. The speeches emphasize the cementing role of marriage and the mutual hospitality of the intermarrying groups. Sometimes it is stressed that this is a rare, distant tie to another tribe; at other times, that there has been regular and friendly exchange with the neighbors within the tribe, and visiting should continue. After the mutual expression of good will and the dispersion of the payments, the bride's group will try to send her back if she runs away from her husband, and the husband's group will try to see that he treats her well. Still, many women have several short-lived marriages before they settle down, and many men can recount a number of temporary marriages, some of which fail because the first wife drives newcomers away, or a man sends a lazy woman home. Only a few men fail to keep any wife.

A successful marriage is followed by exchanges, visits, and gifts between the agnates of the bride and the agnates of the groom. A formal gift to the infant's matrilateral kin is made after each birth, and older children often visit matrilateral kin. The bride is visited by her siblings and parents, who often remain for years at their kinswoman's husband's home.[9]

A younger girl of her own group often joins a bride and may later marry into the same group. This practice is favored because the bride is lonely without some of her old friends, and women from the same group married to another often work and live close together. These ties are sometimes seen in the next generation when the children of these women are close friends.

The ties of kinship within the clan which result are an additional factor in intraclan solidarity and mutual aid. We found several instances of land gifts to fellow clansmen linked to the donors by nonagnatic ties. A married woman may rarely be able to visit her matrilateral kin and female agnates who have married at a distance from her husband's home, yet she may cooperate closely with a clanswoman who has married into

[8] Brown, 1964: 344.
[9] Brown, 1962: 64.

her husband's subclan. In contrast, the ties of men are more easily maintained: male agnates remain together, their sisters return to visit them, and they visit their kin in other clans. It is the removal of a woman from her natal group which begins to break her kinship bonds.

The exchange pattern between affines may be carried into the next generation, but it is not perpetuated long: there is no special relationship with the mother's father's, or father's mother's, or mother's mother's group. Payments at death, to a married woman's agnates and to a man's, boy's, or unmarried girl's mother's agnates serve to settle debts, although some exchange relationships may continue among the survivors.[10]

Marriage is neither restricted to near or friendly groups nor deliberately spread to distant ones. But a summary of cases shows a concentration among nearby clans (Table 1). Some peculiarities are notable and can be attributed to the special hostility between the Naregu and their Nauru neighbors to the south. Naregu tradition states that they are recent migrants to the region from the northeast, and the Nauru speak a different dialect. The filling in of territory has not brought friendly relations, visits, and exchanges. Gamgani, a small clan in Naregu, has intermarried with Nauru for some time; but the only marriages with other Naregu have occurred recently as a result of both groups attending the same mission, being together in the Local Government Council established in 1959, and visiting with Gamgani friends and kin. Kinsmen form a link whereby young people visit; courting parties are arranged so that they can meet members of more distant groups and also kinsmen are called upon for information and liaison with other groups having marriageable girls. Thus further marriages between the more distant kin and associates of one married pair are common.

During my period of observation, children rarely came early in marriage. Probably, nearly all women are over nineteen before they have their first child, and the men are usually over twenty-two. Since about 1950 most young men have left their home communities for labor on coastal plantations or in the New Guinea highlands for periods of two or more years. This practice delays the beginning of reproduction and interrupts reproduction of married people. Considering children who survived for one year or longer, we found that married women aged 16–30 years had an average of 0.9 children and that women of thirty-one and over had an average of 2.3 children.

[10] Brown, 1962: 64.

In common with many New Guinea highland people, the Chimbu believe that close and continuous contact with women is dangerous to men.
Husband and wife did not share a house in the past and this is still rare.
A woman's house usually has one section for pigs and one for the woman
and her young children. Men and boys over seven years normally sleep
in communal men's houses and visit their families for meals and work,
occasionally remaining overnight.

Chimbu women consume plants believed to have contraceptive properties
or to induce abortion. They sometimes use physical means to abort and
sometimes kill newborn infants. The traditional birth practice is to
build a small house to which a woman retires when in labor. Infants
are born with some assistance from neighbors in conditions of filth.
There are no specialist midwives. Birth in government or mission hospi-
tals is rare. In these conditions we can expect high neonatal and infant
mortality.

After the birth of a child, the couple abstains from intercourse, normally
for at least a year, while the infant is breast fed. This serves to space
successive births; when an infant dies intercourse may resume. These
conditions are consistent with a low birth rate and small family size.[11]

We found an average interval of 3.8 years between children and
a child/woman ratio of .520.

Polygyny is not very common now since the mission to which most
Naregu adhere strongly discourages it. The earliest census records and
other evidence suggest that in the past about 50 per cent of men were
bachelors and half the married men were polygynists. Spinsterhood is
unknown. I did not encounter any seriously physically or mentally
defective women and imagine that they may be killed in infancy or
childhood. All girls are married by the age of twenty. A few defective
men have never been married, but most of the single men over the
age of twenty-five we knew had formerly been married to at least one
wife.

Widows are strongly urged to marry again and a young woman
with or without young children often remarries. Widowers and other
unmarried men of her husband's subclan are the favored second husbands as they will foster the children and protect their land rights,
but a determined woman may marry any man of her choice, even in
another tribe, or remain on her husband's land, or return to her

[11] Brown and Winefield, 1965: 176–77.

Table 2. POLYGYNY AND WIDOWHOOD AMONG MINTIMA MEN[a]

	Number	Total	Per Cent
Men Without Wives		19	9%
Never Married or Deserted	6		
Widowed	13		
Men with One Wife		166	81
Married to One Woman	156		
Polygynous, Widowed, One Wife Remaining	10		
Men with Two Wives		18	9
Married to Two Women	17		
Polygynous, Widowed, Two Wives Remaining	1		
Men with Three Wives	3	3	1
Total		206	100

[a] Brown and Brookfield, 1959: 11.

own agnates. If she leaves her husband's group the children, especially sons, will be pressed to join their true agnates later on. They will be offered land and assistance with marriage payments by both their agnates and the man with whom they live. The conflicting pull of agnates and nonagnatic kin is very clear in these cases.

I did not systematically investigate separation and divorce frequency. It was possible to note separations and divorces during field work, but some instances of short-lived marriages which occurred between field trips were certainly missed. Case histories were unsatisfactory since older men informants did not clearly distinguish between a girl's visit to his group and marriage with full payment and accompanying ceremony. Lively and prominent old men can often recall ten or more girls who came to them while ordinary men rarely name more than two or three.

Separation and divorce are more common early in marriage before the young wife has been settled into her own house and has children. Disagreement and failure to work in gardens or care for pigs are the commonest causes given. A later separation, after children have been born, usually occurs after a violent quarrel, accusation of sorcery, or serious illness or incapacity of the husband. The frequent migration of young men to work may delay marriage or may occur at the beginning of a marriage. It seems as though going away to work is today a common means of avoiding responsibility of marriage. During the husband's absence, a young wife often leaves his group and returns to her parents. Thus, when he returns this abandonment may become an excuse to sever the marriage. Such girls sometimes go to other men in the interval. Demands by the husband and his kinsmen for repayment always follow but this is never complete. Such circumstances of desertion and separation in the old days were the causes of fights and extensive hostilities. Nowadays what cannot be settled between the parties may be taken to the Native Affairs Officer or mission priest for adjudication, but it rarely reaches the judiciary.

When tempers run high because payment or recompense seems inadequate, many men say "We won't marry them any more; we have sent many of our daughters to them but they don't treat them well." However, I could not see any evidence that these resolutions were followed. Some marriages, especially now, are initiated by the young couples themselves, but the marriage is not recognized until payments are offered by the groom's people and accepted by the bride's family.

Chimbu do not use distinct terms for persons of married or unmarried status. A girl, *ambai*, becomes a woman, *ambu*, when she marries. A young man, *kumugl*, becomes a man, *yagl*. Old men are sometimes also called *kumugl*. But this is not a matter of precisely recognized status. Divorced and widowed persons do not revert to the status of youth. Once married, a woman widowed or divorced does not again engage in courting parties. Men, on the other hand, may continue to attend them after marriage and the song leaders are often somewhat older men.

Divorce is not always definitive; it usually begins with a woman leaving her husband and going to her parents. Such visiting is very common and may last for days, weeks, or months. Visits may be made because of loneliness, illness, fear of sorcery or accusation of sorcery, quarrels, or for many other reasons. It is only after some time when no return or reconciliation has taken place that the question of a permanent separation arises. When asked, people say "I don't know, perhaps she will go back." The situation may not be certain until the woman takes some step toward remarriage. Some women become attached to other men in their husband's group with little ill-feeling between the men.

After divorce a man or woman with no obvious defects may be married to a second spouse who was never before married. But if the second marriage also fails, kinsmen are unwilling to provide the large marriage payment and ceremony for yet another. Thus these persons usually later settle down with a widowed or divorced mate, perhaps adopting children of the wife and a former husband with only a token payment and no ceremony.

No man can take a full part in political and economic life without a family. Older widowers sometimes have gardens and raise pigs with the help of a daughter or daughter-in-law, and thus keep their social positions. Widowers of all ages seek widows to marry; only the men who have in several attempts been unable to keep a wife do not continue to seek mates. The ideal of maleness includes taking a strong and active part in all public affairs, and this requires the support, food production, and cooking by wives and other women. The attachment of a widow need not include sexual relations—it is more a companionable and helping relationship with the normal sexual division of labor. Men who remain single are never fully a part of adult social relationships.

The general dominance of men in public social relations and political and economic affairs suggests that women have by contrast an inferior position which they resent. Yet this is belied by women's behavior. A young girl has a controlling role in her relations with young men—she invites them to court her and may choose to visit their families. She can refuse to marry the man chosen by her parents, or, once married, she can run away. But she may be forced to return. Suicide was a fairly common reaction to family coercion or difficult domestic relations.

The bride is welcomed by other women in her husband's group; as she grows older, she enjoys her family and social relations with other women. Chimbu man and wife traditionally work and sleep alone or with members of their own sex, coming together irregularly. Nowadays, separation of the sexes and separate dwellings are less evident than they were even a few years ago. It is becoming increasingly common for husbands and wives to share a single house or a cluster of buildings rather than be apart. The use of central men's houses is declining, as is the average distance between the houses of husband and wife. This decline in sexual separation and the abandonment of initiation and seclusion of young men seems to have occurred as part of the general trend of political and economic change.

Marriage Among the
MANGA[1]

E. A. Cook

INTRODUCTION

The Jimi Valley is located in the northeastern sector of the Western Highlands District, Territory of New Guinea. The valley, open on the west, drains ultimately into the Sepik; it is bounded on the north by the Schrader-Bismarck Mountains and on the south by the Wahgi-Sepik divide and it terminates in the east at the base of Mt. Wilhelm where the two mountain chains meet. The area is geologically youthful and is characterized by sharply V-shaped valleys in the middle and upper Jimi and by frequent earth tremors and landslides. In terms of land systems and associated vegetative communities, the middle Jimi (Narak area) appears to be intermediary to the Bismarck and Pira land systems described by Haantjens, Reiner, and Robbins (C.S.I.R.O., 1958).

Europeans first penetrated the Jimi in 1933 and 1934 (Souter, 1964: 187; Leahy and Crain, 1937: 170, 258). However, for the next seventeen years there was little interest and less traffic in this valley. The first official contact with the peoples of the middle Jimi occurred in 1951, but the initial census was not conducted until 1953. In 1955, warfare (previously endemic in the area) erupted along the north wall of the Jimi. Several groups were routed from their lands. This precipitated the establishment of a patrol post at Tabibuga in 1956 and effective implementation of the *Pax Australiana* to the 23,000 or so indigenes of the valley.

In this essay I am primarily concerned with one of the two clans of Manga phratry.[2] The Manga, located at 5°30' South, and 145°10'

[1] Field work in New Guinea lasted from September 1961 to August 1963 under tenure of a Predoctoral Fellowship MF-11,543 and Research Grant M-4895 and M1-04895-02S1 from the National Institutes of Mental Health, U.S. Public Health Service.

[2] Residence with the Manga extended from December 1961 through December 1962. After that I resided with the Morokai, neighbors of the Manga. The ostensible purpose of this research was the conduct of a study in minimal acculturation.

East, are one of the seven Narak-speaking phratries (Wurm, 1961; Cook, 1967b) and are closely related culturally and linguistically to the Kuma of the Middle Wahgi (Reay, 1959: 1).

Manga are swidden cultivators utilizing an altitudinal range varying from 2,200 to 5,200 feet. The principal tuber is the sweet potato though they also rely on yams, taro, and cassava. Other crops include bananas, corn, pandanus, sugarcane, *Saccharum edule, Saetaria palmifolia, Acanthacae Rungia klosii,* beans, pumpkins, cucumbers, peanuts, a large variety of bush, tree and vine leaves, papaya, mangoes, and breadfruit. The major domestic animal and source of meat is the pig. Other domestic animals include chickens, dogs, cats, and cassowaries. Women plant and maintain most food crops and attend the pigs.[3] Men prepare gardens, hunt, build houses, and trade. Ideally, men are the managers, women are managed.

Manga practice residential segregation. Each married woman has her own house in which she rears pigs and children. Males from about the age of seven spend more and more time sleeping in their fathers' collective men's house. The settlement pattern varies from a single village for the entire clan to familial hamlets. The predominating pattern at any time largely depends upon the cycling ceremonial activities involving the pig festival which, in turn, depends upon the size of the pig herd (Rappaport, 1967; Cook, 1967a: 63).

Each of the seven Narak-speaking groups is a segmentary society. Each phratry[4] comprises two or more ideologically exogamous, patrilineal, patrilocal clans.[5] Each of the total of sixteen clans is divided into moieties with complementary ceremonial and warfare functions. I call these units clan-moieties. Each clan-moiety may be divided into at least two but usually not more than six subclans. Subclan divisions may also occur. There is, therefore, a maximum of five levels of segmentary organization. Each of the 185 Narak segments has a proper name.[6]

---

[3] There is a division between "male crops" and "female crops." In general, women plant those crops in which the edible portion develops underground; men plant bananas, sugarcane, and pandanus. The specific location of a garden may be due to several variables including type of crop, soils, residence, availability of land, etc.

[4] Typologically speaking, Unjika and Korika are not phratries; each is itself a single exogamous clan.

[5] Morokai, three clans; Manga, two clans; Okona, two clans; Kaulaga, two clans; Moluma, five clans; Unjika and Korika. Mean phratry population size = 534 (median = 514). Mean clan population size = 197 (median 200).

[6] There is a set of lexemes in Narak that signifies the various levels of the segmentary organization. The segregate label (Conklin, 1962: 121) is /yua ka/ "man lines," which I translate as "patrilineages."

In 1962, 344 individuals resided within the territorial boundaries of Manga phratry (Figure 1). Of these, 188 resided within the boundaries of KulakaeNgeyka clan. Manga envision the clan as a stable male organization to which previously nonrelated females become attached in marriage and from which "sisters" are sent away in marriage. The extent to which this ideal is achieved in practice is revealed in Table 1. Here I present the composition of this clan as derived from genea-

Table 1. KULAKAENGEYKA CLAN, GENEALOGICAL SUMMARY

	Males		Females		Totals
	Dead	Alive	Dead	Alive	
A. Agnatic Core	128	84	74	72	+358
B. Agnatic Emigrants	5	12	36	46	−99
C. Immigrants	4	2	6	3	+15
D. Descendants of Immigrants	16	29	10	15	+70
E. Immigrants Who Left	—	2	2	7	−11
F. Wives Incoming	—	—	102	63	+165
G. Wives Leaving	—	—	5	13	−18
Totals	143	101	149	87	480

logical inquiry and encompassing a total span of five generations. The table reflects the developmental processes at work in the formation of the clan as a population unit. The agnatic core (A) comprises individuals who are agnatic members of the clan by right of descent. This core may be depleted or augmented. The agnatic core is depleted (B) primarily by the marriages of clan women to males of other clans. Seventy-seven of the eighty-two emigrant females fall into this category. Of the remaining twenty-two agnatic emigrants, eight are the descendants of four female spouses who returned to their natal territories and ten are the descendants of two brothers who moved to their sister's husband's territory.

The clan is augmented by immigrants (C) and their descendants (D), though not all of these immigrants will remain in their "adopted" territory (E). Of the eighty-five immigrants (C & D), nine are returning "sisters" and sixty-two are sister's children and their descendants, which collectively accounts for 83.4 per cent of all immigrants. The remaining immigrants and their descendants are distributed fairly equally among sister's husbands (2), sister's husband's brother (1),

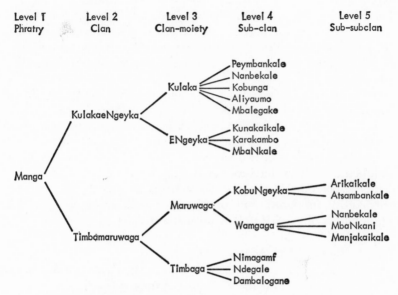

| Level 1 Phratry | Level 2 Clan | Level 3 Clan-moiety | Level 4 Sub-clan | Level 5 Sub-subclan |

Figure 1. SEGMENTARY LEVELS OF THE MANGA PHRATRY

wife's brother (2), and mother's sister's son (1), and their descendants (8). Out of this total of eighty-five immigrants, eleven have subsequently emigrated. Nine are females who have married out and two are males who have returned to their father's clans.

The only remaining alteration to the agnatic core is the accretion of wives (F) and the subsequent return to their natal residences of some of these women (G). There is little correspondence between the total number of wives acquired (F = 165) by KulakaeNgeyka men and the total number of women (77 + 9 = 86) sent away in marriage. It should be noted that there is an imbalance in the sex ratio of the agnatic core (A), because agnatic females in ascendant generations, e.g., FFZ, FFFBD, are more apt to be forgotten than affinal females of the same generation, e.g., FM. This selective forgetting may well be a function of the prescriptive marriage rule.

MARRIAGE

A Manga may not marry any individual recognized as a consanguineal or an affinal kinsman, /wuna tsiNga/ and /wuna kmba/. The prohibition excludes all zero-generation first cousins but not non-coresident zero-generation second cousins; that is, the descendants of non-coresident first cousins consider themselves unrelated. Marriage prohibitions largely depend upon previous marriages. These marriages establish kinship ties which ideally last for a specified two generations, after which the descendants are again regarded as non-kinsmen, /keu wuna/.

Within the span of the five generations available for analysis in the genealogies, 156 KulakaeNgeyka males of marriageable age acquired wives, while only sixteen remained bachelors. Twenty-two men have been polygynous (14.4 per cent), though no man has ever been known to have had more than two wives simultaneously. From the women's standpoint, however, forty-four of the 159 women (27.6 per cent) originating from outside the clan have spent at least a part of their married lives in a polygynous union with a KulakaeNgeyka male. The total number of marital unions for males is 178 (134+22+22).

Table 2. MANGA WIFE ACQUISITION[a]

Method	Number of Cases
A. Courtship	29
B. Sister-Exchange	32
C. Marriage Rule	5
D. "Gift"	6
E. Other	5
F. Unknown	86
G. Levirate	18
H. "Incest"	1
Total	182

[a] There are more "Methods of Wife Acquisition" (182) than actual male marital unions (178) because four women are listed under two categories each. For example, one woman listed under both B and C was acquired by the rule and also as an object of sister-exchange. Three of the women in the category "other" were acquired by an Australian patrol officer from the neighboring enemy phratry and given to the Manga as war reparations. The single case of "incest" was between members of the same clan-moiety, Kulaka, but of different subclans, Aliyaumo and Nanmbekale. At the ensuing trial, it was decreed that if the man moved to the natal territory of his father's father (the opposite clan of the phratry) the marriage would not constitute incest. He did so.

There are several methods available to a Manga male for acquiring a wife (Table 2). Exclusive of the large numbers of "unknowns," [7]

[7] This is due to Manga genealogical ignorance. Of the eighty-six women in this category, fifty-six are in the senior generations of the genealogies.

sister-exchange is the most common method of wife acquisition, with courtship second. Few marriages follow the prescriptive marriage rule. By "Gift" I refer to the practice whereby a leading man acquires rights of marital disposition over some woman through his own affinal linkages, which he then confers on someone else, usually a dependent coresident of his own men's house.

Courtship is initiated by the girl, who sends word or speaks directly to the young man of her choice. The young man can only strive to appear attractive. He greases his skin and wears fancy decorations. Most of these individual dates result from the more formal /kananta/, in which a group of girls of the same exogamous unit collectively invite young men from some other exogamous unit to come to the girls' village for a courtship session. This may be held in a men's or woman's house, though the former is preferred. The young men arrive *en masse* at about dusk.

In the house, the girls sit cross-legged and the men, two to a girl, sit cross-legged facing them. A man begins the verse of a song and is joined in a standardized chorus by the others. Several songs are sung during the evening and the singing continues until daybreak. As the men sing in a nasal falsetto they gently sway toward and then away from their joint partners. Girls may or may not sing; they may simply gaze unconcernedly into the fire, smoke cigarettes, nibble food, or carry on a jocular repartee with each other.

As the night progresses, however, a girl's participation becomes more intense. She has surveyed the men and made a choice, or perhaps wishes to play off one man against another. She sings now, and as a "round" concludes she sways, back and forth, toward one then the other of her partners (or she may ignore one altogether). When the song terminates she may choose to "cook nose" with one. This involves the girl's pressing her forehead against the man's forehead so that as they rotate their heads, their noses are mashed together. Mihalic claims that orgasm is frequently achieved in this fashion (1957: 56); I was never able to confirm this. A good nose, not too broad or too narrow, is a mark of great beauty.

After several rounds have been sung, there may be a general changing of partners, although not in any orderly progression. In the early morning when younger girls have either left or fallen "asleep," and as the firelight gets weaker and weaker, the daring male may fondle a breast and the girl may solicit greater intimacies (to be consummated later in the bush) by surreptitiously reaching under the man's apron to grasp his penis.

At these evening courtships a girl frequently arranges for a young man to meet her the next day or week for daytime courting, which differs in style. The boy and girl sit side by side. She then places both her legs between his, as they joke, talk, and perhaps sing softly to themselves. Sometimes the youth is so handsome that the girl persuades him to take her away, in effect, to "marry" her. Sometimes he makes elaborate promises of huge bride prices, never-ending pork banquets and, most influentially, the promise of one of his "sisters" for her "brothers" to marry. While a girl is encouraged to have many suitors, her showing too great an interest in one may upset the plans of marriage made for her by her kinsmen.

The young man's role in courtship largely depends upon his attractiveness and he uses a great deal of magic to this end. Girls do not desire short and ugly men. However, some men prefer short, stocky wives, maintaining that the durability and stamina of these women are greater than that of taller girls, and that their breasts do not sag so early. Participation in courtship is not limited to single men. Many young married men also engage in them. However, should their wives discover that they are doing so, or are contemplating acquisition of an additional wife, they become angry.

During courtship, a girl, impressed by the attractiveness of a young man or swayed by his extravagant promises, may propose that they depart at once for his home. This is not as easy as it sounds, because all courtship in houses is chaperoned by members of the girl's own exogamous unit; they are quick to forestall elopements because marriageable girls represent a capital asset to the clan. Should the young couple escape, however, the man takes the girl to the house of his own mother or to the wife of an influential man from whom he can expect support.

Since the woman's contributions, in terms of the produce of her labor, ultimately determine the prestige of her husband, the importance of being married cannot be overstressed. Courtship is only one of several methods through which a man may acquire a wife, and it is certainly the most hazardous. Not only are financial arrangements by the groom's kinsmen with his potential affines never begun until after the elopement, but he also risks being shot while running away with the girl. When a girl is missing, her immediate kinsmen quickly grab their weapons and set out in pursuit. Should they overtake the couple before they get to the young man's home, he is likely to bolt into the bush, abandoning the girl to her relatives. But should he succeed in getting her home, a day may elapse before her patrilateral kinsmen appear in a body in that village. The kinsmen's problem is to find where the girl is hidden. Given the number of houses and the dispersal of the population, it might seem that her kinsmen would never locate her. But this is not the case, because inevitably affinal connections of some sort are already established between the groups and serve as an effective communication leak. When her kinsmen learn where the young girl is, they proceed to that house to retrieve her. At first they plead with her, saying that her actions have caused much trouble and that her parents are distraught. If they are unable to persuade her to return willingly, her kinsmen may attempt to pull her bodily out of the house. This, however, usually precipitates violence and occasionally people are killed. On the other hand, successful negotiation may follow between the girl's and boy's kinsmen and the union is thereby sanctioned.

The severity or intensity of these reclaiming activities depends largely upon the marital arrangements that have already been made by the girl's kinsmen in contrast to the potential utility of a marriage based on the *de facto* situation. Sometimes, the right of ultimate disposition of the girl in marriage is sold at birth. This contract is made between two consanguineally unrelated persons. The purchaser is obligated at that time to pay the seller at least one piglet (female) and a pearlshell or two. As the girl matures, the conscientious purchaser should continue to make small prestations to the seller, and when the girl is mature she is transferred to the purchaser. The seller, in this arrangement, has not excluded himself totally from sharing in the final bride price, but his share will be minor. Thus, a man can be presented with a wife who has been partially prepaid. The new husband still owes a bride price, but it goes to the purchaser of the original contract.

Another form of wife acquisition is through sister-exchange. In this, two unrelated men exchange sisters with each other and thereby acquire wives. The significance of bride price in terms of the transfer of wealth in plumes and shells for certain rights in women is highlighted by the fact that, in marriages effected through sister-exchange, no such transfer of wealth ever occurs. The arrangement for this sort of marriage may be made by the girl's brother or by another, more senior, kinsman.

For the Manga, thirty-two women (20.1 per cent) of the 159 acquired as wives from other exogamous units over the period covered in the genealogies were acquired through sister-exchange. If the two senior generations in the genealogies are excluded from computation, the number of women acquired by sister-exchange is thirty out of ninety-six, or 31.3 per cent. It is difficult to interpret the contrast in these two figures. First, as previously noted, most informants are unable to state the method of wife acquisition by males of the two senior generations, in which case the different percentages are simply an artifact of genealogical ignorance and the incidence of sister-exchange may have been just as high several generations ago. Second, it is also possible that sister-exchange is actually declining in occurrence. I have no evidence to prove either of these two interpretations true or false. A third possible interpretation is that the difference in percentages may indicate that the system of marriage arangements is actually changing toward a greater reliance on direct sister-exchange as a method of wife acquisition. There are at least three possible contributing factors to such a change; the incursion of the /kananta/ courtship complex, declining clan size in terms of gross population, and reaction to Administration policy.

The courtship complex of /kananta/ was first practiced among the Manga about two generations ago. It is not yet practiced in the lower Jimi River area and remains more prevalent to the south and southeast of the Manga, i.e., toward the Kuma and Chimbu areas. I suggest that when women begin eloping, as is common in areas where /kananta/ is practiced, much more emphasis is placed upon immediate reciprocation of a woman. That is, as women attempt to exert more control over their own marital destinies, their fathers and brothers more firmly demand reciprocity.

It may also be that the increasing incidence of sister-exchange (if such is the case) is a deliberate effort to initiate continuing affinal alliances by a clan which is diminishing in size and importance. In cases of direct sister-exchange there is no bride price, which works to the advantage of the smaller clan, since its economic resources are not as great as those of a larger clan. Sister-exchange marriages are more durable, since the return of one man's wife precipitates the return of her exchange.

A third factor may well be the effect of Australian Administrative policy. Since 1956, Patrol Officers have upheld the right of a girl to choose whomever she wishes to marry and, at the same time, have denied men the right to make this decision for a girl. In sum, it is currently impossible to tell whether a change occurred or not and, if there is change, in what direction it is moving. Neither can accurate comparisons with other New Guinea highland societies be made at this time, since there are no figures available from other areas on the incidence of sister-exchange. Sister-exchange is nonexistent among the Mae-Enga (Meggitt, 1965: 93), and the exchange of real sisters is relatively rare among the Kuma (Reay, 1959: 66). Among the Manga, 65.8 per cent of the women given in sister-exchange are biologically full or half sisters and an additional 18.8 per cent are father's brother's daughters. This comprises 84.6 per cent of the women given in sister-exchange.

The negotiations for sister-exchange are most frequently carried on by men at the clan-moiety level. Whether the negotiations are or are not conducted at this level is, however, ideologically irrelevant to the Manga since sister-exchange is always referred to as having occurred between clan-moieties. Such affinally linked units are referred to as "brother-brother" units. In other contexts, the phrase may also refer to the paired clans of the same phratry as well as to the affinally linked clans of different phratries. The affinal kinship terminology includes all members of the opposite affinally linked "brother" unit, which dictates, in effect, that no additional marriages may be conducted with that unit for at least one more generation. This results in a wide distributon of women among other clans. The 159 Manga women sent in marriage have gone to at least sixteen different phratries, none of which is located more than five miles from their own territory. Almost one fourth (24.7 per cent) of all marriages have been contracted with the opposite clan of the Manga phratry. The second greatest percentage of marriages (14.6 per cent) has been contracted with clans of the Yuomban phratry. Those phratries with which marriages are most frequent are also those which are spatially the nearest to the KulakaeNgeyka. It is significant that the ideal of reciprocity has been least attained with the neighboring Yuomban phratry and it subsequently initiated the war with the Manga.

A breakdown of the distribution of marriages between Kulakae-Ngeyka and other phratries in terms of subclans of both the wife-giving and wife-taking phratries reveals no significant variations. That is, a subclan of one clan-moiety does not appear to have any exclusive affinal connection with particular subclans of other clan-moieties of other clans. In spite of this, the prohibition against males of the same clan-moiety marrying females of the same generation of some other clan-moiety is frequently violated. However, either the two men or the two women will not both be members of the same subclan, though they may be of the same clan-moiety. Thus, for purposes of adherence to this marriage prohibition, the actual referent unit is the subclan; not the clan as stated in the rule.

In those cases where a marriage arrangement has been satisfactorily concluded, the groom makes to the bride's parents a small payment, /kon kunoN wordndo/, consisting of a single pig, three to five pearl-shells, and perhaps a steel axe or a couple of bush knives. Full bride prices, /ana koluma/, are normally paid for all females except those acquired by sister-exchange. Manga say that a bride price ought to be paid at the time a man initially acquires a woman he intends as wife. In fact, however, bride prices are seldom paid before the couple has at least two living children well past the age of weaning. A wife does not formally determine when the bride price is to be paid; most bride prices are paid or received during the pig festival. She can, however, put pressure on her husband and induce him to fulfil his financial obligation to her parents. Since a man stores most of his valuables in his wife's house, she has a constant gauge by which to measure his efforts to accumulate sufficient wealth. If she feels that her husband is lax in these matters, or that he already has enough wealth accumulated, she may attempt to force him to pay for her. She may do this by berating him constantly, withdrawing sexual privileges from him, attempting adultery, refusing to cook for him, or by threatening to return to her parents.

In the course of any bride price payment and subsequent repayment by the affines,[8] there are two sets of contributors and two sets of recipients. I shall only mention the figures for bride price payments. Only slightly more than 50 per cent of all the contributors and recipients are members of the same subclan. Their average contribution constitutes over 70 per cent of all payments and they receive about the same percentage of all distributions. Less than 10 per cent of the contributors to a bride price belong to a different clan-moiety. The husband personally contributes approximately 50 per cent of the total payment. Additional contributions by nonmembers of the husband's subclan come from political leaders and aspirants, coresident non-agnates, and friends. The payment of the bride price effectively "defines" a marriage. At any time prior to this, the woman may, at the slightest provocation, return to her parents or run off with some other man. And, in fact, this is common. Most males who are now married

---

[8] After the bride price has been paid, the bride's kinsmen make a reciprocal payment to the groom's kinsmen. In the Narak area immediately adjacent to the Manga, this payment may be equivalent to 40–50 per cent of the original bride price payment. The further upriver one goes, the higher the percentage of bride price repayment and, conversely, the further downriver the lower the return. The significance of this is not treated here.

have had temporary liaisons with as many as five or six females before they acquired one who stayed and bore the requisite two living children. But once the /ana koluma/ has been paid, the woman is considered fully the property of the purchasing group (subclan), though the rights to sexual intercourse are solely the husband's.[9] Should the woman seek refuge with her patrikinsmen or some other man for some real or imagined slight, she will probably be returned to her rightful "owner." Should her husband die, the rights to her disposal in future marriages are retained by his subclan "brother." The children remain members of their father's clan. If the man dies before making the bride purchase payment, the woman may return to her original home, where her own father or brothers may again dispose of her in their best interests. However, a "brother" of the deceased may be acceptable to her and to her father or brothers, in which case, he makes her parents a small presentation of wealth and assumes the obligation to pay the full bride price in the future. Of eighteen men who acquired women in this manner, eight were genealogically traceable brothers of the woman's deceased husband, three belonged to the husband's subclan and six belonged to different subclans of the same clan. However, a woman in this position is able to control mate selection within certain limits. She may elect to remain unmarried, especially if she has mature sons, or she may accept an economic arrangement with a senior male of her deceased husband's subclan; she provides pig husbandry, gardening, and food preparation services in exchange for his labor, but normally without sexual union. Any male of the same clan as the deceased may offer himself by leaving bundles of firewood at her door. If the husband thus acquired is a member of a different subclan, he must make a payment of a pig and a few shells to the deceased's brothers, but if he is a member of the deceased's subclan, there is no payment. The new husband also inherits obligations to his wife's agnatic kinsmen and has to continue the wealth presentations to affines at the births and deaths of his children by her, and at her death.

Wives may also be acquired through the exercise of the marriage rule. The peculiarity of which is that it only applies to a man's eldest daughter. The father refers to this type of union as /nambalo konye pi/, meaning, among other things, that his eldest daughter has been married to a man of her generation of her father's mother's patrilineage. Among the nearby Tsembaga of the Simbai Valley, this prac-

[9] This also applies to women acquired through sister-exchange.

tice is known as "returning the planting material" (Rappaport, personal communication). Under this rule, an eldest daughter may expect to marry her FMBSS, or an equivalent. Should the father fail to give his daughter to his mother's patrilineage, he can expect the wrath of his mother's spirit to fall upon his own head. The rule may be circumvented. The father may simply gamble on the possibility that his matrikinsmen will not survive the next fifteen or so years and will therefore be unable to exercise their rights, a likely occurrence given the prevalence of warfare in precontact times; or he may negotiate with them to accept a younger daughter, a course which they sometimes accept; or he may follow the most certain method and "buy his mother." In this last, according to some informants, he makes a payment to his matrikinsmen, ostensibly for his mother (whose bride, child, and death payment his father has already made) but actually to purchase the right to dispose of his eldest daughter as he wishes. This is a difficult enterprise, especially if he already has a daughter born to him; therefore, such payments are usually made in full prior to the birth of any children. Such transactions are relatively uncommon since they presuppose the possession of more wealth than is usually available to a man at that time. Further, his own wife is usually against this practice since she sees the wealth, which could have been her own bride price, disappearing. One aspect of the acceptability of this course to the matrikinsmen is that he too may not live another fifteen years, much less produce a daughter.

The presence of such a marriage rule invites inquiry: Is the rule patrilateral or matrilateral? Is it preferential or prescriptive? Further, since there are only two ideal forms of marriage, sister-exchange and marriage by the rule, I have devised a model incorporating these features.[10] The model itself raises other questions: Is such a system unilateral or bilateral? Is it symmetrical or asymmetrical? What relationship does the model have with actual marital patterns? Does the model reflect any structural relationships of other aspects of Manga society?

Types of laterality in marriage rules are usually based on whether the wife was kin to her husband through either his father or his mother. But is our anthropological bias of regarding a male in the role of bride-taker valid in the analysis of a system in which the

---

[10] For some analytical purpose, marriages for which bride price payments are due may be regarded as a result of not having met the reciprocating ideal of sister-exchange without bride price. In fact a good case can be made for regarding all other forms of Manga marriage as transformations of these two basic types.

future husband's role in the acquisition of his spouse is negligible? In the Manga marriage rule, different interpretations of the type of laterality depend upon which kinsman is regarded as the focal point in the genealogical linkage. The rule is patrilateral if considered from the point of view of either of the marriage partners, since both are linked through their fathers. The rule is matrilateral if considered from the point of view of the father of the bride, i.e., the individual to whom the negative sanction for noncompliance will apply. And last, the rule is again patrilateral from the point of view of the father of the groom, i.e., the individual who claims the girl as a bride for his son. In sum, the possibilities are three to one in favor of regarding this as a patrilateral marriage rule.

The second question concerns the status of this rule as either preferential or prescriptive. I intend to use the term "prescriptive" in the sense promoted by Needham (1962: 9). A marriage rule is prescriptive if "the category or type of person to be married is precisely determined, and this marriage is obligatory." This is a more rigorous definition than that proposed for the Siane by Livingstone. He defined prescripitive "in the sense that it is not desirable or economic to keep sending women to another group with no exchange" (1964: 56). For Livingstone the Siane prescriptive system is also patrilateral though it is not based on exact genealogical reckoning. As Livingstone says, "To obtain a wife a man negotiates with the 'father's sister's' clans" (1964: 56), even though the marrying kin may not be genealogical cross-cousins. Among the Manga, reference is precisely genealogical hence the two cases are not totally comparable.

On these bases I conclude that the Manga marriage rule is a prescriptive patrilateral marriage rule. If the cousins getting married were regarded as kinsmen, which they are not, they would be parallel cousins in accordance with the definition of parallel in the Manga kinship terminological system (Cook, 1966). In a marriage of this type (Figure 2), the claimant (D) of the girl (E) is a terminological cross-cousin to the girl's father (C). That is, marital rights in the girl are transferred by the girl's father (C) to his mother's brother's son (D) who gives the girl, in turn, to his own son (F). In contrast, among the Kuma, the girl's FMBS may take her as a wife for himself.[11] For the Manga, a man (D) may solicit wives for his son (F) along several affine roads but he has a legal claim only on his FZSD (E).

[11] Professor Reay recently informed me that the marriage preference among the Kuma (1959: 57) which is so similar to the Manga rule has now become prescriptive in the sense I have used.

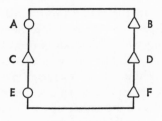

Figure 2.

In cases where sister-exchange has occurred involving A and B (i.e., B's sister marries A's brother), C and D are bilateral cross-cousins and therefore have legal claims on each other's daughters. If effectively concluded, then F's sister and E's brother would also marry; these marriages would symmetrically reunite the two patrilineages after one generation. The resultant pattern, as it continued over the generations, would be one of alternate generation patrilateral parallel cousin marriage with sister-exchange. However, in order to be complete, the marriages of C and D must also be shown as part of this ideal system.[12] In Figure 3, I propose a model which incorporates the two ideals of sister-exchange and the Manga prescriptive patrilateral marriage rule.[13] It must be remembered that this is a model of normative statements and is not one describing the "observed distribution of marriage" (Romney, 1961: 225–26).

The following five conditions exist in the model: (1) There are 2 exogamous clans designated "A" and "B." Note that in the Manga phratry, as in two of the remaining six Narak phratries, the phratry is divided into two clans. (2) The designations "A^1" and "A^2," "B^1" and "B^2" mark a moiety division of each of the clans. Note that each of the six Narak clans has a moiety division. (3) The model spans five generations. The limit of actual kinship reckoning is five generations. (4) All marriages in the model are by sister-exchange. (5) In G^0 and lower generations, each female marries her FMBSS. The model can be extended to include additional senior generations and still retain this feature.

The resultant system of paired exogamous clans, with each clan split into clan-moieties, results in a continuous closed system which does not violate any of the marriage prohibitions and fulfills both the

[12] It is significant that a model with three descent lines is inadequate.

[13] In tracing kin types on the model that incorporates a same sex sibling link, it is necessary to move from one descent line to the opposite descent line of the same clan.

ideal of sister-exchange and the prescriptive patrilateral marriage rule. In spite of the fact that the relationships "wife-giver" and "wife-taker" alter between the marrying patrilines every other generation, "a man would know which descent groups were givers and which takers *vis-a-vis* his own in a particular generation" (Maybury-Lewis, 1965: 216). Further, for an ego of either sex, the model segregates a

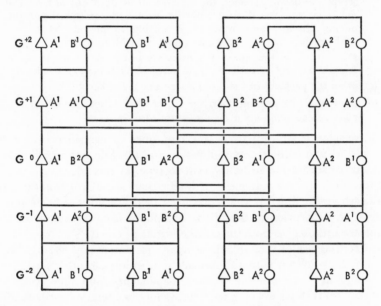

Figure 3. MANGA MARRIAGE MODEL

class of four second cousin types of the opposite sex, one from each of the four possible collateral descent lines. This segregation is effected by the intersection of clan-moiety membership and a type of genealogical second cousin,[14] i.e., Seneca cross or parallel (Pospisil, 1960; Lounsbury, 1964; Cook, 1966).

[14] Of the four kin types for a female ego, only two are correct mates, FMBSS and FFZSS. In order to analytically exclude the remaining two male second cousin types it would be necessary to construct an eight-section system and perhaps matrilineal "ghost moieties." It may be that the ultimate infrastructure, or one of the possible protostructures, of the Manga system exhibits parallels to such a model. However, I have elected to construct a model which is not so removed from social reality. Since the Manga prescriptive rule is only applied through two males who are first cross-cousins in the first (MBS/FZS) ascending generation from a female ego, the kin-types MMBDS and MFZDS would automatically be excluded.

DIVORCE

Normally, a woman may reside with a man in the following circumstances:[15]

(a) From the time she elopes with him until her agnates arrive.[16] If these accept the down payment, she remains. Most (four out of five) elopements do not pass this step, usually because the prospective husband or his kinsmen are unwilling or unable to provide an exchange bride, or because he is young and does not wish to marry yet.

(b) From the time the woman's agnates accept the down payment, /kon KunoN wordndo/, until the bride price, /ana koluma/, is paid.

(c) From the payment of the bride price until his or her death.

(d) As a result of leviratic marriage, which may follow either (b) or (c) above, dependent upon circumstances already noted.

I consider separation to be relevant only to coresidence of type (b) and (c) and divorce only to types (c) and (d). I do not regard either divorce or separation to be relevant to type (a) coresidence since this condition is more a statement of intent than actual cohabitation. In cases where the down payment has been paid but not the bride price, any separation prior to the birth of children usually terminates the contract and there is no return of the initial payment.

In coresidence of type (b), the woman, no matter how she has been acquired, is housed with the groom's mother or a brother's wife for a period of three to nine months, dependent upon how well she "settles" in. If she is working well, caring for pigs, tending gardens, and feeding her husband, he constructs a separate house and garden for her. The man who wishes to be married cares for his wife well during this period and defends her when other women, including her cowives, criticize her abilities or otherwise harass her. If he does not, she is apt to return to her own agnates. As Reay (1959: 85) remarks, men frequently say they sent the woman away because she was derelict in her duties, but as the women are no longer available for comment, there is seldom a way to establish the truth of the matter. I suspect that the men are as much, if not more, at fault but their vanity will not permit them to admit it. When a woman returns to her kin, the

---

[15] I heard of only two spinsters. One was killed by her brother for overt prostitution; the second had leprosy and lacked her nose and several digits and was regarded as too ugly.

[16] The practice of formally sending a girl to reside with the kin of a potential husband for a few days, after which she is returned with gifts to her own agnates, occurs occasionally among groups east of the Narak.

method of acquisition becomes significant. If she had been acquired under the rule or by sister-exchange, her agnates urge her to reconsider. I know of a few cases where a woman acquired in these circumstances who persistently ran away was killed by her own agnates. If, on the other hand, she has been acquired by courtship, she may be welcomed by her agnates. Then her husband must pay a shell or plume to her father or brother before she will be encouraged to return to him.

I have records of only five cases of separation occurring after the /kon kunoN/ payment but before the /ana koluma/. In one instance, the woman returned home with her two children but died before any settlement was reached. In the second case, the woman was the man's second wife and his first wife made her life so miserable that she returned home. No effort was made to secure her return. In the third case, the man left for a two-year work period on the coast; when he returned he learned that the girl's father had reclaimed her and exchanged her with members of another phratry. In the fourth case, a man was forced to marry a girl he had impregnated but did not wish to marry because he was enamoured of her "sister." Under duress he paid the /kon kunoN/ but thereafter ignored her. She bore the child which she claimed was stillborn, though I suspect infanticide, and returned to her parents. He then acquired the girl of his choice. In the fifth case, the girl was supposedly being exchanged but after a few weeks became dissatisfied with her treatment by her intended husband and returned home. Neither side of the exchange was completed and the issue is now regarded as dead.

As children are born to a couple (at least one out of two children die before the age of five), the wife begins agitating for payment of her bride price. Since child prices for the two living children are also paid at the same time as the bride price, the children are legally the wife's until the /ana koluma/ is paid. After a woman has had two children she is unlikely to seek a divorce, but before this she may initiate separations by returning to her kinsmen; such tactics are designed to hasten payment of bride price. However, barrenness is not grounds for divorce. If the husband can obtain additional wives, he may retain the barren wife since her labors in pig and garden tending are highly valued.

It is my impression, though I have no precise quantitative data, that permanent separation leading to divorce is rare after bride price has been paid. Among the KulakaeNgeyka, after bride price has been paid, serious delicts are severely punished by the husband. I know one woman who, although a chronic adulteress, was retained by her husband. Formerly such women were liable to have the tips of their noses cut off or their thighs slashed. Nowadays adultery within the phratry precipitates a lengthy court case (opportunities for a woman's adultery outside the phratry are rare). Wives may also be punished for any of the additional reasons cited by Meggitt (1965: 143), though they are seldon if ever dispatched permanently to their kinsmen.

Leviratic marriages are fairly stable, though they are certainly regarded by many as fraught with danger. For example, there is often the suspicion that the woman herself caused her husband's demise. Also the ancestral spirit of the deceased may regard the copulation of his widow and brother as adulterous and exact retribution. For these reasons, 30 per cent of all leviratic marriages recorded have been effected with men who are not members of the deceased husband's subclan. Of the remaining twelve, nine were by men who already had wives and the rest were by older men who were still single.

In three cases, women married leviratically within the deceased husband's subclan, have subsequently established themselves separately as widows supported by a real or classificatory son, on the grounds that the husband failed to provide adequate houses and gardens for them.

CONCLUSION

Most recent treatments of social structure in the highlands of New Guinea have been primarily concerned with the structure of descent groups and the possible correlates of varying degrees of adherence to descent principles. Nevertheless, the descent model as applied in the New Guinea highlands has come under severe criticism (e.g., Barnes, 1962, 1967; Brown, 1962; Langness, 1964; Pouwer, 1966). With few notable exceptions (e.g., Salisbury, 1956), little attention has been directed to the institution of marriage; nor has there been much effort to approach highland New Guinea societies with an alliance model in mind, since there have been no societies for which a marriage prescription has been reported.

In models of alliance systems, "the segments are articulated into a logically interrelated system by the descent rule, the mode of classification of kinsmen, and the relationship of perpetual alliance between segments" (Schneider, 1965: 58). In models of descent systems, "segments are defined by the descent rule, exogamy, and the variable bounding of the segments in terms of specific functions (domestic, jural, political, residential, territorial, and so on) . . . marriage is but the residuum of exogamy" (Schneider, 1965: 58–59). Schneider also remarks that in the writings of alliance theorists, it has been difficult to distinguish between "marriage as an *expression* of alliance, and marriage as *creating* alliance" (1965: 34).

For the system described here, I regard sister-exchange as the *creative* aspect of alliance and the prescriptive marriage rule as the *perpetuative* and *expressive* aspect. Manga marriage has these two ideological forms: sister-exchange which is by its nature symmetrical, and a prescriptive marriage rule that is, in a certain sense, asymmetrical. If both ideals are adhered to the result is as represented in Figure 4.

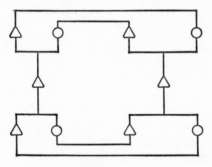

Figure 4.

Certainly, Livingstone's criticism (in Schneider, 1965: 36) that a society ordered by such rules is difficult to live by in real life is valid. But this does not mean that people won't *attempt* to live by such rules. In fact, the common New Guinea expression "we make war with our affines" reflects just such an inability to do so. Poor marital exchange relations between contiguous groups were one of the most frequently invoked overt rationales for conducting warfare. Returning to Figure 4, when the model is completed to account for the similar marriages of the intervening males, the result is the Manga marriage model, Figure 3, a model that also reflects the top three levels of the segmentary organization.

In the marriage model, each woman comes from a "wife-giving unit" (Schneider, 1965: 76) but she is not segregated as a potential spouse by the application of a kinship term. "Choice," as I use it, means that the eldest daughter has no options with reference to alternate types of marriage available to others. In this kind of society, it is the intersection of rules of marriage in conjunction with the existence of corporate segments that define the categories of kinsmen to be married. The kinship terminological system is not totally adequate for this purpose. The corporateness of these segments at various levels in the segmentary structure is verified by their possession of estates which, among other things, can be women. It is at this level of corporateness that alliance theory becomes relevant; but, of course, I have admitted a tenet of descent theory, i.e., segments are defined "in terms of corporate character" (Schneider, 1965: 50).

Hence, in this system, descent-ordered segments are constantly coming into and going out of a state of relatedness with each other, but in a systematic manner. As a result, this is neither a simple case of marriage between units that are already related, i.e., descent (Schneider, 1965: 58). Here it appears that marriage both defines segments and maintains alliances.

If we accept Schneider's notion (1965: 47) that in alliance theory the concept of "segment" implies the *concept* of "unqualified commitment," i.e., nonoverlapping memberships, of the individual, whereas in descent theory the unqualified commitment of the individual to a segment must be *concretely* demonstrable, then I think we may have one of the reasons for the variety of analytical treatments of highland New Guinea societies. Analysts concerned with descent variations in actual group composition are often led into a consideration of the decision processes by which such groups come to be organized, and one consequence of this has been the proliferation of various notions of "descent" (e.g., Sahlins, 1965; Scheffler, 1966). Conversely, the alliance theorist rests a large part of his case on the *ideology* of descent and an *ideology* of marriage prescription.

Manga do not fit well into either polar analytical type, but this exercise suggests that their system can be presented in a profitable manner by employing aspects of both the descent and the alliance approaches.[17]

[17] The lack of a single mythological clan or phratry founder in some highland groups is often supplanted by an ideology that states descent from a pair of brothers, while in other cases a single ancestor has two sons from whom the living members are then descended. In either instance, it may be seen that the model developed here reflects this as well. Also, readers familiar with the literature of the New Guinea highlands will recognize that the model developed here reflects the organizational duality that so many authors have noted.

Marriage Among the
MARING

Roy A. Rappaport

THE MARING

The domain of the Maring speakers straddles the mountainous border between the Western Highlands and Madang Districts of the Australian Trust Territory of New Guinea.

Linguistic and botanical evidence suggests the Maring came from the south, occupying first the middle Jimi and then the middle Simbai Valley. According to Wurm (1964: 79) the Maring language is a member of the Jimi Subfamily of the Central Family of the East New Guinea Highlands Stock, a linguistic grouping which includes most languages of the East New Guinea Highlands (Micro) Phylum. The Maring area is the most northerly occupied by speakers of Central Family languages; the lands to the north and west are held by speakers of the distantly related Karam and Gants languages. To the east and northeast lies a great tract of unoccupied virgin forest.

Government records indicate that patrols first entered the area in 1954; the Maring were officially classified as uncontrolled until 1962, although they were pacified by 1958. Indirect contact began earlier. A few steel axes arrived over trade routes in the late 1930's, but steel was scarce until the middle of the 1950's. Illness also followed trade routes, the dysentery epidemic of 1940 killing perhaps one fifth of the population. Mission activity commenced in 1958; by 1963, when my fieldwork ended, most Maring remained unmissionized, but there were six Papuan-manned stations of the Anglican mission among the Maring local groups. Labor recruitment was negligible until 1964.

The Maring area differs from those occupied by linguistically and culturally related people south of the Wahgi Divide; it is lower (2,000–8,000 feet), more rugged, and more heavily forested. Maring subsistence also differs from that to the south. It is based upon "classical" swiddening. New gardens are cut each year in the secondary forest which forms the cover up to altitudes of 5,500 feet in the

Simbai Valley and 6,000–6,500 in the Jimi Valley. Cropping continues for fourteen to twenty-six months, depending upon how fast the trees grow again, then the site is abandoned to a fallow of eight to forty or so years. The most important staples are Colocasia and sweet potatoes; but five species of yam, Xanthosama, and manioc are also raised. Other important crops are sugar cane, bananas, *marita* pandanus, and greens. Pigs are reared and a few cassowaries are also kept.

Women bear the greatest burden in gardening and tending livestock. While men fell trees, raise fence, plant certain crops, and help the women clear underbrush, the women plant tubers, weed, and do most of the harvesting for their families and pigs.

LAND AND SOCIAL STRUCTURE

The 7,000 Maring speakers are divided into twenty or so autonomous local groups, ranging in size from about 100 to 900 persons. This paper is based on data collected among one local group, the Tsembaga, and its statements are therefore localized and tentative. When A. P. Vayda publishes his survey of over 2,000 Maring marriages some modification may be necessary.

The Tsembaga occupy a territory of a little over three square miles on the south wall of the Simbai Valley. In 1962–1963 they numbered 204 persons. Although gross population density was thus about sixty-five persons per square mile, not all Tsembaga land is arable. Reckoned against land more than marginally fit for horticulture, density stood at 124 p.s.m. The population comprised 114 males and only ninety females, but the disparity was located mainly in the youngest age categories. Above the estimated age of twenty, there were fifty-seven males and fifty-four females.

Tsembaga is a cluster of five named, putatively patrilineal clans (*kai*/"root" or *yu kai*/"root of men"). These clans, the most inclusive units claiming common ancestry, range in size from fifteen to seventy-eight residents, including in-married wives. The two smallest clans are unsegmented, but the three larger clans are each divided into three smaller named segments or subclans, also termed *kai* or *yu kai*, ranging from seven to thirty-seven residents. In each segmented clan, the subclans are named Wendakai ("oldest root"), Amangai ("middle root"), and Atigai ("youngest root").

Tsembaga are a corporate entity in warfare and in the major rituals, in which they participate jointly, and with respect to the nondomesticated resources found on the territory. Any Tsembaga may hunt, trap, and gather anywhere in the territory; nonTsembaga may not.

Although any Tsembaga may take game or wild plants wherever he wishes, portions of the territory are claimed by less inclusive groupings. Ideally these should be clans, for in the Tsembaga view locality is strongly associated with patrilineal descent. But, although there are five clans, the major division of Tsembaga territory is tripartite, the three subterritories being adjacent strips ascending from river to ridgetop. Two of these subterritories are claimed by the two largest clans, the third is held jointly by the three remaining clans. The three subterritories are further divided into smaller areas to which less inclusive units (clans or subclans) claim primary rights, but in which their coordinate units maintain residual rights. Each smaller unit holds a number of noncontiguous tracts scattered throughout the subterritory. Within these tracts individual men claim primary rights to particular garden sites by virtue of clearing the virgin forest or by patrilineal inheritance. Inequities in holdings are quickly corrected by land transfers among all members of the subterritorial group. Moreover, many men make some of their gardens on subterritories other than their own. In a sample of 381 gardens made in 1961, 1962, and 1963 the male gardener used land of another subterritorial group in ninety-four (24.7 per cent) of the cases. In other words, while Tsembaga recognize titles to three distinct areas to be vested in three distinct groups, the gardens of the three groups are intermingled. The part that marriage plays in producing this intermingling I discuss in the last section of this paper.

As the agnatic ideal is violated in land holding, so it is violated in marriage. Ideally, exogamy is associated with patrilineal groups, and clans should form the most significant exogamous units; however this is not the case. On the one hand the clans which share a single subterritory are presently antigamous to each other. They are, or believe themselves to be, related by connection through females in ascending generations when intermarriage is thought to have occurred. That is, members of the three clans regard each other as cognates, although actual connections cannot always be traced. Elsewhere (Rappaport, 1968) I have called this structure a "cognatic cluster."

On the other hand, the subclans of one of the other two clans have intermarried in the past. Informants say this practice began during a period of high population, when the land of the subclans was becoming segregated. Exogamy, in practice, corresponds more closely to the subterritorial unit than to the clan.

FREQUENCY AND RANGE OF MARRIAGE

The Maring say that all adults should marry, and suggest that anyone who does not must be in some way defective. In fact, most people do marry. Of the thirty-five males estimated to be over thirty years old in Tsembaga territory in 1962–1963 the only one who had never married was a cripple. Another Tsembaga bachelor, perhaps forty-five years old, resided sororilocally among the Tuguma, an adjacent group, where his sister was married to an important man. He was considered to be a "rubbish man" (because he was short, ugly, and dull), and it was said he would never marry.

While most Tsembaga men do not marry until late in their twenties, girls usually marry in their late teens; all women above the estimated age of twenty-five had been married at least once. Any woman who can fulfill her wifely duties of gardening, cooking, child-rearing, and pig-tending is unlikely to remain a spinster. Even physically handicapped women find mates. One married woman who died some years ago had apparently been an achondroplastic dwarf but, I was told, she could garden as well as a normal woman, could carry as heavy a load, and was skilled in the care of pigs. On the other hand, some informants doubted that one young woman who had been twice married (once divorced, once widowed) would ever marry again. They observed that her first husband divorced her because she was a poor gardener and domestic manager, and that her second would, perhaps, have also divorced her had he not died. The woman seemed to be mentally deficient.

Divorces are frequent in the early months of marriage, and men usually remarry after an early divorce. Widowers remarry less frequently. Of the thirty-nine Tsembaga men resident in 1962–1963 who were or had been married, eleven had been widowed. Of these, only five had remarried, although one or two of those who had not would probably marry later.

Widows may remarry more frequently than widowers. In 1962–1963 there were fifty women who were or had been married to Tsembaga men; twenty-two of these had been widowed (one twice and one three times). Of those widowed once, nine had already remarried. Six of the others were middle aged or younger and had lost their husbands recently. Funerary services owed by a wife to a deceased husband are protracted and upon their completion it was likely that these women would marry again. The remaining seven widows were old and hence unlikely to remarry.

Of these fifty wives and widows, twenty-two were Tsembaga by birth and eleven were from the Tuguma, a friendly group immediately to the east. The remaining seventeen women came from fifteen clans in nine local groups across the Simbai River or across the Bismarcks in the Jimi Valley.

Forty-one married women of Tsembaga birth were known to be alive during the same period. In addition to the twenty-two married to Tsembaga men, seven were married to Tuguma men. The remaining twelve were married into seven local groups located across the Bismarcks and across the Simbai.

The preference for marriage within the local group and to the neighboring Tuguma is explicit as well as statistical. Parents prefer their daughters to marry men residing close by so that they may be assured of proper funerary services, a duty of women. Conversely, girls prefer to marry within the local group or nearby so that they can make some of their gardens near those of their mothers, to whom Maring women are usually close. A woman's agnates sometimes admit to less sentimental reasons for preferring that their sisters be married locally. I shall discuss these in the last section.

While unions between men and women of a single local group are generally preferred, the Tsembaga recognize certain advantages in marriages to members of other local groups. Allies are recruited through affinal ties, and in case of warfare relatives in other local groups provide refuge. Moreover, unions with groups north of the Simbai River and south of the Bismarcks strengthen trading relationships. Bird-of-paradise plumes and shell ornaments are still obtained from these groups and until the mid-1950's stone axes from the Jimi Valley were traded for salt manufactured in the Simbai Valley.

Most nonlocal marriages are with members of other Maring-speaking groups, but four of the fifty living wives and widows came from Karam groups nearby. Two Tsembaga women were married to Karam speakers and another to a Gants man. While no Tsembaga were married to Narak speakers before 1963, marriage between Jimi Valley Maring and Narak speakers nearby is frequent (E. A. Cook, personal communication).

There are unmistakable indications that pacification, completed in 1958, will extend the marriage relations of Maring local groups. A Tsembaga man, for instance, was planning in 1963 to enter into a sister-exchange with a Simbai Valley Maring group which had previously been inaccessible because of intervening enemies. All informants agreed that there would soon be exchanges of Tsembaga women with the Kundagai immediately to the west, with whom the Tsembaga had been enemies for many years.

RIGHTS IN WOMEN

All members of a subterritorial group share in the pork which accompanies the bride wealth. Indeed, people often relate the antigamy of a subterritorial group's constituent units to this commensality, saying that they do not marry each other's women because they all "eat the same bridal pork." But despite such ritual food sharing throughout the entire subterritorial group, and despite the references to "our women" which accompany it, it is within the minimal agnatic unit, the subclan, or clan, that rights in women are actually held.

Within this group rights in any unmarried female are graded. In the case of a widow, primary rights reside in the deceased man's true brothers, and the oldest unmarried brother has strongest claims in a maiden. He decides to whom she will be sent in marriage, and he benefits most from her marriage. He receives the bulk of the bride wealth given for his sister and has the right to wed the girl who is sometimes sent in return for her. If he chooses not to marry this girl but instead to give her to a clan brother or even to someone outside his clan, he, as well as her agnates, should receive the bride wealth. If a girl's brother is only a child when she reaches marriageable age, her father or his surrogate may decide whom she should marry; but it is understood that he acts for her brother.

Sometimes, when his daughter becomes old enough to make gardens by herself, a man who has no sons selects a young man of his subclan, one whom he calls "son," to act as his daughter's marriage-linked "brother." I know no Maring term for this relationship, but it is recognized and it carries responsibilities. At the time of his selection, or shortly thereafter, the young man presents to his marriage-linked "sister" a small gift of beads or an orchid-fibre waistband and gives her father a few valuables. Henceforth he cooperates with them as if he were a true son and brother, plants most of his gardens with them and helps in housebuilding and collecting firewood. He may also take most of his meals at their hearth. For his gifts and services the young man obtains primary rights in the disposal of his marriage-linked "sister."

The rights of agnates in their women are, however, not absolute. A girl's mother's agnates also retain rights in her (for they have supplied the "planting material" out of which she grew) until they have received child-price (*wamba mungoi*). A woman may send a daughter to live with her own agnates if she or her daughter have not been paid for, and if wealth is still not forthcoming, these kinsmen plan the girl's marriage and benefit from its proceeds. Although a woman's agnates rarely exercise their residual rights in her children, during my residence members of one Tsembaga clan did bring back from another local group the twelve- or thirteen-year-old daughter of a female agnate. They said they had never received wealth for either the girl or her mother and would keep her until they did. The girl was still there five months later.

Rights in women may proliferate. Anyone who cares for a girl for a protracted period has some claim in her, and often a girl spends her early years living with groups other than the natal clan of her father. For instance, before 1958 when warfare was frequent, refugee men often fled with their families to the agnatic groups of their mothers, wives, or sister's husbands. If a man remained permanently with such a group they, rather than his own agnates, claimed superior rights in his daughters; even if he returned to his own land, those who had sheltered him and provided him with garden land continued to claim some rights in his daughters.

Warfare was not the only event that could multiply rights in girls. If a widow's children are young, she may raise them among her own natal group. Nevertheless, her deceased husband's agnates retain some claim in her children. Such plural claims are often settled when the children are still young.

In one case a woman of Tsembaga birth, after being widowed, returned to her natal clan with her small son and daughter. Her agnates later gave her deceased husband's agnates four valuables and a cooked pig in full payment of their claim in the children, who were henceforth considered members of their mother's clan.

Another case was settled differently. Arum was married to a man of the Tsembaga clan.[1] After his death she and her three children were cared for by her own brothers, members of another local clan, Kamungagai. Subsequently, Arum's son, Togle, moved into the men's house of his own agnates. At the pig festival of 1963 Togle's agnates gave to Arum's agnates nine valuables in full payment of the latters' claim to Arum's daughter, Nowa, a girl of thirteen or fourteen. These valuables were presented to Arum's older brother but in the name of his son a boy of twelve or thirteen, who otherwise would have enjoyed

---

[1] "Tsembaga" is the name of both the local population and one of its five constituent clans. The other clans are Tomagai, Kwibigai, Kamungagai, and Merkai.

primary rights in Nowa. Nowa's agnates said they were making the presentation to recover Togle's unimpeded rights in his own sister.[2]

[2] The plurality of rights in women and the possibility of conflict between the wishes of a woman and of men who have rights in her are nicely illustrated by the case of Momum. When she was about six the Kundagai routed the Tsembaga. Momum and her mother fled to her mother's natal group, the Mogli, while her father and his other wife took refuge with another group. Although her mother soon died Momum remained among the Mogli for six or seven years, and was cared for by her mother's brother, Mndngn. The Tsembaga reoccupied their territory in the 1950's, and when Momum was twelve or thirteen she rejoined them. At the 1963 pig festival her father, Muk, presented seven valuables and some pork to Mndngn for his claim in Momum. After the presentation Mndngn addressed Momum:

When you were very small your mother left Muk and brought you to my house. I gave you food and made gardens for you and your mother. Your mother died, and I saw to her burial; I cared for you after her death. When Kiap grew older he remembered that he had a sister living among the Mogli. He decided to come to Mogli to fetch you, thinking that if I were hostile he would leave without you. But I said "she is not my daughter. She is Muk's and he did not abandon her. She and her mother left him and came to me. I have cared for her but she is your sister, and I cannot hold her if she wants to go with you."

Kiap brought you beads and gave them to you, saying "put them on—they are for you." He said that you could stay with me, but I said "no, you go with your brother and he will look after you!" You went with him and came back and stayed with me a little. Finally I gave you a bush knife and told you to remain with your brother permanently. Since then he has cared for you, giving you the flesh of animals he has shot and marking plots for you in the gardens he has cut. He has given you half of his pork and when he has obtained ornaments he has adorned you with them. Now he has grown; he is a man and he will begin to look for a woman. When he finds one, he will come to you and say that he has found a woman and he would like to exchange you for her. When he speaks thus, you must not say, "our mothers were different women and you cannot exchange me. I shall marry a man of my own choosing." You say to Kiap, "all right, you may exchange me, for although my mother left our father and took me to her people, you came and got me and you have cared for me." Kiap will decide to whom you are to be sent. You must not consider running off with a man of your own choice.

I am not an old man. I will come and see you after you are married, and you will tell me that your husband was chosen by Kiap, and I shall then be well disposed towards you. But, if you run off to some man without his permission, I will not eat food from your gardens or the flesh of your pigs, nor will I accept valuables from your husband, and neither will Kiap. If some man asks you to run off with him, do not listen. If you run off, I will never come to see you, nor will Kiap. You yourself will eat the produce of your gardens and the flesh of your pigs. [Enmities and grievances are frequently accompanied by, and formalized through, the assumption of taboos against eating food raised by the antagonists.]

I will hold the valuables given me today by your brother and father; I will not dispose of them now. When I have heard that Kiap has sent you in marriage to a man of his choice, then I shall use these valuables.

The exercise by men of their rights in women is not automatic. Women have, in fact, a great deal to say about their marriages. A man usually takes into consideration his sister's wishes, and sometimes a girl herself starts proceedings which culminate in marriage. Not all, but many marriages follow courtship, and women rather than men initiate courtship. It is said that a man should not approach but should entice women, and it is usually the woman who invites, through intermediaries, a man who has attracted her to come to court. While invitations to courtship may receive the approval of a girl's male agnates, in some instances she extends them without the men's knowledge or consent. This can result in an elopement which effectively abrogates the men's rights. I discuss this in a later section.

MARRIAGE RULES AND PREFERENCES

A Tsembaga man, like other Maring, may have several wives simultaneously, but monogamy prevails. Of the thirty-three married men resident on Tsembaga territory in 1962–1963, only four had two wives at any time, and none had more. One man among the neighboring Tuguma had three wives simultaneously. A. P. Vayda (personal communication) reports that one Fungai man had four and that a Tsinginai man was the only Maring he knew to have five wives.

A man's choice of mates is subject to the following explicit rules:

A. Rules Applying to all Tsembaga:
   No Tsembaga man may marry
   1. Any woman of his own clan.
   2. The actual or classificatory sister of a deceased wife.
   3. Any woman of his mother's clan or the clans of mothers of his clan brothers.[3]
   4. Any woman of the clan of his own mother's sister's husband.
   5. Any woman of the clan of his father's sister's husband, or the clans of father's sisters' husbands of any of his clan brothers.
   6. Any woman whom he calls grandmother (apo), mother (ama), daughter or granddaughter (wambnan), or father's sister (aria). [The term apo applies to all consanguineally or affinally related females in the second ascending generation, and to wives of sons and grandsons. The term ama includes the actual and classificatory sisters of

[3] One informant stated that these prohibitions include only women of the clans of mothers and fathers' sisters' husbands of subclan brothers. Another said that only women of the subclans of mothers' and fathers' sisters' husbands of subclan brothers may not be married. I believe the basic rules to be as I have stated them but because of the fluidity of Maring social structure the details of the rules vary.

one's own mother, the mothers of clan brothers, and their actual or classificatory sisters. The term *wambnan* is extended to all consanguineally and affinally related females in the first and second descending generations, with the exception of sons' and grandsons' wives. The term *aria* extends to mother's sisters' husbands' sisters.]

B. Special Rules:

7. Men of the Tsembaga, Tomegai, and Kwibigai clans (which share a single subterritory) may not take wives from each other's clans.

8. Men of the Merkai clan may not marry the widows of deceased clansmen. Men of the other four clans may. (Merkai say that the widows of clansmen ought to be offered to cross-cousins [*wambe*].)

A few comments are in order. The restrictions on choice enunciated in rules three and four do not extend from one to another of the three antigamous clans. That is, although a Tomegai man may not marry a Kwibagai woman, he may marry women prohibited to Kwibagai men under rules three and four. If as I believe, antigamy among these clans is to be explained in terms of fusion, the fusion is not complete. I will discuss this in the last section.

In addition to subterritorial exogamy the most obvious effects of these rules are generational endogamy and antigamy between intermarrying clans in alternate generations. It is in connection with the latter that the role of the one prescriptive rule among the Maring should be seen. This rule states that one of a woman's granddaughters (a son's daughter) should marry into her natal subclan. This is called "returning the planting material."

Despite these restrictions, the number of clans from which a man may properly take a mate is large. Among the twelve local groups with which the Tsembaga have intermarried in the past few generations, there still existed over fifty clans in 1962–1963, and a number of others had become extinct. Thus, the limitations upon the choice of mates by marriage rules are not sufficiently restrictive to guarantee the renewal of marriage ties between clans in alternate generations. However, although the Tsembaga do not state that "returning the planting material" insures the renewal of ties between clans established by earlier intermarriage, this would be the effect of this prescription. Moreover, they do recognize a special relationship between two clans that have renewed their marriage ties, saying that they form a "pig-woman road."

In a sample of seventy-five marriages (including, in addition to extant marriages, those to decreased spouses of individuals living on Tsembaga territory in 1962–1963), I know of fifteen violations of the rule stated above.

The rule of clan exogamy was broken in five cases. All of these marriages were between members of the Merkai Atigai subclan on the one hand and the Merkai Amangai and Wendegai subclans on the other. I mentioned earlier that intermarriage between the Merkai subclans began during a period of high population when the lands of the subclans were becoming segregated into separate subterritories. I thus take these intraclan marriages to indicate that fission was occurring (cf. Meggitt, 1965:16, 96). This process seems to have been arrested and reversed probably as a correlate of the recent severe depopulation of the Merkai. At any rate, informants say that there will be no more intermarriage between the Merkai subclans. I accept their prognostication if only because the Merkai Atigai are virtually extinct.

Two of the ten apparent violations remaining were of rule 5, and eight were of rule 3. These rules prohibit marriage to true or classificatory first cross-cousins. However, it is not clear whether violations actually occurred in all of these cases. In at least four cases the groom was irregularly affiliated to the patrilineal clan in which he claimed membership and in terms of which the prohibited field was defined. Knowing the Maring propensity for invoking connections to alternative kin when it is convenient, I suspect that these men rationalized their ostensibly improper marriages by claiming for the nonce their proper (rather than their *de facto*) patrilineal identity. The same manipulation of patrilineal identity is possible in the case of brides, and in at least two cases of apparent infringement the bride was irregularly affiliated to the group from which she was married.

OBTAINING A WIFE

Marriages are entered into in several ways. I describe these below and indicate the relative frequency of each mode in a sample of seventy marriages.[4]

1. *Sister Exchange.* According to informants, sister exchange is the ideal way to obtain a wife but it occurs in a minority of cases. Only fifteen of the women in the sample were obtained in this manner. In eleven of these cases the exchange of women was simultaneous, while in the other four considerable time elapsed, in one instance more than a decade, between the movement of the two women.

[4] The sample size here is seventy rather than seventy-five, which was used in an earlier section. Information relevant to the present argument was available only in seventy cases.

2. *Prescribed Second Cross-Cousin Marriage* ("returning the planting material"). This has been described above. Its occurrence seems to be rare. Only three of the women in the sample had been returned for their grandmothers.

3. *Bride Purchase.* I use this term to refer to instances in which a woman is obtained, with the consent of the men claiming rights in her, in exchange for valuables rather than in exchange for another woman. Fifteen of the women in the sample were obtained in this way.

In these first three types of marriage, the grooms usually arrange them themselves, although older brothers or fathers sometimes obtain brides for young men without consulting them in advance. The groom arrives one day at the house of his mother or a brother's wife to find a bride awaiting him. His reaction, which shows itself sometimes in flight, is discussed in a later section.

4. *Blood Debts.* Women figure in the composition of blood debts in several ways. Sometimes the agnates of a homicide victim give women to nonagnates who have avenged the homicide by slaying a member of the killer's local or agnatic group. Five Tsembaga men obtained five wives in this way. Occasionally a slayer's group seeks to offset vengeance by offering a woman to the victim's agnates. One woman in the sample was obtained in this manner. Another was obtained in compensation for an insult grievous enough to induce a threat of homicide.

In warfare the principal antagonists are responsible for the deaths of their own allies and should compensate by giving a woman to the agnates of the victim. However, allies seldom suffer casualties, and only one woman in the sample was a replacement for a man thus slain.

When peace (not mere truce, cf. Rappaport, 1968) is made between warring groups, each of the slain should be replaced by one of the enemy's women. In 1963 the Tsembaga were planning to exchange women with their former enemies, the Kundagai, but stated that replacement of every one of the slain by a woman would be impossible; too many (perhaps seventy or eighty) had been killed during their long enmity. It is well to note, however, that ideally the number of marriage ties between former enemies is directly correlated with the severity of their enmity as expressed in the number of deaths they have inflicted on each other.

5. *Levirate.* I said earlier that four of the five clans permit, but do not require, widows to marry their husband's agnates. The sample

includes four instances in which women married men of the deceased husband's subclan and one instance in which the widow was taken by a different subclan of her deceased husband's clan. In three of these cases the deceased husband's true older brother married the widow.

6. *Rearing the Bride.* The sample includes one woman of Karam birth who was sent when young to her future Tsembaga husband's agnates, who cared for her for some years before she was married. Tsembaga say that sending a bride to the groom's parents is a custom of the Karam speakers north of the Simbai River.

7. *Stealing the Bride.* Tsembaga and other Maring use the term "stealing" to refer to marriages entered into without prior consent of the men claiming rights in the bride. Stealing occurs in twenty-two of the seventy cases in the sample and is the most common means of obtaining a bride.

In most cases about which I have information the bride and groom eloped to the house of his mother or another woman married into his subclan; but sometimes a girl appears uninvited at the mother's house of a youth she admires. Bride stealing frequently follows the all night dances which occur during festivals. I have argued elsewhere (1967, 1968) that these dances are, among other things, epigamic displays (cf. Wynne-Edwards, 1962:17): the girls are presented with eligible young men of local groups with which they may otherwise be unfamiliar. The context, moreover, permits the young women to discriminate among the young men in terms of strength (shown by how vigorously and how long a man continues in the competitive dancing) and wealth (signified by the magnificence of his shell and feather finery). Several Tsembaga men say their wives were first attracted by their dancing on festival occasions.

Usually the male relatives of a stolen bride set out in her pursuit as soon as they discover her absence. In 1963, four or five years after pacification, the ensuing confrontations by her group and the groom's group were touchy affairs; they must have been explosive in preadministration times. At the least they involved much shouting and threats, and often violence erupted. The long and bloody enmity between Tsembaga and Kundagai grew from an occasion when a member of a party of Kundagais came to Tsembaga to recover an eloping girl and was killed by one of the locals. Such confrontations, nevertheless, usually come to an amiable, or relatively amiable, conclusion. Sometimes the girl is sent home, but usually the marriage is regularized. After the girl's relatives have ranted sufficiently to demonstrate a proper amount of belligerence and ferocity, they permit themselves to be persuaded that the marriage is not intolerable. Often they are influenced by the promise of a bride in exchange in the future or by the promise of a large and prompt payment of bride wealth. Indeed, one informant suggested that the threats of an eloping girl's kinsmen are as often directed toward extracting large payments quickly from the groom's group as they are toward recovering the girl.

AFFINAL PRESENTATIONS

All marriages should be bound by presentations of valuables by the groom to the males who have rights in the bride. Even men who have received brides in reward for avenging a homicide or in compensation for suffering should present valuables to the bride's kin. In the case of sister-exchange identical valuables move reciprocally and sometimes simultaneously. I know of only one recent case of a Tsembaga man who never gave valuables to his affines; his reason was that immediately after his marriage his brother was killed in an ambush in which his wife's brother participated. Among an earlier generation nonpayment was more frequent, for when hostilities broke out during the 1900's between Tsembaga and Kundagai, who had long exchanged women, affinal prestations between them ceased.

When brides are stolen, the groom's group often makes substantial prestations to the bride's group then or soon afterwards. In the case of marriage by permission of the bride's responsible kin, however, only small prestations are made immediately or else none at all. Those made are likely to consist merely of the shell ornaments that adorn the bride when she goes to her husband, and usually much of this finery is borrowed for the occasion and must be returned. Generally among the Maring the first substantial payment is likely to be delayed at least until the bride and groom are harvesting a garden they have made together. Among the Tsembaga, and perhaps some other groups, it may be delayed for years until the next Kaiko or pig festival. Tsembaga prestations to affines seem to be made most frequently at these festivals; nineteen were made at the culmination of a festival on November 9, 1963.

Some men, particularly those who have recently received bride wealth for a sister, are able to make an affinal prestation with little or no assistance from kinsmen. Bride wealth in most cases, however, is quickly distributed among agnates and perhaps other kinsmen to meet their claims in the bride, to repay assistance previously given, or in response to requests for assistance in meeting obligations. Therefore, most men require help in making affinal prestations, particularly the first or second, of which one at least should be handsome. Assistance comes mainly from the groom's subclan, but other members of his clan and even nonagnatic kinsmen may contribute valuables.

The first payment is always called *ambra poka* or *ambra mungoi* ("woman price," "woman wealth"). Later payments are sometimes, but not always, referred to as *wamba poka* ("child price") rather than *ambra poka*. Nevertheless, Tsembaga do not distinguish sharply between presentations for the wife and those for the children. A man has received a woman from his affines, and she has borne him children. He therefore stands in a generalized debt-relation to his affines, and throughout his wife's life he must continue to compensate them for their favor to him. Some men make five or more prestations to their affines. I do not know, however, whether a man would continue to make payments for a barren woman. In all cases of second or later prestations about which I have information, the woman had borne at least one child before the payment was made. A small final prestation is made when a woman reaches old age or dies. Unlike earlier ones, this prestation involves a counter-prestation which may match it in size.

All prestations are composed of the class of items termed *mungoi* ("valuables"). In 1962–1963 the valuables most prominent in bride wealth included shell ornaments (both gold-lip and green sea snail), steel axes, and bush knives. Bands of cowrie shells, important ten or twenty years earlier, still appeared but were considered old-fashioned and insignificant. Marsupial fur headbands played a minor role. Until the mid-1950's thin bladed "ceremonial," "dance," or "bridal" stone axes played an important part and heavier bladed utilitarian axes a lesser part in bridal payments, but by 1962 both had dropped out completely. Trade beads and money were appearing. Men of middle age say that in the time of their grandfathers, before shells first appeared in the area, the teeth of dogs and marsupials were of great importance, but these no longer have any value. Bird-of-paradise plumes, although highly regarded and included in the category *mungoi,* are not included in affinal prestations by or to Tsembaga and other Simbai Valley Maring. However, informants said they are occasionally part of prestations in the Jimi Valley where such birds are rare.

In affinal prestations connected with most forms of marriage the flow of valuables is asymmetrical, although bride's groups occasionally make small counter-prestations. In the case of sister-exchange, however, there should be reciprocal prestations (sometimes simultaneous) of identical valuables between the doubly linked affines.

I mentioned that nineteen Tsembaga men made prestations to affines on November 9, 1963. Five of these were death or terminal prestations and involved two to twelve valuables. In four of the five cases, the prestation was reciprocated simultaneously and fully or almost fully. Two of the prestations were to men who had only secondary rights in the bride. Both were small, and included only two valuables. Another two were to affines who had cared for unmarried female agnates during some portion of their lives, and whose rights in these girls were being bought out. In one case the prestation included seven valuables, in the other nine. The remaining ten prestations were to agnates of women still active; their average size was about ten valuables, the range two to forty-two. The sample included three first prestations (five, ten, and forty-two valuables respectively) and one third prestation (nine valuables). The rest were second prestations.

Live pigs are not included in affinal prestations by the Tsembaga or, to my knowledge, other Maring. All the prestations included in the sample were, however, accompanied by cooked pork in amounts ranging from one side of an adolescent animal to the entire carcasses of two full grown pigs.

The sample is too small to allow definite statements, but informants say that prestations are especially large in cases of sister-exchange, and nineteen men helped the groom to make this prestation. None of the other men making prestations was assisted by more than four others. Probably men are eager to participate in prestations associated with sister-exchanges because they know that the valuables they contribute will soon be returned.

Statements by Tsembaga men suggest that there may also be a correlation between the amount of bride wealth and the needs of the bride's agnates. Thus, one old man, a member of a declining clan and without sons of his own, told his daughter's Tsembaga husband to give him no valuables for he had no need of them, and two other Tsembaga men told me that they had given little for their wives because their wives had no brothers.

TRIAL MARRIAGE AND DIVORCE

Maring men and women live apart. During 1962 and 1963 the Tsembaga men's houses, which accommodate males above the age of seven or eight, had from two to fourteen occupants. In contrast, each married woman or widow has a separate house where she resides with her unmarried daughters, small sons, and pigs.

Rarely does a man construct a house immediately for a new bride. Instead, she resides initially with the groom's mother, if she is alive, or the wife of one of his true or classificatory brothers. Tsembaga men say that it would be a mistake to build a house or assign pigs to a woman before it is clear that her marriage will last. If the union endures long enough (about six months) for the couple to harvest root crops from a garden they have planted together, it is said that they are likely to remain together permanently and the groom then thinks about building a house. My evidence is insufficient, but I believe it is later that he entrusts her with the care of pigs.

The Tsembaga thus recognize that marriages in their initial stages are brittle. I do not have comprehensive figures indicating the number of women each Tsembaga man has taken and quickly lost or returned, but I believe the rate to be high. Several Tsembaga men report taking two or three women from whom they were soon separated. One important man from the neighboring Tuguma group, who was still under forty years old and who had two wives in 1963, reported having had seven others at various times. These had either been sent home or had left him within months, weeks, or even days after their arrival. My limited information (twelve cases) suggests that more often the woman, not the man, is responsible for early termination of marriage. In all cases the bride came from outside the local group and may have had trouble adjusting to strange people in strange surroundings as well as to a husband whom she had not previously known well.

Tsembaga say men are too afraid or too ashamed to commence sexual relations with their brides immediately. In the case of stolen women, intercourse probably begins when the woman comes to the man, if not before, but, in sister-exchanges and other properly arranged marriages, it is likely that there is a delay. The behavior of new grooms suggests this. In 1963 two young men, when they discovered that their kinsmen had obtained brides for them, immediately left Tsembaga for several days. On returning, they avoided the houses in which their brides resided and refused even to acknowledge that they had wives. They soon stopped avoiding their brides but continued for months to insist that they had no wives. I was informed that it would be impolite, in conversation with these men, to allude to the women as their brides. In view of this delicacy as well as the grooms' reluctance, and considering the delay in beginning sexual relations, setting up separate domiciles, and making prestations to brides' kinsmen (as well as the likelihood of an early termination of the union), one may well ask whether it is proper to say that a marriage has occurred when a bride takes up residence with a groom's group. It might, indeed, be better to refer to a union as a "trial marriage" until the harvesting of a garden, and perhaps until the birth of a child.

While trial marriages seem to be brittle, marriages become stable after the birth of children. Only two divorces after the birth of children occur in the sample of seventy marriages and these took place in exceptional circumstances. In both cases the woman was the second wife of a polygynist, and both followed the Kundagai rout of the Tsembaga in 1953. In one case the woman did not wish to join her husband in taking refuge with his first wife's agnates. In the other the woman refused to join her husband in taking refuge with a group too far from her natal group. Both women fled with their children to their own natal groups, where one soon died. The other never returned.

MARRIAGE, POPULATION DISPERSAL, AND GROUP DYNAMICS

In the second section of this paper I described the formal structure of the Tsembaga and how constituent groups were dispersed over the total territory in 1962 and 1963. I believe that the structure then was a more or less transitory state in a continuing process of population dispersal over available land and that marriage is an important part of the mechanism which effects this dispersal.

I said earlier that 44 per cent of the fifty wives and widows resident on Tsembaga territory in 1963 were of Tsembaga origin, and that another 22 per cent were from Tuguma, immediately east of Tsembaga. When the natal groups of husband and wife are adjacent, as in 66 per cent of the Tsembaga cases, the bride's kinsmen usually grant a garden site to the groom once it is clear the marriage is an enduring one, and they are likely to make further grants of land to him throughout his life. These grants, which confer rights only in specified sites and not in the entire estate of the grantor, do not require the recipient to take up uxorilocal residence, and he is unlikely to do so. In most cases a man continues to reside patrilocally and rely upon his patrimonial lands, but, whether or not he needs the lands granted by his affines, he uses them, for he is under pressure to do so. Most women like to make some gardens on the lands of their natal group so that they may visit there frequently; sentimental ties between mothers and daughters are particularly strong. On the other hand, a woman's agnates wish her husband to garden on their land for less sentimental reasons. From their point of view the affinal grant enables them to exploit some of the woman's labor after she marries. The sites granted to a woman's husband usually adjoin those cultivated by her agnates. A married woman can thus conveniently assist a widowed father or unmarried brother with his gardens.

Affinal land grants are said to be made in perpetuity, but it is not surprising that they often revert to the donor or his heirs after one generation. The pressures that induce a man to cultivate land received from his wife's agnates are absent from his relationship with his mother's natal group. If, however, the lands received by his father through affinal transfers are conveniently located, a man is likely to continue to use them, with the result that garden sites claimed by members of adjacent subterritorial groups become intermingled. Among Tsembaga this intermingling has proceeded so far that the subterritories of the cognatic cluster and of the Kamungagai clan to its west are fusing. Many younger men are ignorant of the location of the border. Older men know where it is but invariably state that it no longer means much.

I call such structures, consisting of two adjacent subterritorial groups whose lands are becoming intermingled through affinal grants, "affinal clusters." I have argued in detail elsewhere (Rappaport, 1968) that cognatic and affinal clusters may represent two points in a continuous process of land amalgamation. The garden land of members of adjacent subterritorial groups becomes intermingled through grants of land in perpetuity. There is full or partial antigamy between the groups in alternate generations, but the intermingling is maintained because sons tend to maintain rights in sites ceded by their mothers' brothers to their fathers when these sites are convenient to their patrilocal residences. More intermarriage ramifies the web of cognatic relations for descending generations and produces further intermingling of the land. People come to regard the territories of the two groups as one and the boundary becomes indistinct. It may be that at this stage cognatic connections begin to replace affinal connections as the preferred means by which rights in land are acquired from the other group. Thus, four of the ten grants in perpetuity made between the two subterritorial groups comprising the affinal cluster in 1961–1963 did not rest upon new affinal connections but on affinal connections in ascending generations, that is, cognatic connections.[5] The number is small, but it may indicate a process which is completed with antigamy developing between the constituent subterritorial groups. Affinal clusters may thus be transformed into cognatic clusters. The kinship terminology facilitates this transformation. It is Iroquois in ego's generation and bifurcate merging in the first ascending generation, but generational in the first descending and second ascending generations. Terminological distinctions between one's own exogamous group and groups with which it has intermarried are obliterated in two generations. Whereas the children of affines refer to each other by special cross-cousin terms, the children of cross-cousins refer to each other by sibling terms although they may, and sometimes should, marry ("returning the planting material"). This may be a terminological concession to group dynamics. At any rate, previously separate intermarrying groups can become single exogamous corporate cognatic groups, or cognatic clusters, without requiring people to change terminological usage. Terminological usage also facilitates the transformation of the cognatic cluster into the putatively agnatic descent group of which it is a functional equivalent. Terminology masks the distinction between cognates and agnates in two generations and, given the shallow genealogical reckoning, it may be that common agnatic descent eventually comes to be assumed (cf. Meggitt, 1965: 31ff.). Naturally, it is impossible to obtain evidence from informants concerning what they have forgotten.

As previously intermarrying groups may become antigamous during the process of fusion, so may previously antigamous groups begin to intermarry during the process of fission. There is evidence that clan fission correlates with population pressure, and I have suggested elsewhere (Rappaport, 1968) that as critical density is approached or exceeded land claiming groups at all levels discourage the cultivation of their lands by members of coordinate units. Marriages between the subclans of a clan may be part of the associated strategy. Such marriages transform clan agnates into affines (affinal terms are employed), and affinal land grants may replace the recipients' residual

[5] In addition to the grants in perpetuity between members of Kamungagai clan and the cognatic cluster, twenty-three grants in perpetuity were made between members of these two subterritorial groups and members of the third subterritorial group, the Merkai. The remaining sixty-one of the ninety-four instances of men gardening on the land of subterritorial groups other than their own involved in most cases usufructuary grants. Most commonly these were made by men to their wives' brothers, but various connections were employed.

rights as agnates in the subclan estates of the donors with the more limited rights of affines in specific sites while leaving intact or ambiguous, at least for a while, the donor's rights in the land of the recipient. Leach's assertion (1961: 305) that "kinship systems have no 'reality' at all except in relation to land and property" seems to be an accurate judgment which is applicable to Maring descent groups and Maring marriage.

Marriage in
MELPA

Andrew and Marilyn Strathern

OUTLINE OF GROUP STRUCTURE

In the Hagen Subdistrict of the western highlands of Australian New Guinea the chief dialects spoken are Melpa and Temboka (Wurm, 1961; Bunn and Scott, 1962); the former predominates to the north, the latter to the south of Hagen township. The Europeans discovered Hagan in the early 1930's, had stopped warfare in most parts by 1946, and have since spread mission teaching widely.[1]

Our demographic data relate mainly to Northern Melpa of the Kawelka, Tipuka and Minembi of the mountainous Sepik-Wahgi Divide and to the Central Melpa Elti of the grasslands of the Ogelbeng Plain (CSIRO, 1958). The Elti are among the groups described by Vicedom (1943–48) as Mbowamb.

The major groups throughout the Melpa area and much of Temboka we call tribes. The tribe has a creation myth, which links it to an origin-place and to a mystical quasi-totemic divination object, *mi* (Strauss, 1962). Many tribes have expanded, contracted, split, and scattered from their origin-places, owing to pressures of warfare and ecology. Tribes thus vary greatly in size and population density. Of fifty-three censused by the Administration, twenty-six have populations less than 500, eleven 500–1,000, twelve 1,000–3,000 and only four between 3,000 and 7,000. The largest tribes and highest densities are among the Central Melpa and on the slopes of Mount Hagen (densities: 118–270 per sq. mile; sizes: Ndika, 6,749; Mokei, 6,199; Kumndi, 5,414).[2] The lowest densities are in the Northern Melpa area (60–70 per sq. mile). The average size is 1,200.

[1] We carried out seventeen months of field work in Hagen during 1964–65, under the auspices of the Emslie Horniman Anthropological Scholarship Fund and with the help of other grants from Cambridge University. Five months were spent at the Australian National University, Canberra.

[2] Figures include wives and children and exclude married sisters, owing to patrivirilocal residence at marriage.

Tribes formerly took concerted action in warfare against traditional enemies, and nowadays they occasionally synchronize activities for a pig feast or a spirit cult. Usually they are linked in pairs; the pairing may be important or it may have little contemporary significance.

Tribes divide into major sections (and occasionally subsections), clans, clan sections, subclans, sub-subclans, and small lineages or quasi-lineages. Tribes below 500 are sometimes exogamous; above this figure, rarely so. More often exogamy is placed at the level of the clan or sometimes the major section.

Agnatic "dogmas of descent" (Barnes, 1962) apply with varying force to all these levels of segmentation. The tribe's origin myth may identify its original father and his sons, who are eponymous to the sections or clans, but tribesmen emphasize equally their common name, origin-place, and *mi*. Clansmen most strongly assert common descent ("one father") as the charter for internal social control, co-operation in warfare, and joint responsibility for compensation payments and *moka* ceremonial exchange.

A clan usually has its paired clan. The two are often closely intermarried and may form one exogamous unit. Ideally they avoided internal warfare and were firm allies in the past; now they should co-operate in *moka*. However, if one enlisted the other in battle and the ally lost a man, reparations had to be paid (cf. Glasse, 1959); the two clans were "war root man" and "war dead man." Paired clans and other allies still express mutual opposition by demands for such reparations.

Enemies in battle were either major, traditional enemies ("war red bird-of-paradise man," from the plumage of warriors) or minor enemies ("little fight man"). Clans paid direct compensation for killings only to minor enemies, for these might be allies against a traditional enemy. Cross-tribal alliances occurred, owing to the imbalances of power within tribes.

The clan's "one father" is often said to have married several wives, each of whom founded a subclan, but this is not intended literally. Clans and subclans do not always possess comprehensive genealogical frames. Instead, men emphasize that subclans are separate *rapa*, "men's houses." Their men do not actually live in a single house, but they do hold joint discussions for *moka*, perhaps in a house at the head of their ceremonial ground. Clans invariably, and subclans often, have such grounds. Sub-subclans ("little men's houses") do not, unless a Big Man (*wua nyim*) within them has laid out his own. A clan has a few *wua nyim* who are outstanding in energy and shrewdness, and others of lesser eminence throughout its segments. Subclans make *moka* on behalf of their clan, or even independently.

Clan-sections are recognizable as higher level groups than subclans in that between them (1) rules of marriage apply differently (see section 2); (2) there is a sharper opposition; and (3) the "war root man"–"war dead man" relationship may hold.

Only the lineage consistently has a named single ancestor or brother pair of ancestors and a genealogical framework. The founder is rarely considered to be more than two generations up from living adult men. The lineage is called "one penis, one semen"; but, despite these agnatic concepts, its composition is rarely completely patrilineal.

Divorce, uxorilocal residence, and the return of women with their children to their natal groups all augment lineages with nonagnates, and 20 per cent to 50 per cent of a clan's adult males may in fact not be agnates. Lineage members attached via their mother are *amb-nt-mei* ("woman bearing"), those through their father *wua-nt-mei* ("man bearing"). The sons of *amb-nt-mei* men become *wua-nt-mei*. *Amb-nt-mei* members suffer no formal inferiority (although uxorilocal affines may) but sometimes in practice lack sponsors to help them marry.

Clans usually have bounded territories. No clansman may alienate clan land, but rights of gardening and coresidence are readily granted to kinsfolk, as to refugees and refugee groups in the past. There is residential intermingling between subclans of a single clan. Settlements are simply consolidated homesteads, occupied by elementary or extended families, polygynous or otherwise, or by a number of immediate brothers with kinsmen and affines. Except in the largest tribes, sub-subclans and lineages are not territory based, but individual land claims tend to be inherited within the lineage.

From the tribe to the sub-subclan all groups are named. Lineages are simply the "sons of" their founders. With population growth, new lineage and sub-subclan or subclan names often emerge, through splits between leaders or the advantages of division for receiving *moka* gifts. Clan and tribe names are more stable; but groups at all levels gradually change their segmentary status, a factor which complicates the analysis of marriage rules.

MARRIAGE RULES

Except for widow inheritance, there are no marriage prescriptions; but two rules prohibit intermarriage: (1) persons who share blood may not marry, and (2) *rapa* (sub-subclan or subclan) groups linked directly or indirectly by a remembered marriage may not contract further marriages.

THE DEFINITION OF BLOOD AND RAPA TIES

Persons who share a genealogically traced or putative common forbear are of "one blood." All immediate cognates thus share "blood," as do clansmen, who are putatively of "one father." [3] The idiom extends to all of one's immediate mother's clansmen and to all of one's clan sisters' immediate children. Moreover, if a clan comprises sections, its men may in fact marry the daughters of female members of the opposite section from their own: this is an important stage in clan fission. Further, it is expected that after three or four generations a marriage is forgotten, as are the cognatic ties issuing from it. Intermarriage thus becomes possible. In any case the blood of the common ancestors of cognates is thought to be diluted in each succeeding generation, so that after four generations it is scarcely a bar to intermarriage. A man thus shares more blood with his mother's clan than with that of his grandmother, and hence he may marry into the natal clan of the latter, although not into her subclan.

The last point is also covered by the *rapa* rule. Once two *rapa* intermarry there should be no more marriages between them till the resulting blood ties are forgotten. Thus, direct sister-exchange is precluded, nor may siblings marry into the same *rapa*.[4] Further, a man may not marry affines or cognates of his lineage or *rapa*-mates of his own affines or cognates. Thus from ego's viewpoint, some prohibitions fall under both rules, some under only one. For example he may not marry a cross-cousin (rule 1) nor any woman of the cousin's *rapa*, including the cousin (rule 2); nor again his wife's sister (rule 2 only). Nor may he marry his male cross-cousin's wife's sister, whose lineage is linked to his via his cross-cousin's marriage (rule 2, indirect linkage).

Flexibility in the application of rule 2 rests on the fact that the term *rapa* can refer to groups of varying size and segmentary level. An individual learns the rules through his knowledge of the names of groups he may not marry into. In a given group there are different

[3] It is said that the mother contributes "blood" to her children, the father "grease" and bone, and "blood" (*mema*) ties can thus mark off matrilateral (or generally cognatic) kin from agnates; but, in the context of marriage prohibitions, the idiom applies to all kin relationships.

[4] Except that, if his wife dies childless, he may marry her immediate sister as a "replacement," giving new bride wealth for her.

extensions at different levels: thus rules about marriage with FZD apply to all the "FZ" of one's clan; about ZHZ, to one's subclan "sisters" only. Moreover, levels are deliberately reinterpreted in order to rationalize "improper" marriages. Such flexibility can result in disagreements between informants on individual applications of the rules. Moreover, to present all the theoretical applications of the rules would be cumbersome. We give, instead, first a tentative paradigm of applications for the category of cross-cousin, and second more extensive examples of prohibitions resulting from the *rapa* rule and its subrules. As the first paradigm shows, classificatory extensions may fall at any point along the string of genealogical categories denoting a particular kin type. In the second paradigm we group the categories so as to show the differences between extensions for affines (narrow) and those for cognates (wide). It should be emphasized that the denotata and their arrangements which we give are only a selection from the total set which could be generated from the rules. Thus, the asterisked cross-cousin prohibitions in Table 1B correspond to only two lines in the paradigm in Table 1A. Where we omit brackets for extension specification, the extensions are at a minimal level of segmentation or below this.

There are two supplementary rules:

1. It is dangerous to marry a woman from a *rapa* which had a man killed by one's clansmen. The fear is not so much that of ghost revenge (cf. Meggitt, 1965: 100) as that women can carry poison on behalf of their natal groups; a sister might avenge a dead brother by marrying into the killer's subclan and poisoning him.

2. Close clansmen of a dead man expect to inherit his widow, or at least to retain her and her children within his clan territory. If so, the inheriting husband need pay no new bride wealth, but he should "compensate" his subclan or clan-section mates, and appease the previous husband's ghost with pork ("pig of the widow's bridge"). An immediate brother may be reluctant to inherit, for fear of his dead brother's jealousy.

SANCTIONS AND SECONDARY FORMULATIONS

Persons related by blood or *rapa* ties should be ashamed to marry or have sexual relations. Moreover, to do so ignores or shows disrespect for the intermediary kinfolk. For example, if a man married into his mother's brother's subclan, he would be ignoring the fact that he already has a close tie, viable for exchange partnerships, with that group through the mother's brother. The mother's angry brother might then ask his ancestors to punish his nephew with sickness.

Table 1. MELPA MARRIAGE PROHIBITIONS

A. *Complete Paradigm for Cross-Cousin Categories*

Ego May Not Marry His:

1. Immediate M Clan or Section BD = M(BD)
   F Other W (= M) Subclan BD
   Lineage M Sub-Subclan BD
   Subclan M Lineage BD
   Clan M Immediate BD (Disagreement About This)
2. Clan or Clan-Section FZ Immediate D = (FZ)D
   Subclan FZ Sub-Subclan or Lineage D
   Sub-Subclan FZ Lineage D
   Lineage FZ Subclan D
   Immediate FZ Clan D (Disagreement About This)

B. *Examples of Prohibitions for Other Categories*

Rule	*Extensions*	
A Man May Not Marry:	*Wide* *(Clan Level)*	*Narrow* *(Subclan Level)*
I. Female Clan Members	(FZ) (Z) (D)	
II. Into *Rapa* into Which Woman of His Own *Rapa* Have Already Married	(FFZ) D *(FZ) D, (FZ) SD (Z) D, (Z) SD (D) D	(FFZ) HZ (FZ) HZ (Z) HZ (D) HZ
III. Into *Rapa* with Which He Has a Genealogical Connection; Nor into the *Rapa* or Smaller Groups into Which His Connections Have Married	(Z) DD	(FFZ) DD, ZDHZ (FZ) DD, ZSWZ FZDHZ FZSWZ
IV. Into *Rapa* from Which His *Rapa* Has Obtained Wives	M (Z) *M (BD) M (BSD)	W (FZ) W (Z) W (BD) FM (Z), FM (BD) SW (Z), SW (BD)
V. Into *Rapa* with Which He Traces a Connection Through Persons Indicated in IV; Nor into Their *Rapa* (or Smaller Group) of Marriage	—	MM (BD), MMZD FM (BD), FMZD MZ (D), MFZD WM WMBD, WFZD WMZD, WZD WBWZ, WZHZ MZHZ, MBWZ MBDHZ, MBSWZ MZDHZ, MZSWZ

Similarly, to marry a cross-cousin's wife's sister would be to ignore one's cross-cousin, through whom one already has an indirect link with his wife's *rapa*.

Where there is some suggestion of impropriety in a marriage, a mechanism of protest exists. This is likely to be employed only if the relevant kinsman is not consulted as the appropriate intermediary for the negotiations. Hence the boundary between "improper" and "proper" marriages cannot be defined simply by reference to "rules." Should the kinsman be neglected, he may light a fire in the path of the bridal party. The groom's father should then pay him a leg of pork or a pearlshell in compensation.[5]

Doubt over the propriety of a marriage can arise where groups are expanding and segmenting, where Big Men push the rules to their limits, and where nonagnates make marriages which strengthen the ties between allied *rapa* groups. However, if close cognates wish to marry or have intercourse, no compensation can make their union "proper." Intercourse between such persons is thought to bring them rapid sickness, sent by their affronted common ancestors. By contrast, ordinary adultery is simply an offence against the woman's husband, who should be compensated. Only if it remains unconfessed (as with all wrongs) will the ancestors eventually punish the adulterers with sickness.

Rapid sickness results from intercourse with:

1. FZ (up to subclan level), Z, and D (both up to lineage level only), also with M and other senior women married into one's subclan; and with one's immediate MZ (classified as "mother"), MBD and FZD (*pelpam* = cross-cousin), MB's and FZ's children's daughters (*pepa* = distant cross-cousin; or *mboklam* = daughter), mother's sister's daughter (*kimun* = opposite sex sibling), sister's daughter (*pam*), and sister's son's daughter (*pepa* or *mboklam*). These are all persons with whom one's blood ties are strongest. There may be extensions to the cognates of half-siblings.

2. *affines*:
   (a) wives of kinsmen: MBW (*amb ape*), MBSW and FZSW (*kimɸm*), BW (*kimɸm*), and SW (*amb kulpam*).
   (b) wife's female kin: WM and WMZ (*amb kulpam*), WZ (*kimɸm*) and WFZD and WMBD (*kimɸm*).

In type 1 the pair share a common ancestor, who sends sickness to either or both of them. In type 2a they do not, but the adulterer and the woman's husband do, and the ancestor here attacks both the adulterer and the adulterous woman. The offended husband's an-

[5] Similar demands for compensation may also be made by a disappointed suitor.

cestors thus control his wife and can punish her (as fits a norm of patrivirilocal residence). But, in 2b, where the offence is against the ancestors of the innocent wife, sickness cannot be visited on her guilty husband, but only on her children by him or on the wife herself. Here the sickness indicates that her ancestors pity her and will eventually remove her from the husband who chooses not to treat her as a wife. The death of persons thus afflicted by sickness can sometimes be avoided through sacrifices and confession.[6] In all these cases the ancestors are said to be angry at the neglect of critical kin and affinal relationships, just as the kinsmen themselves are angry when they burn the protest fire.

BRIDE WEALTH

First marriages

Twenty-four of 35 women said they married before their first menstruation; boys marry at a later age, between eighteen and twenty-five. Boys and girls of, or approaching, marriageable age join in courting ceremonies (*turnim hed*). At these, presents may pass privately between partners,[7] but sexual advances should not be made; premarital intercourse is not so common as among the Kuma (cf. Reay, 1959: 31–32). Men say they dislike marrying girls who are not virgins, though little public emphasis is placed on this. Often a girl herself comes to stay at the homestead of her chosen young man. After two weeks or so the embarrassed parents of the boy either persuade her to return home with compensatory gifts, or they raise bride wealth for her. Whether one of the pair chooses in this way or the marriage is planned by senior kin, formal negotiations have to take place, with the help of related intermediaries who provide a "road" for the marriage.

The parents of the groom stress the importance of choosing a hard-working and steady girl, as affinal exchange relations will depend on the later stability of the marriage. The girl's parents ask for a generous immediate display of bride wealth but are not over-concerned with the general economic standing of the groom's family. Yet bride wealth exchanges are only the first of many which affines make. Men see the bride wealth as soothing the hearts of the bride's kin, so that they will neither grieve her departure nor "grease" her to

[6] Sexual relations between immediate B–Z, M–S, and F–D are considered the most heinous. We have cases of the (latter) two (as of MZS–MZD), but not of immediate B–Z incest (nor of incest between immediate cross-cousins). In type 2b sickness could be visited on the wife's kinswoman, but it seems that she is not held responsible to the wife for her adultery.

[7] Formal betrothal gifts for young girls are rare. (Cf. Strauss, 1962: 322).

return, and so force the groom to pay more items in order to recover her. Instead, the payments should lead into reciprocal *moka* exchanges.

The girl's parents and often her close cognates should be acknowledged in the allocation of bride wealth items. The bride's father makes the detailed distribution to different relatives subsequently in private, but one large pig is publicly set aside for the mother—a favorite category for disputation, for the mother may secretly tell her daughter to run away if the pig offered is too small. The bride must be asked formally if she agrees to the marriage, and she can wreck negotiations simply by walking off. Return gifts are made by the bride's kin to prevent the providers of bride wealth from resenting the need to be generous.

We summarize the typical sequence of events (among Northern Melpa) for a woman's first marriage:

1. The groom's kin make an initial display of bride wealth: live pigs, pearlshells, and Australian money. Cassowaries and bamboo tubes of cosmetic oil may be added. Argument on the total amount and on the allocation of items to different persons proceeds.[8] Amounts vary from eight to twenty-four pigs, ten to sixty shells, and c. $A10 to A$200. A total average payment represents c. $A400. If it is the groom's first marriage, he contributes much less than his clansmen. Perhaps 80 per cent comes from them, and two thirds of this from his lineage mates, especially his father.[9] For subsequent marriages he

[8] The Dei Councillors (Northern Melpa) have attempted to curb inflation by fixing the total number of items, apart from money, at thirty, e.g., ten pigs and twenty shells.

[9] A nonagnate who has a sponsor can expect him and his clansmen to contribute as much as his own agnates might have done.

Source of Contributions	Groom an Agnate (Per Cent of Ten Cases)		Groom a Nonagnate (Per Cent of Four Cases)	
Sponsor and Close Associates and Groom	69%		58%	
Subclansmen, Clansmen and Pair-Clansmen of Sponsor	18	87%	29	87%
Nonsponsoring Kin	5		9	
Affines	8		4	
Totals	100		100	

There is no statistical difference between the mean size of bride wealths paid on behalf of agnatic or nonagnatic grooms.

negotiates and contributes more by himself. At the first showing men decide which items to meet by equivalent return, which will "die on" the bride (i.e., will simply be taken by her kin), and which pigs will be equivalents of pigs to be cooked and presented to the bride's kin at the next stage. Discussions are helped by subclan and close cognatic relatives on each side. Close kin of the bride agree to reciprocate for some of the items. Her father may provisionally allocate three-quarters of the pigs and shells to her closer clansmen (including himself) and further items to her immediate mother's brothers, provided these formerly cared for her with gifts of clothing and decorations.

2. After two days the bride's people receive the groom's kin who bring cooked pigs for the *penal kng* ("pig for public distribution"). The total bride wealth is displayed before a wider range of the bride's kin. The groom's party load the bride with a full netbag of pork, which she carries to her own clansmen. The return gifts are then announced and made, and the final speeches take place just before the gift of pork is distributed to the bride's clan and other visitors. Pigs equivalent to half of the live bride wealth pigs, and to all those cooked, may be returned, also a quarter or half of the money and a few of the shells. For larger initial prestations proportionately more is returned. The bride's father retains the money for later distribution. Special portions of meat may be deposited in the bride's parents' house for their private consumption, and the father takes perhaps 10 dollars from the money.

3. Usually about a week elapses from the first showing to the *penal kng*. Perhaps a fortnight after that a more private transaction, the "pig of the house" (*mangal kng*), occurs. The groom's family and close lineage mates cook two to six pigs and take these by night to the bride's family. In return the bride now receives a personal dowry of netbags, oil flasks, and breeding pigs, and ideally a return is also made for the cooked pigs. After the *penal* the bride stays at the groom's settlement but will not have intercourse with him nor begin routine work until after the *mangal kng*.[10]

4. The bride now begins cooking for the husband and may harvest a part of her mother-in-law's gardens. She sleeps in her mother-in-law's house initially, where she may keep her own pigs. Women do not

---

[10] For a previously married woman no *mangal* is given. A man making his second marriage may be bold enough to take his bride after the *penal*, but a younger man, who in any case acts with embarrassed indifference during the bride wealth proceedings, is too shy to do so.

regard having their own house as a special mark of status and are often willing to share indefinitely;[11] but each woman insists on independent claims to garden land and pigs. Where there are cowives with children, husbands tend to separate these in housing also.

5. For the next few months the groom and his father are solicitous to send portions of cooked pig to the wife's kin. Reciprocal exchanges begin, which may develop into formal *moka* gifts if the bride settles down.

THE DISSOLUTION OF MARRIAGES
AND INHERITANCE OF WIDOWS

Jural divorce depends on the return of part of the bride wealth. Outstanding items from the initial prestation and the *mangal* should be returned. In the past, when wealth was scarce and warfare endemic, it was hard to secure repayment; and nowadays it still involves protracted litigation through the Local Government Councilors. If the husband tells his wife to go, he has to accept an incomplete return, or none if he retains the children, although no precise adjustments are made for the number of children. Moreover, if the marriage has lasted some years, the groom finds it difficult to press any claims, whatever the circumstances. However, where a wife leaves her husband after only a few months, her kin should not only return outstanding items but also add another pig "to make the skin smooth and clear from debts." Men say that marriages break up either owing to the obstinate caprice of the bride or because of pressure exerted by kinfolk who are dissatisfied with their share of the bride wealth. In an attempt to stabilize marriages the Dei Councillors have now ruled that no second bride wealth can be taken for a divorced woman. The new husband of a divorced woman need thus pay no immediate bride wealth for her, but at the birth of a child he makes unusually large growth payments for it, both to demonstrate his paternity and to establish exchange relations with his affines. Growth payments are required for a first child, whether bride wealth has been paid or not. They are made to enlist the interest of the maternal ancestors in the child's growth and to prevent their wishing it ill.

If a wife dies, no return of bride wealth is made unless she has

---

[11] Of twenty-four cases where the groom's mother was alive, the bride slept in her house and received gardens exclusively from her in sixteen cases. In the rest she shared housing and gardens with other women of the settlement as well as with the mother-in-law.

lived predominantly at her natal place. If the husband dies, his widow should remarry within his clan, but such marriages are often unstable.

Table 2. DISPOSAL OF MELPA WIDOWS

A. *Inheritance of Widows, Initial Situation*
(*Kawelka Sample Only—Two Clans, Both Divided into Sections*)

Wife Remarried within Dead Husband's:	Clan	Clan-Section	Sub-clan	S-Subclan or Lineage	Sibling Set, Close Lineage	All
Number of Cases	2	11	6	14	6	39*

B. *Wives of 172 Men Now Dead*
(*Excluding Divorcees—Two Samples from Northern and Central Melpa, Combined*)[12]

Type of Disposal	Number of Cases
1. Wife Predeceased Husband	66
Situation Uncertain	39
2. a. Remains with First Husband's Clan, But Has Not Remarried	77
b. Remains with Husband's Clan, Remarried within It*	49
c. Has Returned to Natal Home	18
d. Has Remarried Outside Husband's Clan	6
Total	255

* Eight of these women afterwards divorced their new husbands; the remaining thirty-one are in category 2b.

Rarely, a cross-cousin of her husband, not necessarily one living with the husband's clan, may claim the widow. If she remarries a clansman (or cross-cousin) of the husband, no further bride wealth goes to her kin, although the pig her new husband gives to the clansmen may be called "bride wealth." The deceased husband's children, but not his widow or the new husband, may share in this pig. The latter two should cook a smaller pig and offer its liver to the widow's ancestors, signifying the new husband's duty to sacrifice to them on her behalf. Prayers used to be spoken over the liver, telling the dead husband not to be jealous of the new man and not to attack the

[12] The two samples differ significantly in the pattern for the short-term, but not the long-term situation of widows, which is shown in this part of the Table.

children or his widow. The widow should observe some months of mourning before remarrying.[13] The new husband may also make private courtesy payments to the widow's kin. These become new bride wealth payments if she remarries outside her first husband's clan. The latter will try—not always successfully—to prevent this, otherwise they have no further claims either on her kin or on the new husband.

RATES OF POLYGYNY AND DIVORCE

Marriage and social status

Big Men in Hagen are polygynists who have shown ability in *moka* ceremonial exchange; but not all men obtain even a single wife. Orphans without an able sponsor within their clan or their mother's

Table 3. MARITAL STATUS OF LIVING MELPA MEN

Tribe	Currently Married		Previously Married		Never Married			
					Above Twenty-five (Age)		Under Twenty-five (Age)	
	Num-ber	Per Cent	Num-ber	Per Cent	Num-ber	Per Cent	Num-ber	Per Cent
Kawelka (North Melpa)	184	71.6%	20	7.7%	30	11.7%	23	8.9%
Elti (Central Melpa)	76	67.8	18	16	5	4.5	13	11.6

clan, youngest sons whose fathers die before they reach puberty and men who have physical or mental disabilities are less likely to marry. Bachelors often attach themselves to related Big Men in hope that these will provide bride wealth in return for services. There is no difference between the two samples in the proportions of men once married ($\chi^2 = 0.77$, df $= 1$, p 0.10), although fewer Elti men remain married ($\chi^2 = 4.25$, df $= 1$, p 0.05). Men of both samples thus stand

---

[13] Until the final "death house" pigs are cooked to establish the first husband's spirit in the world of the dead.

marrying, but Elti men are more likely to lose
urn to near-bachelor status.

nber of current wives per married man is 1.25
he mean of all wives per ever-married man ranges
4) to 1.8 ($^{171}/_{94}$). There are no significant differences
samples here, nor in the ratio of polygynists to other
en (15%–19%). However, it is usually among the larger
al Melpa tribes (e.g., Ndika, Mokei) that outstanding polygynists
with eight or ten current wives are found.

Table 4. NUMBER OF CURRENT WIVES PER MARRIED MELPA MAN

	0	1	2	3	4	5	No. Men
Kawelka	20	150	24	8	2	—	204
Elti	18	64	5	7	—	—	94

A third of the Kawelka polygynists have wives dispersed in separate
homesteads; another quarter are permanently "separated" from one
wife. Typically, such "separation" means that the two continue to
cohabit, and the wife rears pigs and children for the husband; but she
does not regularly cook for him, and she withdraws from daily
competitive interaction with her cowives. She may live and garden
at her parents', brother's, or married daughter's home. However,
there is no regular "terminal separation" (cf. E. Goody, 1962). Moreover, all wives make temporary visits to their natal homes, and
husbands become anxious about these absences. Such visits are common in the early months of marriage, when divorce is most likely.[14]

The Rights of Marital Partners

Individual components of the bride wealth are not closely linked to
the transfer of specific rights, although the pigs for which no return
is made are called "pigs for the girl's vagina" and mark the husband's
exclusive sexual rights over her. The husband should provide gardens
for and allocate pigs to his wife and should exchange *moka* gifts

---

[14] Of sixteen first marriages contracted by girls in 1964, two were ended by divorce
in four to nine months, two were fragile, and in four others the wife spent her
time with her natal kin. In the remaining eight, the wife lived with her husband,
and the marriage appeared to be stable.

with her kin. He should also fetch firewood for her. The wife should plant, weed and harvest her gardens, cook her husband's food, rear his pigs, and bear his children. For five days during her menstrual periods she should retire to the seclusion hut and refrain from cooking food for males of her settlement. She should warn her husband not to copulate with her if she is menstruating. Her fluids can cause a man's blood to rise to his neck and kill him. Again, she may not offer her husband food for two months after bearing a child.

A married couple should avoid intercourse till the end of the suckling period (average 2½–3 years, range 1–3¼), for the husband's semen, if ingested through the mother's milk, could kill the child. (In the early months of pregnancy, by contrast, semen is needed to mould the foetus into a creature with human features and limbs.) The taboo is given as one reason why men like to be polygynists.

As it is thought that several acts of intercourse are required to conceive and form a foetus, it is assumed, even when a wife has been adulterous, that only her husband has had frequent enough sexual access to her to cause a successful pregnancy. The *pater* of a child should be its *genitor;* and in clear cases of *de facto* separation where the wife becomes pregnant while cohabiting with another man, her child will be his if he makes payments on behalf of it.

Patterns of Divorce

Eighty to ninety per cent of divorces involve childless women. In the remaining cases husbands try to retain the children, but if the children are less than ten years old, the mother is likely to remove them. As they approach puberty, their agnates urge them to return, but this is a matter for their own choice. Children whose affiliation has been changed assume their adoptive lineage's marriage prohibitions, unless their nonagnatic status is invoked to rationalize exchange marriages which are contracted. Provided that the first husband of a remarried woman cared for his children for a short while, they are said fully to share his blood and his semen; they can be sent sickness by him and they will observe prohibitions resulting from their "blood" connections.

Perhaps 40 per cent of all litigation concerns marital disputes. Women are more likely to protest to their local councilor than are men. In the past they would have been helped only by their natal kin, who were expected to be "sorry" for them, within reason (contrast Meggitt [1965: 157] on the Mae Enga). If the husband wounds his wife, he should compensate her kin. Rarely, a wife may compensate her husband with her kinsmen's resources (e.g., for polluting his food), but spouses are expected to tolerate offences which in others would be actionable for compensation. In most disputes with outsiders, the husband should meet his wife's debts.

A husband tells his wife to go only if he suspects her of planning to poison or pollute him; but women may leave their husbands for preferring a cowife or for not making gifts to their kin. Once affinal exchange relations are established, the exchange partners are likely to discourage divorce; but many divorces occur before successful exchanges have been made. Even if mediators are successful the woman continues to feel the tensions of her "intermediary" situation, which may lead to quarrels over the allocation of valuables and pigs. Once divorce occurs, the ex-affines rarely continue exchange partnerships.

If a woman is adamant for divorce, she gets her way. "It is her own strength of will," men say. The anxiety that men display about the possibility of women exercising this "strength" results from their dependence on them for rearing pigs and children and as links with their exchange partners. Discussion often centers on promiscuous women who pass from man to man in a series of short unions, although these constitute no more than 5 per cent of all women. Offspring of such women have no clear *pater* and may lack a firm clan affiliation.

Table 5. DETAILS OF MELPA DIVORCE RATES

Ratio of Divorces to:*	Eltl	Per Cent	Kawelka	Per Cent	Difference
All Marriages	$\frac{42}{173}$**	24.4%	$\frac{56}{330}$**	16.9%	Insignificant
Completed Marriages	$\frac{42}{78}$	53.8	$\frac{56}{100}$	56.0	Insignificant
All Marriages Less Deaths	$\frac{42}{137}$	30.7	$\frac{56}{286}$	19.5	$\chi^2 = 5.77$, af = 1, p .025

* For calculation of divorce ratios, see Barnes (1949).
** Both samples include wives who divorced but later returned to their husbands, so that the total number of marriages is 330 and 173, but the number of wives is 328 and 171.

The samples here are based on current and previous marriages of living men. The difference between the samples for ratio C is confirmed by other figures based on women's marriages. Within the two samples the ratios of the rates for men do not contrast with those for women.

Table 6. MARITAL HISTORIES OF CURRENT WIVES OF LIVING MEN

Wives (Tribes)	Previously Unmarried	Previously Widowed	Previously Divorced	Previously Promiscuous	Uncertain Status	Totals
Kawelka	157	29	33	2	9	230
Elti	61	10	16	6	2	95
Totals	218	39	49	8	11	325
χ^2	.68	.16	.11	6.03	—	
		Insignificant		p .025		

Wealth in valuables came from Europeans to Central Melpa before it reached Northern Melpa, and this greater wealth may have forced a slightly faster circulation of women among the former. Valuables are now more evenly distributed; but whereas the Northern Melpa circulate theirs intensively in *moka* exchanges, among the Central groups the bride wealth nexus remains heavily loaded.

PATTERNS OF INTERMARRIAGE BETWEEN GROUPS

The Spread of Marriages

Clans tend to avoid marrying their traditional enemies. Courting and visiting in such enemy areas entail dangers of poisoning, particularly as there are unavenged killings between enemy groups. Affines should visit and be exchange partners, and the tendency to establish intense *moka* exchange relations with allies and former minor enemies fits with the clustering of marriages between them.

Propinquity by itself does not determine marriage patterns, although it influences them. A clan often has both friends and enemies along its boundaries. Thus a clan-segment is likely to intermarry heavily and share territory with neighbors in a former minor enemy clan but not with neighbors in a traditional enemy clan. The pattern is complicated by cross-cutting ties of military alliance between isolated clans of formally traditional enemy tribes.

Rates of intratribal marriage depend partly on the size and segmentation pattern of the tribe. Shrunken tribes of 500 members or less may form a single exogamous unit. The Kawelka (Northern Melpa) tribe forms three exogamous clans of 200 to 360 members; 13.7 per cent of their junior and 16 per cent of their senior men have married Kawelka women (cf. A. J. Strathern, 1965: 188). The figures for two clans of the larger Tipuka tribe (2,419) show 30 to 40 per cent of intratribal marriages and for the Welyi (1,250) they reach 55 per cent. A small tribe like the Kawelka (860) tends to "marry out," to keep up extra-tribal alliances; whereas the Welyi, beleaguered in warfare by their Tipuka neighbors, decided to "marry inside" to prevent their women bearing children for their enemies.

The wider relations of the Kawelka are in Table 7.

Table 7. DISPERSION OF MARRIAGES MADE BY MEN OF KAWELKA CLANS

Marriage (Dispersion)	Mandembo	Membo	Kundmbo	Totals
Intratribal Marriages	22	21	14	57
Marriages with Bordering Tribes	65	79	75	219
Marriages to the South	6	28	24	58
Marriages to East and West	13	9	8	30
Marriages with Jimi Groups to the North	9	6	—	15
Marriages with Non-Hagen Women	—	1	—	1
Totals	115	144	121	380

Most wives are taken from neighboring groups. Within this category we distinguish (in Table 8) between (a) traditional enemies, and (b) minor enemies *cum* allies.

Table 8. MARRIAGES AND ENMITY AMONG MELPA

Wives Taken From:	Mandembo	Membo	Kundmbo	Totals
(a) Minembi and Kombukla Clans	10	25	51	86
(b) Tipuka and Klamakae Clans	54	55	24	133

The pattern for the Kundmbo clan reverses that for the other two; this fits the cross-tribal alliances the Kundmbo have always had with their Minembi neighbors, especially with the Minembi Kimbo clan

with which they are paired in opposition to the Membo and Mandembo pair within their own tribe. Many of the more detailed patterns
are obscured in our simplified presentation,[15] but for Membo and
Mandembo clans many more marriages have been made with their
allies than with their traditional enemies.

Exchange Marriages

Vicedom (1943–48, vol. 2: 201) says, "The (Central Melpa) Mbowamb
like to exchange women. If a clan has given one of its daughters to
another, it is happy to take a girl back from that clan, if one of its
young men is ready to marry. It is through this double bond that the
clans first become properly tied to each other."

Barnes (1962: 8) has suggested that in the highlands "matrimonial
alliances are either concentrated or deliberately dispersed" and that
the latter alternative is more common, in keeping with the emphasis
on fresh interpersonal connections rather than on intergroup solidarity.
However, in Hagen there is both concentration and dispersion. A
certain spread of affinal ties is useful, in order to draw in wealth
from diverse sources when it is needed. But the shape of political
relations and the need for security of investment both induce a
clustering of marriages between paired clans and ex-minor enemies.
Such unions should not break the usual marriage prohibitions, but
nonagnates can facilitate exchanges by marrying into groups from
which their agnatic lineage mates are debarred. Direct reciprocity
between two lineages or *rapa* groups may be impossible, but at the
clan level it becomes feasible. Fifty-two per cent of the boys and
sixty-six per cent of the girls in the younger generation from one
Kawelka clan have married into clans with which a clan F or FZ
had earlier contracted a marriage; and in seventy per cent of these
cases both a clan F and a clan FZ had married into the group. The
lower-level segments actually arrange marriages, but it is the clans
that are said to exchange women (*amb rop roromen, amb aklwa
etimin, amb timb ak°k ngoromen*). The last phrase means "they
harvest their footsteps and give," i.e., they retrace their steps, which
they planted in carrying a bride wealth to a group, in order to claim
a bride wealth back.

Despite the idiom of "harvesting footsteps," there are no precisely
reckoned debts in women existing between clans, and thus there is

[15] Further analysis is given in A. J. Strathern, 1965: 210 ff.

no question of marriages being arranged to meet such debts.[16] The idiom is in fact a *post hoc* evaluation of existing marriages. Moreover, there is great flexibility in the way individual "exchanges" are reckoned. Informants readily list pairs of marriages, in the form: "Woman X went from our clan to clan B and woman Y came back." They choose pairs which are known to them and involve persons closer to them than to others; and the citation may be a charter for their own friendship with the groups they mention.

The divergence in pairing which results can be seen from the following table:

Table 9. Exchange-Marriage Pairs Among Melpa

Tribe	Number of Pairings	Number of Marriages	Number of Informants	Number of Identical Pairs Cited
Elti	63	97	7	0
Kawelka	90	139	7	5

The reference group cited varies also, from the whole of a small tribe (Elti) to clans or subclans; but this also can be an outcome of the individual informant's interests. The variation makes it even clearer that such paired marriages are not arranged beforehand; they are evaluations after the act.

As exchange marriages are not regularly arranged on a "debt" basis, we must look elsewhere for the significance of the idiom of "exchanging women." We suggest this must be done by analogy with *moka* relations. In the *moka* former minor enemy groups maintain an alternation between friendship (or equality) and modified hostility (or inequality), by means of exact or overtopping reciprocity in wealth. Men think in the same way about reciprocity in women. Exact reciprocity implies equality and peace, and it is thus appropriate that intermarriage between groups was in the past appealed to in order to halt warfare. For example: "We fought them in minor warfare only, and when we were tired we thought of our sisters who had married their men and theirs who had married us, and of the sisters' sons who were now in each clan, and so we used to make peace." In this formulation reciprocal marriages and extra-clan kinship are seen as interlocking factors facilitating peacemaking between groups.

[16] Contrast the debts in women among the Kuma (Reay, 1959: 97 ff.), and the precise debts in wealth incurred in the Hagen *moka* system.

By contrast, imbalance in reciprocity implies superiority and a measure of hostility. To the Mbowamb, however, superiority is gained not by giving but by taking more wives from the other group. It is the group which has been "strong" and provided more bride wealth payments than the other which gains prestige. Essentially, it is the imbalance in bride wealth, and not in women, which is the focus here. Even a small group, such as the Elti, can assert superiority over the very host group which saved them earlier from extermination in warfare, by claiming to have married all its daughters and so to have won over it.[17]

[17] Yet, from the hosts' point of view, the giving of wives, and the subsequent attachment of Elti children to them as their sisters' sons, may be regarded as a means of gradually "incorporating" the Elti into their own group.

Marriage in
MENDI

D'Arcy Ryan

THE SETTING

The Mendi people occupy a rugged mountain valley about twenty-five miles long in the Southern Highlands District of Papua. The land lies between 5,000 and 7,000 feet above sea level, bounded by ranges rising a further 1,500 to 2,000 feet. The valley widens from about two miles across at its south end to about twelve miles where it rises into the northern ranges. The terrain is broken: swift, rock-strewn streams tumble through gullies whose walls rise steeply from 50 to 250 feet. Thus, the whole valley floor is a network of gullies and ridges which define territorial boundaries of the localized social groups.

The valley has a temperate climate, but its northern higher parts are subject to severe frosts. The rainfall averages about 108 inches a year, varying from six inches in June to over twelve inches in September.

The valley was first visited by an exploratory patrol in 1936 and by a mapping expedition in 1938. The war intervened and there was no other outside contact until 1950, when the Australian Administration established in the lower valley an airstrip and a station which became the administrative headquarters of the Southern Highlands District. In the same year, the Methodist Overseas Mission established a post near the government station, and in 1955 the Roman Catholic Capuchin Mission also acquired land nearby. Until 1958, when I last visited Mendi, mission influence was negligible.

The Administration followed its usual practice in new areas: it prohibited interclan fighting and began to build roads. The first motor vehicles appeared about 1954 and by 1958 negotiable roads ran north and south of the station. But as late as 1966 the only access from the rest of New Guinea was by air or foot-track.

The people living close to the station had some contact with Europeans and with native government employees from other areas.

When this study was made, a few had acquired a smattering of English and some grasp of the *linguae francae,* Pidgin and Motu. Native traders had introduced steel axes and knives some time before the first European visits and, by 1958, these had replaced the stone working-axe; this had some effect on the local economy (cf. Salisbury, 1962) but in other essentials the traditional culture was untouched.

Wurm (1960 and 1961) classifies Mendi with the Mendi-Pole subfamily of Highland languages. The Mendi valley is situated on the eastern edge of this linguistic area, adjacent to that of the Hagen subfamily. Dialects differ markedly over short distances but are mutually intelligible; differences do not seem to affect marriage alliances. Wurm (1961: 9) estimated that 33,800 people speak dialects of Mendi. They refer to themselves as the Mendi River People as compared to the Lae River People or Nembi River People, but this designation does not imply any political unity.

The physical type is common throughout the New Guinea Highlands: short, muscular, and well proportioned. The men average about five feet one inch and the women four feet eight inches. Skin color varies from dark brown to light olive. Some young men prefer lighter skinned brides, but skin color seems to have no other social significance.

The people are subsistence gardeners using a combination of swidden and fallow. The staple crop is sweet potato, supplemented by bananas, sugar cane, taro, beans, edible gourds, and leaf vegetables. Pigs are economically important but prohibitions limit their consumption. They are important items of bride wealth.

The predominant feature of the economy is the elaborate series of ceremonial wealth exchanges that accompany every important group activity. The exchanges occasioned by a marriage are particularly complex and continue for the duration of the marriage. No serious discussion of Mendi marriage is possible without detailed reference to these payments.

SOCIAL STRUCTURE

The Mendi have a segmentary social structure based on a system of localized agnatic clans. The clans are divided into patrilineages, usually four to six generations deep. The size of the clans and lineages varies but there appear to be optimal limits within which they can function. Most clans of more than 300 members, for example, strain their territorial resources and become unstable and potentially fissive.

Lineages of more than 100 members reach a similar state, but for different reasons (Ryan, 1959: 262ff.). At either level of segmentation the clan or lineage splits along the usual agnatic lines of cleavage, forming new units. When a lineage degenerates (e.g., through disease or warfare) it can no longer perform certain essential functions (of which the payment of bride wealth is one) so it either fuses with a co-lineage or amalgamates with a stronger unit.

Although the lineage model is agnatic and patrivirilocal, there exists, nevertheless, considerable mobility in both residence and lineage affiliations. Some people leave their agnatic territory for a variety of reasons and go to live with a cognatic or affinal relative who may grant them some of his garden land. Such a change is often permanent and land acquired in this way follows thence the usual rules of agnatic inheritance. In the course of two or three generations, the descendants of such an immigrant assume full agnatic status, gradually falsifying their genealogies to strengthen their position. At any point in time, however, the population of a clan territory comprises an agnatic core, together with a number of affiliated non-agnates of various kin categories.

Before the Administration imposed a general peace, warfare was endemic among these people, and whole clans were driven by enemies from their territories and dispersed. In such circumstances, the survivors (as lineages, or as individual families) took refuge with clans among whom they had affinal or cognatic ties. The necessity to establish such ties as sources of potential refuge had some influence on the patterns of marriage.

These dynamic processes of constant fission and fusion, fragmentation and amalgamation, common to lineage systems in general, are an essential part of the Mendi social structure (cf. Meggitt, 1962).

FREQUENCY OF MARRIAGE

No transition rites mark the passage from youth to adulthood and there is no generally accepted marriageable age. Men marry for the first time in their mid-twenties and the dozen or so brides I saw were between fifteen and twenty-two. As they did not try to reckon their ages, more precise estimates were unobtainable. In general, a man marries when he can afford his bride price, and few men voluntarily remain single.

Ideally, the Mendi are polygynous, and the ability to instigate and maintain the economic exchanges accompanying a number of coterminous marriages is a sign of wealth and hence an important mark of high status. A sample of sixty married men had contracted an average of 2.1 marriages each, with an average of 1.5 contemporaneous wives; 64 per cent of these men married once only, and 70 per cent had only one wife at a time; only seven men (12 per cent) had more than two contemporaneous wives. Informants knew of no man with more than seven living wives. In practice, therefore, the polygynous ideal is severely limited by economic factors.

COURTSHIP

Acquaintance between the sexes begins most often with an accidental meeting, usually at a dance or, today, at the government market, but sometimes on bush tracks. The significant point is that most initial meetings appear to be fortuitous. The young man may ask the girl's permission to come and sing to her. This is a matter of pride to both. A desirable young man must have entrée to as many girls' houses as possible, and the girl's prestige demands that she attract male singers. A popular girl has between six and a dozen courtiers and an enthusiastic young man attends regularly a similar number of girls. Courting parties take place in the evening in the girl's house. She sits against the wall while her visitors sit facing her over a long fire. She usually has a couple of female chaperones and sometimes a brother as well. One guest sits cross-legged beside the girl, their shoulders touching. In a soft nasal falsetto, he sings a courting song; the words may be part of a general repertoire or self-composed, but the tune is always the same. When the song is finished, the young man moves back across the fire and another takes his place. There is some conversation among the waiting men, and sometimes a few whispered words between the singing couple. Often someone plays a jews-harp or, more rarely, pan-pipes. New guests arrive and others leave.

In the course of time, for both boys and girls, the field of prospective mates narrows. The singing parties become smaller and more intimate until at length the girl reaches an understanding with one young man and thereafter receives only him and his clan brothers who come to spare him the embarrassment of courting alone. When the affair has reached this stage, the suitor formally approaches the girl's father or brothers and, if they agree, the marriage payments are arranged. He gives one pearlshell immediately as a deposit.

Although young married men frequently attend singing parties, older men seldom do so. It would be beneath the dignity of an established man to compete for a girl's affection with his juniors. Instead, he negotiates directly with the girl and her parents.

Until the formal consummation of the marriage the couple are supposed to remain chaste, but it is accepted that some intercourse takes place. This is not frequent, as unlawful sex, like overindulgence, can result in a physical wasting away of the man, with loss of hair and drying up of the skin (known as being "eaten by a woman").

CHOICE OF SPOUSE

Marriage is forbidden with members of the following groups:

1. Any lineage with which common agnatic descent is assumed.

2. Any lineage into which a member of one's own lineage has married within the previous five or six generations. That is, one marriage between any two lineages bars all further marriage between them for five or six generations. Theoretically, this prohibition applies for the same period to all descendants of the original two sublineages; in fact, an individual remembers few of the marriages of any ancestors outside his own patriline, and even the lineage name of mother's mother is often forgotten. For this reason, an individual's choice of eligible lineages is in fact much wider than a strict application of the rules would allow.

3. Any lineage into which one's mother's lineage cannot marry under either of the preceding rules.

It follows then that each individual has a number of antigamous[1] lineages in common with other members of his agnatic descent group. In addition to these, he has a further list of antigamous lineages, derived from his mother, which he shares only with his full siblings. The range of potential spouses is determined therefore by personal genealogy. It is not immediately affected by change of residence or even of lineage affiliation; but people residing permanently with lineages of which they are not agnatic members tend to adjust their genealogies to eliminate cognatic ties and to assume putative agnacy. This takes at least two or three generations; but, when the process is complete, the new agnates have more or less severed ties with their former agnatic lineage and they now assume the marriage prohibitions of the agnates with whom they have become affiliated.

---

[1] Antigamy: the prohibition of marriage between specific social groups or categories; hence, antigamous groups: groups whose members are forbidden to intermarry. I have found this neologism useful in discussing marriage systems of this type.

The genealogical rationale of any antigamous prohibition is usually remembered only by older men; individuals tend to remember their personal antigamy lists in terms of lineages rather than of genealogies. After five or six generations, the details of a common descent are forgotten by almost everybody, and this marks the time when the groups concerned are again permitted to intermarry.

Mendi rules of marriage prohibition might have been specifically designed to spread the net of kinship ties and political alliances over as wide an area as possible; mature informants were fully aware of this.

When asked positive reasons for the choice of a particular spouse the Mendi spoke only of the personal attributes of the couple concerned. Women are attracted to men entirely by their appearance, perhaps encouraged by love-magic (but little importance is attached to this); men like women who are tall, straight, and strong. For the young man, his bride's appearance and personality are primary considerations but, as he gets older, he places more value on strength, industry, and skill in tending pigs and gardens. In short, a man selects a woman he likes with the qualities of a good wife, and she will marry a man she likes who is able to pay a good price for her. Always, it is emphasized that the personal qualities of the two parties are the only factors of importance. Nevertheless, choice is influenced by at least two other factors.

The Mendi terrain is rugged and broken, and courting takes place at night. After dark, ghosts are abroad in the bush and, until recently, so were enemy ambush parties. If a young man has the choice of two girls of more or less equal attraction, one of whom resides within fifteen minutes easy walking and the other two hours away across deep gullies and mountain torrents, there is little doubt as to which girl will receive his attentions. In a sample of ninety-three marriages, nearly fifty-three per cent were between couples residing less than two miles apart, and the frequency of marriage decreased as the distance increased.

Most men agreed that wealth does not have much influence on the spouses' own choice, but it could influence a girl's parents to try to force her into an unwelcome marriage. The whole question of parental influence on marriage can be answered most simply thus: (a) most marriages are arranged by the couple themselves; (b) where parental pressure is exerted, some children are more submissive to their parents than are others; and (c) resistance is easier for a man than for a girl, but possible for both.

Some lip service is paid to the ideal of premarital chastity, and a new bride is expected to be a virgin although the men assured me that few were. Whatever the private reality, if it became public that a girl had been seduced, her parents usually tried to force a marriage; but the seducer, if he wished, could avoid the match by payment of compensation, the size of which is determined by the relative strength and bargaining power of his kin group and of hers. The girl would be somewhat disgraced and, on the argument that "loose before marriage means loose after marriage," her potential bride price would be lowered. On the other hand, the principle worked both ways, and it was generally agreed that a young man could acquire a wife at a reduced bride price by seducing her first, and also that a young couple could overcome parental opposition in the same way. Actual cases were cited.

MARRIAGE PAYMENTS

Most New Guinea highland peoples operate gift exchange systems of great complexity (cf. Elkin, 1953; Bulmer, 1960; Meggitt, 1965). That of the Mendi area is possibly the most elaborate of all and permeates their whole society. Every social relationship of importance is marked by formal prestations of wealth. Marriage exchanges follow the usual basic direction: the bulk of the payment in pearlshell,[2] pigs, and lesser valuables is made from the groom's kin to the bride's kin, while the bride brings to her husband a return gift, or dowry, of pigs. The dowry is always much less valuable than the groom's payment. The latter varies in size from about sixteen shells, six pigs, and a considerable number of minor items (salt, oil, axes, etc.) to one or two shells and one pig. The scale of the other payments in the exchange is in proportion and depends on the age and desirability of the woman and the economic and political status of the respective kin groups of bride and groom.

Notwithstanding the variation in the size of marriage payments, the phases of exchange follow a prescribed sequence: (1) A good faith deposit of one or two pearlshells paid immediately on betrothal by the prospective groom to his fiancée's father or brothers or to other representatives of her kin. This is refundable if the betrothal is broken by the girl. (2) A series of small betrothal gifts (mirrors, beads, etc.) to the girl herself. (3) The private display of pearlshell (and, usually

[2] A valve of the large pearl oyster *margaritifera-margaritifera* polished and cut in a crescent shape.

a few pigs) to those of the bride's kin who ultimately share her bride price. This takes place in the house yard of the groom or of a close kinsman who has been acting as his agent.[3] Representatives of the bride's kin inspect the marriage payment, and if they approve, they ceremonially offer the girl two of the shells. She takes them, faces the spectators and then hands them back, thus stating publicly that the bride price has been accepted. This action also signifies that the girl herself is the recipient of her own bride price, that it is hers to dispose of as she thinks fit, and that her kinsmen are acting only as her agents. This assumption of her independence is a distinctive and basic feature of Mendi marriages, and although it is sometimes a fiction, the girl is often allowed to exercise her discretion. (4) A few days later, the bride wealth is publicly handed over on the bride's ceremonial ground.[4] The girl, covered in a gleaming black mixture of palm oil and soot, wearing a bulky blackened net bridal veil and carrying the bride's forked wand, stands alone in the midst of the bride wealth placed there by the groom and his kin, who have retired to one side. The girl then makes the distributions. Item by item, she hands the wealth out among her kin and their affines, calling the name of each recipient. (5) On this same occasion, certain of the bride's kin make a return gift of pigs. The value of these pigs is known in advance, and the groom must add an equivalent sum to the agreed bride price. To build up the scale of the payments in this way greatly increases the prestige of the contracting parties. (6) After the ceremonial distribution of the major items, the bride accompanies her husband to his home bringing with her the return gift of pigs. The marriage should not be consummated for another month (or, as the Mendi say, until the bride's anointment has worn off). During this period, the groom gathers from his clansmen and others the numerous minor items to complete his payment. Meanwhile, he does no arduous physical work, abstains from certain foods, is sexually continent, and acquires and memorizes the antiwoman magic to protect him when eventually he has sexual contact. These taboos are part of the general complex of behavior occasioned by the belief in the dangerous impurity of women found throughout the New Guinea highlands (cf. Meggitt, 1964). The taboos have two sanctions. First, the man who breaks them is "eaten" by the woman

[3] A young man is shy at his first marriage and inexperienced in handling the complicated transactions that go with it, so he asks an older kinsman to act as his spokesman and negotiator. For subsequent marriages, he usually supervises his own arrangements.

[4] A kind of "public square," the social center of her agnatic (or residential) territory.

(i.e., wastes away physically); second, his kin may refuse to contribute the rest of his bride price. Such taboos are more strictly observed at a first marriage than later when the groom is sexually more sophisticated and less dependent economically. The month of abstinence gives the bride time to become acquainted with her affines and adjust to her new life. It is regarded as a trial period. If the marriage is to break, it is thought better for the separation to come then and many marriages are annulled during this period. That marriages are recognized as being initially unstable is shown by the fact that the bride's kin who have received her bride price are expected to keep the goods in their possession for the time being. They do not always do this however; there may be debts to meet or payments to make. If the bride price is prematurely dispersed and the unconsummated marriage then breaks, the groom claims a refund of his bride price and the bride's kin may find themselves seriously embarrassed. In these circumstances they do everything in their power to preserve the marriage, and if the bride leaves her husband they try to force her return. Many marital disputes arise from this situation, which formerly could have led to warfare, but which today are brought in increasing numbers to the Administration court. (7) When the major payment is complete down to the last small item, the groom gives a marriage feast for the bride's kin and all contributors to the bride price. He kills the return gift pigs together with others of his own, and the ensuing pork distribution is both a gesture of friendship by the groom to his new affines and a token of acknowledgement to those who assisted with his bride price. (8) Before the marriage is consummated, the bride and groom perform a small private ceremony in her house. The bride cuts a cooked gourd with a bamboo ritual knife and the couple eat half each. Within the next three days, when the man has performed the appropriate protective magic, the marriage is consummated.

It is expected that for his first marriage a bridegroom should contribute a considerable part of the marriage payments from his own assets, and, indeed, he is not ready to marry until he can do this. Most of the remainder is contributed by his lineage, and to a lesser degree by fellow clansmen or lineage affines. For subsequent marriages, a man receives little or no economic assistance. The Mendi themselves see bride price not as the purchase of a woman by one group from another but as the payment of a woman for her future services. The women do not themselves retain or use any of the forms of exchange wealth. Even when, as in marriage payments, they are the recipients, they immediately redistribute the goods among their male kin. But because, however temporarily, a woman is the actual owner of these goods, she has, in theory at least, the right to say who will ultimately receive them. The reasons for which a girl might exclude (say) a particular brother, were given as these:

1. He failed to give her pork when he killed pigs.
2. Before she married, he refused to make her ornaments to wear or to carve her digging-sticks.
3. He gave her no oil or paint for the dances at which she hoped to attract young men's attention.
4. He wove her no arm bands.

A share in a woman's bride price is thus seen as a material return for certain personal obligations, gifts, and services, rather than as a compensation to her clan as a whole. But these gifts and services, whilst trifling in themselves, have a great symbolic importance, for they signify the girl's attachment to her own kin—the people with whom her main interest and loyalty reside, those to whom she can look for refuge and protection while living her married life among strangers. A brother who neglects his symbolic duties towards her is not merely depriving her of arm bands or occasional scraps of pork but is also, in effect, repudiating his entire relationship to her, thus forfeiting any share in her bride price. The converse of this is equally true. A girl never lightly or capriciously denies a share in her bride price to someone normally entitled to it. To do so would formally sever a relationship which she might one day need. As an informant put it succinctly: "If a girl offend her brothers, who then will give her pork?"

In practice, a woman's right to distribute her own bride price may be modified by her relationship with her father and brothers. A timid girl with a domineering father may, indeed, have no say in the matter. I recall, however, several cases in which the girls' discretion was decidedly and pointedly exercised, to the chagrin of several close kinsmen with whom they had recently quarreled. In the ordinary way, therefore, a girl distributes her bride price to her father and brothers, to her mother (who gives it to her own brothers) and to her married sisters (who pass it on to their husbands or sons). Generally speaking, the people who receive part of a girl's bride price are those who would have contributed to it had she been a man. It often happens that there are not enough major items to satisfy all the people with a reasonable claim to them. In such cases the recipients are determined, through long preliminary discussion, by a complex of personal factors: degree of relationship, seniority, status, need, size and frequency of past contributions and receipts, etc.

Distribution of bride wealth follows a different pattern in two special cases: (a) where the bride does not reside with her patrikin and (b) the remarriage of a widow. In the first case, the Mendi answer is clear and unequivocal: "The men who weave her armbands and give her pork will take her bride price." Bearing in mind the significance of these symbolic services, the statement means that her bride price goes to the men who have reared her, sheltered her, and fed her; that is, to the men of her clan of residence. It is of course possible for a girl to have maintained amicable relations with the men of her agnatic lineage while residing permanently elsewhere; then her patrikin receive some share in her bride price but the bulk of it still goes to her clan of residence.

When widows remarry, the situation is more complicated. To begin with, the individual character of Mendi marriage is again emphasized in the absence of any form of levirate. In no circumstance does a man give his brother access to his wife, and when he dies his widow cannot remarry within his lineage. Indeed, it is considered more proper that she avoid remarrying within his clan, although this does occur. Her bride price is divided equally among her brothers and her children by her previous marriage(s). The payment to the former is seen again as maintaining the important relationship with her own kin, while that to the latter is a compensation to her sons for depriving them of her labor in their gardens. If the second bride price is large, further items will go to the woman's sisters and to her late husband's brothers. The former to ensure her an alternative place of refuge should she leave her husband's people, the latter because they had contributed to her previous marriage payment. This rationale, although stated explicitly, is also expressed in pork-sharing symbolism. But the importance for the woman of maintaining friendly relations in as many different places as possible is always stressed. And while the Mendi clans were in an almost constant state of warfare, this matter of potential refuge was vital.

The eight formal prestations described above do not by any means conclude the payments associated with marriage; in a sense they merely begin them. There are five other categories of payment and exchange which are incumbent on a husband for the duration of his marriage.

1. The husband is obliged to engage in a series of personal exchanges with his wife's close male kin. The Mendi say that "only friends can exchange, and all friends must exchange." Personal gift

exchanges are thus the recognized method of establishing and maintaining personal friendships. It is essential therefore that a man exchange with his close affines to symbolize publicly the friendly relations
that exist between them. Failure to do so is either a deliberate re-
pudiation of such friendship or an admission of economic weakness
unworthy of a sister's husband.

2. On the birth of each child a man pays his wife an honorarium
which she passes on to her brothers.

3. A father must compensate his wife for a miscarriage or for the
death of an infant within its first two or three years.

4. A wife must receive compensation for injury whether deliberately
or accidentally inflicted.

5. A fine must be paid to the wife's kin for any breach of the affinal
avoidance rules.[5]

Detailed analysis of a number of marriages and the associated payments reveals certain facts not otherwise apparent. In the residence
patterns we saw that the occupants of each clan territory were a core of
agnates together with an accretion of nonagnatic kin whom they had
sponsored and to whom they had granted land. As many of the nonagnates were originally refugees whose clans had been dispersed in
warfare, one would expect to find them suffering some social disad-
vantage, and evidence from other areas reinforces this expectation
(cf. Meggitt, 1958, 1965; Vicedom and Tischner 1943–48). The Mendi,
however, stated firmly that this was not so: nonagnates were just as
good as agnates and were not discriminated against in any way. Daily
observations seemed to support their assertion, which conformed indeed to their general ethos of egalitarian individualism. An examination of marriage payments, however, showed that, when compared
to agnates, nonagnates tend to 1. contract fewer marriages, 2. marry
only once, 3. have only one wife at a time, 4. pay less for their wives,
5. pay a bigger proportion of the bride price themselves, and 6. be
assisted by a narrower range of kin. Nonagnates are similarly handicapped in their ability to contribute to other important intergroup
payments, despite the people's explicit assertion to the contrary.

POSITION OF WOMEN AFTER MARRIAGE

One of the basic assumptions of a marriage payment is the maintenance of ties between a wife and her own kin, the people who reared

---

[5] A man must avoid all face-to-face contact with his wife's parents. To her
brothers he behaves formally and avoids the use of personal names.

her. The importance of this is stated explicitly and is also symbolized in many ways, not only by the woman's own distribution of her bride price, particularly on her remarriage, but also by the fact that her husband is expected to conduct personal gift exchanges with her father and brothers. His failure to do so can, and does, result in divorce. The existence of such friendly ties between a man and his wife's people is regarded as an added inducement for him to treat her well. A further constraint is that he has, as it were, invested wealth in her, and she, by wise distribution of the bride price, has maintained potential rights of refuge not only with her own brothers, but with her married sisters too. The husband would therefore be foolish to ill-treat her. If she leaves him she not only has her choice of places to go but if, in addition, she can prove cruelty, he cannot recover his bride price. On the other hand, a woman who runs away from her husband for no adequate reason may forfeit the protection of her kin, who are always reluctant to return a bride price. Nevertheless, the safeguards are such that one might expect a wife to be well treated, and from my own observations this does in general seem to be so.

RELATIONS BETWEEN AFFINES

Writers describing other societies in the New Guinea highlands have asserted that affines are always enemies, a concept familiar in anthropology for over a century (cf. Brown, 1964: 335). The Mendi deny this explicitly: not only do they believe that affines should be friends, but also the marriage exchanges are such that it would be organizationally impossible to instigate and maintain them between enemies. This does not mean, of course, that relations between affines are never strained. Indeed, the existence of potential conflict is recognized in the observance of rules of avoidance and formality between close affines. But the acknowledgement that a marriage might provide a focal point for certain kinds of intergroup hostility does not imply that the groups are recognized as "enemies." If the phrase "we marry our enemies" refers to such a situation, then it is not really meaningful.

WIDOWHOOD

On the death of her husband, a widow usually returns to her own kin, and should she later remarry, her bride price distribution follows the pattern described. If she has young children by her late husband she takes them home with her. The stated norm is that, when old enough to be independent of a mother's care, the children return to their father's people and their agnatic territory. In practice however their future affiliations are decided by ties of personal sentiment. Thus they may (a) return to their father's people, (b) continue residing with their mother's people while retaining formal affiliations with their agnatic kin, (c) affiliate completely with their mother's lineage, severing all ties with their true agnates, or (d) if their mother remarries while they are still infants they may be adopted by her second husband and become affiliated to his lineage.

If the widow is old and unlikely to remarry she may please herself where she ends her days: in the menage of a son or married daughter, or back in her natal territory with her father's people. Once again the decision is guided by personal relationships.

DIVORCE AND SEPARATION

The distinction between divorce and separation is not always clear cut. Certainly, divorce takes place when the bride price is refunded, but there are instances in which the husband waives the return of bride price, or his claim expires, or he is not strong enough to enforce the refund. Nevertheless, such marriages may be permanently dissolved with no sanction to prevent the woman remarrying. A separation may be permanent or temporary and can be instigated by either party, with or without mutual agreement. It is necessary, therefore, to distinguish three kinds of marital separation:

1. *De jure:* a bilateral abrogation of the marriage in which the husband's claim for a refund of bride price (a) is met, either wholly or in part, (b) is waived, or (c) has lapsed.
2. *De facto:* a unilateral abrogation of the marriage, in which, despite the husband's assertion that she is still married to him, his ex-wife has gone through a form of marriage with another man (i.e., her kinsmen have accepted another bride price for her).
3. Separation: (a) the wife has gone to live with her kin (or elsewhere) and may or may not return to her husband or (b) she is cohabiting with another man who either has not offered bride price for her or has had his offer rejected by her kin.

Some women, after being dutiful wives for many years, and having borne their husbands' children, simply decide to go home; in such cases return of bride price is not claimable, as it is held that over the years the husband has received full value from the woman.

Some reasons for dimissal of a wife are: nagging, "eating" sexually, or because she is unlucky. (An old man told me he had dismissed one wife for adultery, but she probably eloped, for women found guilty of adultery were usually executed by drowning.) A woman may leave her husband permanently because she cannot get along with her co-wives (particularly if she is younger and more attractive than they), but this is not common because incompatible wives are usually given separate establishments. Another reason is that her husband disgusts her physically, or she may elope with another man. A runaway wife may or may not be pursued by the husband, depending on circumstances.

Far commoner is the case of the wife who returns home because her husband has failed to meet his economic obligations to her or her kin. If the husband fails in these payments, his wife withdraws her services and returns home until he redeems her by making the missing payments. In deciding how temporary or permanent this separation will be, we must consider the husband's motives. The usual reason given for such defaulting is that he does not have the goods available; but it is sometimes added that the wife was a lazy shrew. The implication is that he refrained more or less deliberately from making the payments and has no immediate intention of redeeming her. In one case, a further explanation was offered. A man who is ambitious, and bent on establishing himself as a "big man," may overreach himself and become involved in a tangle of payments, personal exchanges, and other commitments greater than he can handle, so that he is temporarily forced to retrench. The failure to render an obligatory payment to one of his wives, therefore, suspends his economic relations with her kin until such time as he is ready to resume. In this way, he relieves himself of a whole group of financial commitments by placing them, as it were, in cold storage but without permanently impairing the relationship.

This kind of economic pressure obviously leads to a form of blackmail, with the wife threatening to go home unless the husband makes repeated payments to her kin. This is, however, a risky game—a form of "brinkmanship" which balances the respective political influences of the wife's and the husband's kin groups. If the wife loses, her husband may kill her publicly with a red-hot stone in her vagina; I know of two cases in which this did in fact happen.

REFUND OF BRIDE PRICE

Apart from the exceptions already mentioned, a marriage is properly terminated by the return of at least some portion of the bride price, but the amount cannot be predicted with any exactness. Although the original bride price was arranged in formal and amiable circumstances tending to inhibit argument, the social atmosphere with returning is very different and the parties argue every point in the dispute. It is possible therefore to give only a rough indication of the refund that might be expected, bearing in mind that the final details will, as always, be the resultant of the interaction of individuals.

First, the people agree that all negotiations for recovery are primarily the concern of the husband and perhaps a brother or close friend. Second, cases of complete refusal to refund are rare; only then does the lineage or clan become involved, with the possible result of a clan war.

As we have seen, bride price is thought of essentially as a payment to the woman for certain services she renders to her husband. If she leaves him soon after the marriage, he may claim the return of his bride price in full (less the value of the return-gift pigs, and less any debts he may owe her family). If, however, the marriage has lasted an appreciable time the girl's kin say that, as the husband has enjoyed her services, there must be a corresponding reduction in the refund. The husband admits this general principle and the argument carries on from there. Unless the marriage is recent, only the pearlshells and pigs are returned; minor items are seldom claimed. If the wife has borne children, a further deduction is made; although opinions differ, it is widely agreed that the bearing of three children completely eliminates the refund. (This deduction for children has nothing to do with the childbirth gratuity mentioned earlier.)

The above rules apply whether the marriage is terminated by husband or wife.

ADULTERY

In normative statement, adulterous couples are killed: an adulterous wife is drowned. In practice, however, retaliative measures depend on the relationship between the husband and the adulterer. If the adulterer is an enemy, the wife pleads rape, and the war continues as before. If however the adulterer is a member of a friendly group, the husband can usually be persuaded to negotiate. He then claims compensation from the adulterer and the size of the compensation will depend on their respective bargaining powers.

CONCLUSION

Mendi marriage must be considered on two levels: as a personal contract between two individuals, and as an affinal alliance (which is essentially political) between two groups. The personal elements in the arrangements are indicated by: (a) the freedom of the individual in the choice of spouse (almost complete for men and somewhat less so for women), (b) the man's relative economic independence in amassing his marriage payment (particularly in his later marriages), and (c) the discretion exercised by the woman in the redistribution of her bride price. On the other hand, that marriage is also a political alliance is shown by the mandatory personal gift exchanges which must take place between the husband and his wife's father and brothers. In many instances, this intergroup obligation is extended to include not only the wife's actual kin but also those men who have been major recipients of her bride price. Gift exchange with affines thus represents and supports a network of friendly intergroup alliances brought about by, and focused upon, the marriage.

Political alliances, like all friendly relationships, must be marked by economic exchanges. That is why the pattern of marriage payments stresses the element of exchange by requiring a return gift from the recipients. Thus, the institution of bride price in Mendi is not only a payment for the services of the woman, but it is also a ceremonial exchange of goods marking the establishment of amicable relations between hitherto separate groups. These relations must be reaffirmed at frequent intervals by further economic exchanges for as long as the marriage lasts.

A Mendi woman, even after marriage, preserves strong ties with her own kin. A married woman's affiliation and loyalty remain with her own patriclan or clan of residence and are not transferred to that of her husband. On the latter's death, she is free to return to her own kin and usually does so.

Contrary to the people's own assertion, agnates are in a better marital position than nonagnates in the same local group.

Marriage Among the
TELEFOLMIN

Ruth Craig

COUNTRY AND PEOPLE

The Telefolmin live at the headwaters of the Sepik River about forty-five miles east of the West Irian border and five miles north of the Papuan border.[1] Their cultural affinities are westwards with the people of the Star Mountains and there is no contact with, and little similarity to, the highlanders east of the Strickland Gorge.

The 1,000 Telefolmin, whose population density is three persons per square mile, live in villages on the valley floor, about 5,000 feet above sea level, but most of their gardens are scattered over the surrounding slopes up to 7,000 feet. Village houses are built with two hearths and are usually occupied by at least two elementary families. The elementary family is the basic economic unit and, unlike many highlands societies, a man, his wife, and children live and work together. Ownership of taro, the staple, is individual, and men and women spend much time planting, tending, and harvesting their crops. The kinship structure is cognatic. Descent is irrelevant in most contexts, but the filiative tie is important. A man has full rights in the village to which his father or his mother belonged. Women also retain membership in their natal villages and may exercise their land rights there even if they marry away. Adult immigrants, including affines, are welcomed without discrimination. They are freely given good land, which passes indisputably and with full rights to their children. However, although it is easy to transfer village membership, men rarely do so. Because of the preference for intravillage marriage, for most men the village comprises cognates and affines who were

[1] There are four Telefol-speaking tribes inhabiting adjacent valleys. I use *Telefolmin* to refer to the inhabitants of the valley settled by the original immigrants. The other three valleys were settled later by the Telefolmin through wars of conquest. Each tribe is now autonomous, with its own name.

previously cognates. This produces a strongly solidary unit, a friendship network which people are unwilling to forsake. In one parish, Kialikmin, eighty-three men (98 per cent) are birth members of their village of residence; only two men born there live elsewhere.[2]

Both the village and the parish are political units. Members gather for religious and initiation ceremonies, for social feasts and dances and, formerly, for warfare and communal gardening near enemy territory. Tribal unity is expressed at the most important ceremonies and in large-scale warfare. In all these contexts where there is a need for coordinated activity, Big Men take charge.[3]

This formal structural picture, in terms of kinship affiliations, corporate local groups, and group leaders, obscures the essence of Telefolmin social organization—individuality. Despite the feeling of group pride, there is little practical reinforcement of group unity. Villagers gather only every three to five years for war or ceremony; there are no intergroup food or pig festivals and no gathering of kin or local groups at most life crises. Moreover, as personal obligations are not defined in terms of common group membership or formal kinship, a man cannot rely on others just because they are fellow villagers or are particular kin of his. Rather, it is the number and quality of his personal friendships that count. That is, the Telefolmin do not think in terms of kin and non-kin, but in terms of friends (i.e., kin with whom there is a long history of close association) and strangers (who may be known kin). The way the concept of friendship dominates social interaction emerges clearly in the process of marriage.

GETTING MARRIED

Table 1 shows the frequency of five marriage types and something of the circumstances in which each is contracted.

[2] This parish consists of two villages, about 300 yards apart, with a population of 312—85 men, 89 women, and 138 children. Kialikmin is one of a number of descent names. It is borne by the local group, the parish, because of the descent affiliation of founding members. But not all members of the parish are Kialikmin by descent, and there are many individual Kialikmin residing in parishes with other descent names. Sometimes the name is used with a descent connotation, but more often as a local identification. There are also Kialikmin parishes in other tribes, whose founders were Telefolmin Kialikmin. Of the parish men, 42 per cent are bifiliates (persons whose parents both belongs to the group), 45 per cent patrifiliates, and 11 per cent matrifiliates.

[3] Under European administration their only remaining function is to organize ceremonies, and they concentrate their energies on private exchange activities.

Table 1. TELEFOLMIN MARRIAGE PATTERNS[a]

	Bestowal		Independent		Affairs		Abductions		Runaways		Totals
	−	+	−	+	−	+	−	+	−	+	
Intravillage											
S	18	18	1	7	4	9	2	—	—	—	77
F	4	9	—	—	1	3	—	1	—	—	
Extra-village, Intraparish											
S	7	3	—	—	—	2	1	—	—	—	15
F	1	1	—	—	—	—	—	—	—	—	
Extra-parish, Intratribal											
S	4	2	—	2	—	8	2	—	—	6	35
F	1	1	—	—	1	2	3	—	—	3	
Extra-tribal											
S	1	—	1	1	—	—	—	—	2	—	9
F	—	—	—	—	—	—	1	1	2	—	

Note: −/+ symbols denote pre- and post-European marriages respectively. S/F symbols denote successful and failed marriages (see below).

[a] Based on 136 marriages made by 81 men.

Bestowal

This is the proper way to marry. There are no bilateral, prenuptial negotiations between the bride's and groom's kin. The girl's senior kin meet to decide where to bestow her and escort her to the chosen groom's family house, where she sleeps the night with the women of the household. In the morning she cooks the groom's breakfast; if he takes the taro from her hand, he indicates he accepts her. Sometimes the youth is unaware of the proposed marriage till this moment. More often there is an understanding that a particular youth and girl will marry, but even so his family do not know which night (or week or month) the bride will arrive. The organizers should consult the girl's wishes, but they do not if she opposes their interests. An unwilling girl is lectured and beaten. She may seek refuge with other kin but, unless these belong to the enemy Falamin tribe, she is quickly brought back. Commonly, her relatives tell the chosen groom of her flight and suggest that he abduct her. Many girls submit after this betrayal; others in despair commit suicide.

Independent

These are marriages of convenience between older people, arranged by mutual consent and independently of kin approval. Usually the woman is widowed or divorced. Such women are free to remarry as they choose; neither their own nor their former husband's kin have the right to control, or much interest in, their movements.

Affairs

Ideally, young men should wait patiently till their elders give them brides, and girls should be virgins when bestowed. In fact, premarital affairs are common. If the girl's guardian disapproves the liaison he chastises her, assigns a chaperone, and immediately arranges a more desirable match. Often at the first sign of opposition the youth disavows interest in the relationship. Otherwise he, too, faces censure, perhaps a beating from the girl's "brothers." Sometimes a lad hangs himself in shame after being lectured by the girl's father. But, if the youth belongs to a suitable family and has a good reputation, especially if he has a sister to offer in exchange, the girl's family may wink at the affair until they feel ready to initiate formal arrangements. Then they act as if it were a proper bestowal, and all the formalities— the appointment of organizers, the bringing of the bride, and the ceremonial breakfast—are completed.

Abductions

A man who desires a girl of another parish knows that his suit will fail, if only because her kin prefer her to marry within their own group. So, helped by age-mates, he abducts her, hoping that her kin will accept the *fait accompli*. Rarely is this hope realized unless she has no near kin; nor will his kin seriously resist an attempt to retrieve her. There may be a fight, but the girl is always returned. Or she herself may be unwilling and may escape her abductor. Within the village, however, a disobedient girl who constantly thwarts plans made for her marriage may be carried off. Though not in collusion with her parents, the abductor can feel confident, for her kin are glad to see her settled with any man of the village.

Runaways

A girl seeking to escape an unwelcome, arranged marriage may find refuge with kin in another parish, who, if they are not close friends of her family, encourage her to marry one of them and stay. Sometimes she already has an extra-parish lover and flees straight to him.

Bestowals and independent marriages are regarded as "right" ways of marrying. An affair which is eventually approved is an irregular way to marriage, but at least approval predates cohabitation and the girl's kin manage the proceedings. But they are seriously affronted if she elopes or is abducted, for the formalities are disregarded and no semblance of propriety or authority can be maintained.

FAILED MARRIAGES

The Telefolmin describe short-lived unions of one night to three months as failed marriages rather than abortive affairs because cohabitation is accomplished and permanence intended, either by one or both partners or by their kin. The break occurs before bride wealth has been given and before mutual interests have developed. Most Telefolmin experience at least one failed marriage before settling down.[5] Examination of these unions reveals important aspects of marriage patterns and ideals.

Failure of an arranged marriage may be due to opposition from one of four directions. First, the girl may dislike the groom or the idea of marriage, or may already have a lover; and she may be strong enough to outface reprisals. Second, the groom may repudiate the bride. An unwilling bride, if she seeks no active escape, may be so uncooperative that eventually her husband sends her back; if she is also continuing an affair with a lover, he has a stronger case. Sometimes a man refuses a bestowal because he prefers another woman, but only Big Men and their sons can afford to do this. Third, both young people may reject the match planned by their seniors. Finally, in interparish unions, the women of the groom's village, feeling cheated of a husband by this foreign bride, may force her to leave.

Whether an irregular marriage stands depends on a combination of factors: the consent of both partners and their compatibility; which

---

[5] My figures for failed marriages are certainly underestimates; many informants did not relate all they experienced.

of the girl's kin are alive and whether they feel their interests threatened by the marriage; the relative statuses of the heads of the two families and the friendship between them, if any; and the political relationship of their respective villages. Within the tribe, other considerations rarely outweigh the desire for intravillage marriage, and physical sanctions effectively enforce this. In intertribal unions, the girl's kin are powerless to retrieve her, but circumstances may return her to them. A hasty marriage quickly loses its appeal for a girl who has no close kin in her husband's village, and she is easily persuaded to remain when she makes her first visit home. Also, when war erupted, new brides went home for fear of being killed as representatives of their tribe.

THE CHANGING PATTERN

Today the system of arranged marriage is foundering, and more self-initiated marriages are succeeding. Traditionally, interparish affairs were infrequent because contact was restricted to occasional visits. Spatial containment and kin supervision within the parish effectively monitored the system. No man or woman walked alone; independent movement aroused suspicion. Nowadays, not only is it safe to work and travel alone, there is also more reason for traveling—to visit friends employed at government station and mission, or sick in hospital, or in jail, and also to sell produce and spend the proceeds at the store. With this mobility and diversity of contacts, young people easily form attachments contrary to their parents' wishes. They are also in a better position to thwart those wishes. A girl's kin can no longer retrieve her by force. Men who attempt to discipline uncooperative daughters in the old way find themselves serving a jail sentence for assault. Moreover, the government court favors free choice over arranged marriage on the grounds that unwilling brides make trouble, and opposed kin are usually persuaded to give in. Finally, as well as the traditional bush rendezvous, the houses of station and mission employees provide meeting places where senior kin are unlikely to intrude.

The increasing independence of Telefolmin youth accounts for some modification. Traditionally, a young man's wealth was managed by his father until he married or left home. He depended on his father's contacts for entry into the exchange system, where he could gain economic security and prestige. His father managed his marriage, and he was often ignorant of the content of the bride wealth payment and the identity of contributors, who were his father's friends and contemporaries. His only role was to accept the bride. But today's young men, though subject to moral pressures which limit freedom of choice, are much more independent, economically and socially. Many are wage-earners. With cash they can purchase goods to enter into the exchange system and acquire the wealth and reputation to attract brides. They can also provide all or most of the bride wealth themselves. Even in arranged marriages, the groom and his bride's "brothers" now participate directly, and with increasing frequency manage the entire proceedings.[6]

To sum up, the prohibition on physical coercion, the ease of access to legal settlement, the less restricted social movement and the economic changes all contribute to neutralize traditional sanctions and promote freedom of choice in marriage. Further, bestowal is not the only marriage type affected by these forces. The ease with which affairs are initiated and transformed into marriages renders abductions and runaway matches unnecessary.

PREFERENCES AND PROHIBITIONS

There are no prescriptive rules. The only prohibition is against marriage with close kin. Informants do not agree on the precise limits of the range, though all say that second cousin marriages are improper. Yet such unions are common, and the prohibition is a convenience rather than an enforced rule. Kin opposing a marriage between second cousins will moralize: "You cannot marry your sibling." But if the match is approved, no mention is made of the relationship. Rather, people point out how suitable the union is because the two families are good friends, already members of the same work groups, etc.—a situation directly dependent upon the close genealogical relationship. In effect, the only prohibited spouses outside the elementary family are first cousins.

Neither kinship terminology nor generation level regulates or defines marriage choices. Every cognatic kin term, except those for grandparents, appeared in a tabulation made to determine what spouses called each other before marriage. There were eight second cousin marriages (two with FFBSD, one with FFZSD, two with FMBSD—all called *tenum kayak* = FBD; two with FFBDD = FZD,

---

[6] Also, more contributors are the groom's contemporaries, and many are workmates rather than kin.

nek; and one with MFBSD = MBD, *nek*).[7] In cross-generational marriages the closest relationship recorded was FMBSDD (= FBDD = ZD, *man*).[8] In others, where wives called their husbands FB, or husbands called their wives FZ or MZ, the relationship was untraceable. Thus a bride may stand in any classificatory kinship relationship to her husband, providing that the genealogical relationship is not improperly close.[9]

With no prescriptions and few prohibitions, the system is expressed in three preferences: for equal age of spouses, intravillage marriage and sister exchange.

1. Equal Age

The Telefolmin strongly disapprove of persons of disparate age marrying and few cases were recorded, all in unusual circumstances. A man who does not marry at the same time as his age-mates often finds it difficult to secure a bride. The maturing girls are reserved for youths of the next unmarried age-set, and he may have to wait ten years or more for a widow.[10] In all cross-generational marriages I recorded, spouses were about the same age. Moreover, the age criterion applies to subsequent as well as first marriages. Thus, this preference is a limiting factor in the choice of a spouse.

2. Intravillage Marriage

This is the most strongly held ideal (see Table 1), and a significant number of marriages accord with it; fifty-eight per cent of recorded marriages were intravillage and seventy-one per cent were intraparish. Further, most approved marriages, especially bestowals, occur within the parish; irregular marriages most often contravene the ideal.

[7] A second or more distant cousin relationship is reduced to a first by counting as siblings the parents through whom the relationship is traced.

[8] There is only one term, *man,* for all kin of descending generations.

[9] Prohibitions cannot be based on terminological categories or generation in a system like this where two people may call each other by a number of different kin terms, depending on which particular pairings of their parents they use to trace relationship. Most relationships are regulated by a dominant reciprocal terminology, with alternatives utilized in appropriate social contexts.

[10] Ten of seventeen widows and divorcees who remarried went as brides to men making first marriages. These were mostly unenterprising men who had not been given brides by their unimpressed seniors and who had been unsuccessful in their attempts to gain brides by irregular means. Most had had more than one failed marriage and four were wifeless into middle age.

One reason people give for preferring intravillage marriage is their desire for emotional and social security. One should not marry amongst strangers. Affines should be kin who are also friends, and the spouse in particular should be someone whose character and abilities are well known, a childhood playmate, a frequent visitor at the house, a member of the same work groups. Usually this ideal is met only within the village, more especially within the household. It explains the one recorded marriage between first cousins:[11] their "sibling" relationship proved so compatible they decided to make it permanent in marriage, and no relatives were sufficiently interested in the bride wealth to prevent it. Several men have attempted marriage with FBD, but in each case the couple was apprehended by the bride's kinsmen. The union was not condemned as incestuous, but because "we cannot receive bride wealth from ourselves."

Fortunate are youths whose households contain adopted girls. Marriages with this kind of "sister" are common and approved. There are no bride wealth problems and neither spouse has to endure the unsettling experience of moving house and adjusting to the other's kinsfolk. Moreover, parental insurance against old age seems doubly assured, for there is no daughter- or son-in-law stranger with loyalties directed to another set of parents.

If there is no suitable spouse within the village or parish, a less satisfactory marriage is with a cognate in another parish, where the two families exchange frequent long visits. Reluctance to give a girl out of the village is tempered by the fact of close friendship; the girl's parents have had opportunity to assess the groom and, because he knows their kin and territory well, they may persuade him to remain in uxorilocal residence while they are alive.

There is additional evidence for the preference for marriage amongst friends. Widows and divorcées, who can marry where they please, mostly choose husbands in their own villages. If they marry out, it is usually to be near a special woman friend married into an alien village. Moreover, in all successful marriages where the bride ran away or was abducted, she had at least one close kinswoman in her husband's village. Finally, all Falamin spouses, men and women, belonged to one parish, Falamin Kialikmin, where kin are many and close because of continuous intermarriage over the generations.

But there is more to intragroup marriage than desire for security. In many highlands societies men marry, and send their women in

[11] Three generations ago.

marriage, to establish intergroup relations: the number and quality of such affinal connections are crucial in determining a man's status. But at Telefolmin the accent in intergroup relations is on cognatic ties and inherited partnerships. The original affinal connections which generate the cognatic network, far from being purposeful, normative, or advantageous, constitute a minority of accidental, undesirable, and compromise matches. Because of this and because they do not need each other in any role not better filled by extra-parish cognates, affines from different groups, especially different tribes, rarely meet their marriage payment obligations and often have little to do with each other subsequently. A visitor to a village may ignore his affines to exchange with cognates. Nor do such affines provide safe conduct; in war time they might betray their visitors to others of the group seeking vengeance.

But the quality of the affinal relationship is different within the village and parish. There cognates automatically cooperate to some extent. Normally, they cannot afford *not* to meet their commitments, and once the marriage payments are completed the way is paved for a firm friendship. Thus, when fellow villagers become brothers-in-law they usually join the same work groups, become frequent rather than casual exchangers, and often set up house together. Marriage, therefore, is a way of reinforcing existing relationships rather than initiating new ones. This applies equally to men who choose their own brides, and to marriages arranged to express friendship between the senior men of two families. A marriage between close cognates of different villages is seen in the same light—as a way of "bringing the line back together," of restating family ties which have become spatially and genealogically remote.

Not only are individual friendship networks strengthened; people maintain that the closer the relationships among members, the more congenial and effective are intragroup relations in general. They say that, in sustaining this ideal through frequent intragroup marriage, the problem is to keep girls at home. Women are irresponsible. Sometimes they actively thwart plans for their marriage, and always their basic irresponsibility is accentuated by interparish competition. Relatives encourage a visiting girl to form an attachment among them, and the affair may continue for weeks before her kin at home are informed. This is more likely if she has run away, and if she decides not to stay she may even be constrained physically. In sum, the paradoxical male view, reflecting a concern for group strength, is: keep your own women at home and acquire as many as possible from other villages.

3. Sister-exchange

This is often planned but rarely achieved. Only four out of eighty-five men contracted marriages where actual sisters were exchanged. Twelve others, in six reciprocal transactions, exchanged "sisters" within the second cousin range. All transactions took place within the parish—in fact, all but two within the village.

Sister-exchange may be effected in two ways. A man who desires another's sister approaches him with the offer of his own, and a simultaneous exchange occurs. The other method is delayed exchange. One marriage is made, and some time later—it may be years—the woman's brother, or a kinsman, claims a return bride. He may go through formal channels, or he may abduct a girl from the group into which his sister married. By calling the abduction a legitimate exchange claim, he has more chance of support from his own kin and eventual consent from hers.

Planned exchanges frequently break down during negotiations, either because one girl refuses to go through with the exchange, or because of quarrels over rights of disposal. In one case, the oldest of three brothers had arranged an advantageous marriage for their sister with a Big Man's ward. The third brother was sleeping with this youth's sister, a liaison the Big Man tolerated because of the impending exchange. But, as negotiations neared completion, the second brother gave his sister to his best friend and age-mate, with whom he had an understanding. With the promised exchange bride no longer available, the other connection no longer appealed to the Big Man. He forbade the affair, which led to fighting and precipitated a village split.

Complications arising from claims and counter-claims multiply in the Telefolmin system, where rights of disposal are bilaterally defined and almost any close male relative may attempt to exercise a claim without consulting others. Moreover, closeness of relationship with the bride is not the only factor; it may be modified by the respective ages, statuses, and personalities of rival claimants, and by their place of residence in relation to the bride's. This is not to suggest that in other New Guinea highlands societies disputes do not arise amongst kin over the disposal of their women. But it seems that where there are exogamous descent groups, with rights vested in particular agnates and ultimately in the descent group, claim conflicts do not exhibit the same complexity and are not so frequent and so disruptive in their effects.

Although ideally exchange brides are sisters, so many factors militate against successful negotiation that in practice the institution embraces exchanges of women in diverse categories. Any kinswoman is an asset, in the same way as a sister, as long as a man can make good his claim to rights over her disposal. Even intergenerational exchanges (e.g., one man's sister for another's daughter) are acceptable if the ages of the spouses match.

Individuals transact exchanges, usually acting independently, but people speak of groups as the units of exchange—most often families and extended families. Or representatives of one "line" may claim to be owed a bride by another: the exchange bride may go to any member of the line.[12] The context for exchange claims may even be broader. Members of one village may say that another village owes them brides. One Kialikmin father refused to let his daughter marry a Falamin suitor because, he said, "We have sent many of our girls to Falamin but they do not send brides in return." In its ideal form, then, exchange of brides refers to an exchange of sisters within the village or between closely related families of different villages. In its extension, it is seen in the context of intergroup relations where one group should not gain brides, and increase membership, at the expense of another.

THE MARRIAGE PAYMENTS

Bride Wealth

However a marriage is contracted, it must receive legal recognition through bride wealth transactions. Bride wealth should be presented the morning after the marriage, but weeks or months may elapse, especially if the girl is unhappy or from another village and the groom's people fear the marriage may not last. Some abductions and runaway matches are not legalized for years.

Bride wealth consists solely of valuables, traditionally strings of cowrie and tambu shells, stone adzes, bows, and net bags. Today cash, steel axes, and bush knives are added. The payment should include fifteen items, but in fact the number of items and their total value

---

[12] In this context, "line" is the equivalent of stock. It may be concentrated within the village or dispersed.

vary considerably. Factors influencing variation are the relative statuses and wealth of the two parties and the moral conscientiousness of the groom's people.

I recorded bride wealth transactions for sixty-five marriages, classifying contributors according to their relationship with the groom and their village affiliation. This tabulation showed that: (1) Kinship categories are unimportant; all types of kin, and occasionally, affines make contributions. (2) Close relatives are more likely to contribute, and more generously; but genealogical closeness by itself does not define the obligation, for extra-parish close cognates, even if actual FB, MB, and first cousins, rarely contribute. (3) Village affiliation is more important than kinship. Of the 452 contributors, 340 came from the same village as the groom and fifty-three from the other village of the parish. Only fifty-nine were from outside the parish, and most of these were assisting a few underprivileged men who were forced to solicit contributions from extra-parish kin. (4) But residence and close kinship are not the only factors, for on a number of occasions coresident close cognates failed to participate. Some attributed the failure to alienation due to property disputes and domestic disagreements; others indicated a variety of petty excuses; a few potential contributors gave nothing because they happened to be absent that day. All this illustrates the informality of a system where obligations are not clearly defined in terms of membership of kinship categories or corporate groups. People decide whether and how much to contribute on the basis of friendship with the groom or his father.

When sufficient bride wealth is gathered, the bride informs her mother, who takes it to her house for distribution. Normally, one of the original contributors presides over the distribution and is himself the chief recipient. Recipients are of two classes: those who make a claim by virtue of their close relationship with the bride, and those who had contributed to her mother's bride wealth but had received no return payment.[13]

Whereas personal inclination, and not kinship with the groom, decides the identity of contributors, the recipients are the bride's closest kin. The reason for this difference is clear. Ideally, the transaction is one of equivalence: each contributor should recover the value of his contribution because each recipient should repay the item he receives. In fact, all but the chief recipients can evade this obligation. For this

---

[13] If such claimants die, their heirs may collect the credit. Important men die with many outstanding credits, which they bequeath to sons and daughters in turn to avoid disputes. This is one way women may acquire wealth.

reason, men contribute only when self-interest demands it, for giving may mean the loss of a valued possession, but they seldom waive rights of receiving, as these often entail profit. The difference is evident with extra-parish kin, who rarely come to contribute but regularly appear at distributions. Thus the groom's family may have difficulty recruiting sufficient contributors, whereas claimants on the bride's side usually outnumber the bride wealth items. Hence there is a need to define carefully the eligibility of recipients, which is achieved by invoking the formal criterion of close kinship.

The Return Payment

This is made up of foodstuffs—a whole pig, its carcass heaped with vegetables and fruit—and should equal the bride wealth in value. It should be presented the day after the bride wealth, but usually it is delayed and sometimes not offered at all. The chief recipient should provide the pig, together with additional pork if necessary to recompense all contributors. Other recipients should send pork to the value of the items received; but in my experience minor recipients met their commitments only when they and the contributors were close friends, who completed the transactions privately. As for the main payment, only Big Men and exceptionally moral men fully meet their obligations. Otherwise, the food comes in piecemeal, perhaps over decades.

The exchange of payments constitutes two functionally autonomous but overlapping transactions. The first, the receipt of bride wealth, legalizes the marriage and legitimizes the children by fixing the father's rights in them, and their rights in his estate even if they later affiliate with another group.[14] The second transaction, the return payment, initiates the affinal relationship and emphasizes its chief characteristic, friendly reciprocity. The statement that the bride's people make with the return presentation, that this "kills" (i.e., cancels out) the bride wealth, places the two payments in a meaningful and unitary transaction. The relationship starts as one of equality. Only thus can a satisfactory affinal connection be maintained.

---

[14] The direct exchange of women does not render bride wealth unnecessary. When men exchange sisters simultaneously, each receives a full bride wealth and makes the return payment. Bride wealth is not a substitute for occasions when there is no exchange bride. They are institutions with different functions: exchange of brides is meant to ensure the *status quo* of groups; bride wealth defines rights in women and children.

Normally, the bride's kin do not refuse the return payment; it is a matter of promises and procrastination. But, even if there is a genuine reason for delay, failure to make immediate payment lessens the likelihood of its ever being made. The groom's family can do nothing. If they complain, the affines may return the bride wealth—one of the deepest humiliations a Telefolmin can suffer. Meanwhile, the cognates who assisted with bride wealth are pressing for compensation, and the relationship is strained till they receive it. Men cannot afford such estrangement, socially or economically, so if the bride's people fail in their obligations the groom must compensate the contributors himself. Thus, although the ideal is transactional equivalence, the burden often falls doubly on the groom's family and, as the Telefolmin have few pigs, it is felt heavily.

Failure of the bride's people to render the return payment, then, produces both an affinal relationship of uneasy oneupmanship and potential rifts in cognatic relationships on the groom's side. The frequency with which payment is evaded indicates that affinal relationships, as such, are exiguous. By contrast, the strength of and dependence on cognatic ties are indicated by (1) the fact that the closer the cognatic relationship between affines, the more likely they are to meet their obligations; and (2) the custom whereby the groom himself compensates the bride wealth contributors.[15]

Another, smaller payment devolves on the bride's family. It comprises two to six valuables, depending on the size of the bride wealth, the relative statuses and wealth of the two families and the degree of friendship between them, and is more likely to be made when the affines are close cognates in the same village. Men give it so that a daughter will not feel she has married a "nothing man" whose house is "empty." The husband, who has impoverished himself to provide bride wealth, sees it as a partial reimbursement. Ideally, the couple keep it for their own use but, if the groom has senior kin who made substantial contributions to the bride wealth, they get most of it.

An interesting aspect of Telefolmin marriage ceremonial is the limited interaction of the participants. The bride's and groom's kin do not meet to discuss the marriage. Subsequently, when the two sets of kin need to contact each other, they do so through individual repre-

---

[15] There is an analogy in compensatory payments following war, fighting, or brawling. Initiators on each side compensate their own allies, but not each other. Wounded friends must be compensated, because outstanding debts (in either goods or services) can damage a friendship, but there is no point in compensating enemies or strangers.

sentation. The bride is not dressed up and paraded to the groom's house, but is taken there surreptitiously by one or two kinsmen; only the women of the household greet her. The wife's mother, alone, collects the bride wealth on behalf of the recipients. The return payment is brought to the groom's house by only as many as it takes to carry it, and they depart immediately upon delivery. In the exchange of payments, contributors and recipients do not meet together; they do not even gather as groups. Each man brings his donation or makes his claim individually, in his own time. Thus, not only is a contributor ignorant of the identity of many recipients and what each received; he may not know all the other contributors or what they contributed. Even the feast of the return payment is not an occasion for ceremony. Food is cooked by any contributors who happen to be around then and, when it is ready, each departs immediately with his portion. One cannot seriously talk of kin-based action groups here.

SUCCESSIVE AND SIMULTANEOUS UNIONS

Of the eighty-five men in the sample, seventy-one have currently cohabiting wives while fourteen (16.5 per cent) are wifeless; seventeen (19.5 per cent) women are without husbands. Two bachelors and four spinsters have never married.[16] They do not appear in Table 2, which indicates remarriage of divorced and widowed persons.[17]

Table 2. REMARRIAGE AMONG TELEFOLMIN

	Years Single					
	1–3	*3–5*	*5–10*	*10–15*	*15+*	*Totals*
Men:						
Still Single	3	—	2	2	5	12
Remarried	5	1	3	1	—	10
Women:						
Still Single	6	—	—	7	—	13
Remarried	9	3	5	—	—	17

These figures indicate the long periods for which people remain single, even those who were widowed or divorced in youth.

[16] One woman is an hydrocephalic. The rest are people past marriage age whose marriages have so far failed.

[17] Whether they become single through divorce or death did not prove significant.

Men without wives say that they do not mind being single, and this is not entirely a face-saving remark. Telefolmin spouses share household and garden much more than do most highlanders. They plan the day's activities together and share the jobs to be done. While some tasks are thought to be better performed by women (e.g., weeding, cooking) there is no rigidly defined division of labor. It is a matter of convenience. Men plant, tend and harvest crops, take turns at tending children and piglets, gather firewood, light the house fire, and prepare the evening meal if they come home first. The only task they normally avoid is the women's part in preparing gardens. But in taro cultivation this is minimal, and single men do not grow sweet potato.[18] Thus a Telefolmin man left wifeless finds it no effort to fend for himself.

Some single men do without feminine assistance altogether; others rely on occasional cooperation from women of the same household. Some establish satisfactory quasi-marital relationships with single kinswomen, particularly widowed sisters, who fulfill the wifely role except for sex. This could only work in a social system where many brothers and sisters remain in the same village, sometimes in the same household, throughout their lives (40 per cent of joint householders are brothers-in-law). Even if a woman marries out of her village, she usually rejoins a brother's household when widowed or divorced and she is not pressed to remarry.

Perhaps the most important single factor here is that no payment is due to the kin of a widow or divorcée when she remarries. In addition, the maternal kin wish to retain the children. From the woman's point of view this has several advantages, emotional and economic. The women of the village are not strangers from other groups but her own kin. The land is hers; she did not cease to cultivate it during her marriage. Her children have full rights in the village and need fear no discrimination as they grow up. Finally, widows among their own kin may become respected and wealthy; ambitious, younger kinsmen depend on them for loans, advice, and representation to senior kinsmen.

Despite what men say, they do not like to be single. Although no stigma attaches to the single state, men try hard to remarry. But the freedom of widows and divorcées affects the remarriage opportunities of men whose choice, because of the age criterion, is virtually re-

---

[18] Sweet potato, regarded as inferior food, is used mainly for pigs—and single men rarely have pigs.

stricted to this category of women. A man who loses his wife in the first years of marriage may be given a new bride immediately. Otherwise, his remarriage depends on the presence of a widow or divorcée of approximately his age, who is willing to remarry and is attracted to him.

Simultaneous polygyny is another matter. Ten men in the sample have been married polygynously. Two had three wives simultaneously; the other eight had two each. One of these polygynous unions was an actual sister-exchange, and three were the result of unusual circumstances.[19] The other eight wives were taken by four Big Men, an aspiring Big Man, and a Big Man's son. This suggests a connection between polygyny and social status. There is one, but not after the common highlands pattern wherein polygyny is crucial in becoming a Big Man and an ambitious man seeks more wives in order to grow more crops and rear more pigs.

In Telefolmin pigs are not significant in the exchange system and there are no large pig feasts, so there is no point in accumulating pigs beyond the number needed for immediate personal commitments.[20] More important, pig ownership is not limited by the number of wives; pigs are agisted, and a man with one wife can have as many pigs as a polygynist. Finally, prestige does not accrue to the producer of a surplus, because there is no intergroup feasting where his contribution can be acclaimed. Hence extra wives do not increase a man's wealth. A Big Man does not need more than one wife; rather, he acquires more wives because he is a Big Man. Men eager to secure connections with Big Men offer them their daughters and sisters. Women, too, find them personally attractive, because they embody manly virtues, and value the social and economic advantage of being a Big Man's wife.

Most men, however, assert that polygyny is an uneviable state. The husband's responsibilities are doubled, and the emotional strain is often insupportable. Telefolmin men do not build a separate house for

---

[19] (1) An impoverished man gave his sister in exchange for some taro gardens (2) A loose woman, disowned by kin, attached herself to different men in turn. These were real marriages, each of five husbands compensating the former (3) An amusing accident—two families, unaware of each other's plans, brought brides to the same man's house one night.

[20] Pigs are important but scarce. The average is three per family, the range one to eleven. At one initiation ceremony, attended by about 600 people, only nineteen pigs (one or two from each village) were killed. I never heard of more than twenty-five being killed on any occasion.

each wife, and cowives sharing one house quarrel constantly. If one wife does not leave, the husband usually cannot control the situation and has to send one to live with her relatives. Eight of the ten polygynous households sampled broke up in the first year because of cowife conflict. Thus the normal polygynous marriage comprises one permanently cohabiting wife, the other separated.

SEPARATION AND DIVORCE

All separations I knew arose from cowife incompatibility. The separated spouses occupy different houses but maintain some contact and identity of interest—how much depends upon the attitude of the favored wife. If she tolerates the association, the separated couple may garden together, have a joint interest in pigs and exchanges and have sexual relations, a situation satisfactory for a lifetime. But most separated wives have little to do with their husbands, and the separation is likely to become a divorce.

Divorce is characterized by property division, cessation of sexual relations, and cancellation of all joint interests. The wife identifies wholly with her kin or with her new husband. There were thirteen divorces in this sample: three the result of dissension between cowives, three initiated by husbands, and seven by discontented wives. The contact situation was directly responsible for divorces initiated by husbands—men found that the traditional demands of marriage (especially the preparation of gardens) prevented their continuing in full-time European employment. Apart from this conflict, men see no advantage in divorce. Most are satisfied to beat adulterous, uncooperative, or neglectful wives. It is against a man's own interest to send a wife away, for he has little likelihood of gaining another for years. Thus, divorce is initiated by the wife, who has no other means of redress or retaliation.

A deserting wife's kin may try to persuade her to return to her husband, but they do not persist if she is adamant. This mildness, which contrasts with the violent coercion of an unwilling bride, is understandable; the divorce does not obligate them. Bride wealth is rarely returned after the first few months. Only the original items are acceptable, and these have been dispersed through ceremonial exchange and commercial transaction. Further, a deserted husband is entitled to recover the value of the bride wealth from the next man his wife marries, and her kin invoke this rule when they refuse to return the bride wealth.[21] The amount the first husband collects when his wife remarries ranges from a few token items to the equivalent of the bride wealth and depends on the circumstances surrounding the divorce. But no formal rules fix payment proportionate to blame, even when the facts are clear. The first husband simply extracts what he can. It helps if he has higher social status than the other man and if he has public opinion behind him.

I examined several factors, as well as the cited grounds for divorce, in an attempt to predict situations in which divorce is likely. (1) Parish affiliation seems unimportant. The intra-/ extra-parish ratio in the divorce category (5/13, 38 per cent) is close to that in the total of marriages (29/72, 40 per cent). In only one case did the fact that spouses came from different parishes affect their parting. (2) The presence of children does not seem to be a deterrent, for most divorcées have young children (nine out of thirteen in this sample). A divorcée is free to take her children with her. (3) The time factor may be significant. Seven out of ten divorces initiated by husband or wife occurred within the first three years of marriage.

FREQUENCY OF DIVORCE

In many societies with lower divorce rates, divorce is rare because sanctions apply to those desiring it—sanctions deriving from the need

Table 3. TELEFOLMIN DIVORCE RATES (MEN ONLY)

Ratio of Divorces to:	Number	Per Cent
All Marriages	12/101	11.9%
Completed Marriages	12/30	40.0
All Marriages Less Deaths	12/83	14.5

to return bride wealth and from the complex of exchange relationships built upon affinal connections. Then, unless the offense is flagrant, kinsmen of the disputants refuse to negotiate a divorce. In contrast, Telefolmin divorce is easily obtained. I heard of no man or woman who sought one unsuccessfully. Here, a strong affinal friendship, based

[21]It is easy to understand the husband's anxiety to get an immediate return of bride wealth, rather than wait for compensation from a remarriage that may not occur for years, if ever.

on a cognatic relationship, will survive the break. There is no bride
wealth settlement to negotiate and kin are not so vitally concerned.
In any case, only individuals are involved, not whole kin groups;
divorce is not decided with reference to group interests but is a matter
of personal feeling.[22]

Considering the limited interference from kin, the question is why
so few Telefolmin seek divorce. The conjugal relationship is rarely
harmonious and sex antagonism is strong. The people themselves
rightly see intravillage marriage as a major factor in conjugal stability.
A wife feels secure when her protectors (father and brothers) and con-
fidants (age-mates) belong to the same local group. In a serious quarrel she may confidently call on their immediate support. The wife
may move temporarily to her parent's home, and most wives leave
their husbands several times during the early years of marriage. But
here "going back to mother" is not final—the wife goes to the family
gardens and the children freely visit their father's house. Reconciliation is easy because of the many mutual kin in the village, and "coming back" is not a dramatic event but an unobtrusive move across the
street. People say that knowing they can easily go to their kin makes
distressed wives less likely to act impetuously.

CONCLUSION

Where marriage is a transaction between exogamous descent groups,
as in many New Guinea highlands societies, the ceremonial surrounding it not only affirms and sanctions the intergroup relationship being
formed, but is also a means of demonstrating group worth and wealth
and of acquiring prestige. But at Telefolmin corporate groups do not
exchange brides, and marriage is not seen as initiating intergroup
relations or expressing group unity. Marriages are private family
affairs rather than occasion for public display and feasting, drama,
dances, and speeches. There is no aspect of the ceremonial that requires participants to gather in groups. Rather, interaction comprises
a series of personal, private transactions with key figures.

Compatible with the absence of prescribed group activity are other
differences in personnel, role structure, and the definition and content of jural relations. Where patrilineal descent groups are important,
jural relations in many contexts are defined in terms of agnation.

---

[22] In other highlands societies, divorce and ensuing bride wealth disputes often
lead to bad feelings between already competing groups and sometimes to killings
or interclan fights.

Thus at marriage, the identity of participants and their roles can be predicted and analyzed in terms of descent group affiliation. But among the bilateral Telefolmin, roles are not permanently fixed to particular kinship groups, kin categories, or kin relationships. Depending on circumstances, any role can be filled by any type of kinsman. This informal role organization is interesting, but more interesting is the fact that, although all participants are kin of the bride or groom, kinship *per se* is an unsatisfactory framework of analysis, for on some occasions it has little to do with the definition of roles. More significant interpersonal relations take the form of *voluntary* friendships, the choice of friends being influenced by personal compatibility, residential proximity, status considerations, age-mateship, and inherited friendships.

Not only does friendship frequently determine the composition of Telefolmin action groups and the character of the interaction of their personnel. It also supports the popular preference for intravillage marriage, maintains the idea that marriage is for reinforcing existing ties and not for creating new ones, and justifies the lack of interaction with affines who are strangers.

Marriage Among the
KONDA VALLEY DANI

Denise O'Brien

"Dani" is a linguistic and cultural designation applied by Europeans to a large Papuan population in the central highlands of West Irian. About 200,000 Dani-speaking people (Bromley, 1961: 1) occupy a region of some 6,000 square miles stretching from Ilaga in the west throughout the Grand Valley of the Baliem in the east (Figure 1). The people of the Konda Valley speak a Western Dani dialect which also extends to other valleys in the Swart region and to parts of the Jamo drainage (Larson, n.d.: 24–27; Bromley, 1967).[1]

The Konda Valley, located between 138°24' and 138°32' east longitude and 3°35' and 3°45' south latitude, is one of several contiguous valleys known collectively as the Swart Valley. Dutch explorers first reached the Konda Valley at its northern extremity in 1920. A second expedition in 1921 camped briefly in the Konda on their way to Mt. Wilhelmina (now Mt. Trikora) (Bijlmer, 1923: 255–57, Le Roux, 1948: 6). These contacts had little apparent effect on Dani culture except to create legends about light-skinned spirits who possessed "boom-sticks" but no women. The Konda was left undisturbed until 1957, when two missionaries built an airstrip, established a station called Karubaga, and brought in their families.[2]

The first government post in the Western Dani area opened at Bokondini, about twenty-two miles east of Karubaga, in 1959 (Figure 1). Government influence in the Konda was slight and the Dutch administration classified the Swart region as "uncontrolled territory" until their departure in 1962, even though pacification problems were

---

[1] I carried out fieldwork in New Guinea from October 1961 through January 1963 and from April 1963 until September 1963, on a research fellowship (13,785) and research grant (5124) from the National Institute of Mental Health. Anthropological fieldwork among other Dani groups has been done by: Broekhuijse (1967), Bromley (1961), Heider (1965), Larson (1962), Peters (1965), Ploeg (1966), and Wirz (1924). Earlier drafts of this paper benefited by criticism from Jay Ruby and Mervyn Meggitt; any errors are my own.

[2] The missionaries at Karubaga are members of the Regions Beyond Missionary Union, a Protestant interdenominational evangelical organization.

minimal. By the end of 1962 the missionaries had considerably changed the traditional Dani way of life, most notably by abolishing warfare and indigenous religious ceremonies. My aim is to analyze the traditional marriage system, though some mention will be made of mission-induced changes.

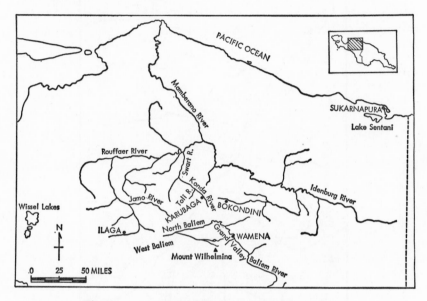

Figure 1. CENTRAL HIGHLANDS OF WEST IRIAN

The Konda is a narrow valley about ten miles long. A mile-long plateau in the center is the only level terrain for several miles. Here, at an altitude of 4,900 feet, the Karubaga airstrip and station were built (Figure 2). The eastern and western valley walls reach an altitude of 6,000 feet, and most of the 5,000 Konda Dani live on the slopes of these ridges several hundred feet above the Konda and Kudage gorges. The ridge slopes, deeply cut by streams and gullies, are covered by secondary forest, open grassland, and gardens. The ridge tops are covered by a primary growth of dense, mossy rain forest, though hamlets and cultivation extend to within a hundred feet of the crests.

The Dani are horticulturists whose economic system centers around pigs, sweet potatoes, and shells which are common in highland New Guinea societies. The sweet potato is quantitatively the most important plant grown in the Konda Valley. Other traditional crops include taro, yams, bananas, pandanus, sugar cane, winged beans, cu-

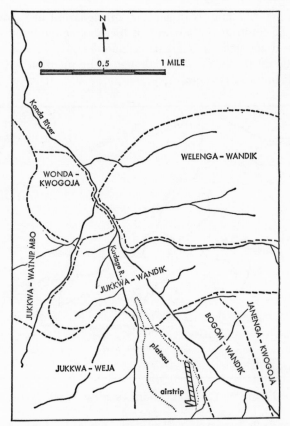

Figure 2. KONDA VALLEY CONFEDERACIES

cumbers, squash, ginger, and tobacco. Men clear and fence the gardens and cultivate bananas, taro, sugar cane, pandanus, and tobacco. Women tend sweet potatoes and all other crops, and care for their own and their husbands' pigs.

The Konda Dani are patrilineally organized and have an Omaha-type kinship terminology. They are polygynous and postmarital residence is usually virilocal. The settlement pattern is one of small dispersed hamlets consisting of one men's house and one or more family houses where women, children, and pigs sleep and eat. The maximal social unit is a dispersed, named, patrilineal clan which is divided into localized patrilineages. There are over seventy-five Western Dani clans extending from Ilaga to Bokondini, of which sixteen have a large membership (i.e., more than 100) in the lower Konda Valley. The clan is ideally exogamous but has no other functional importance. Clans and clan membership, signified by a common name, are important primarily as symbols of the Dani descent ideology. The confederacy is the most important sociopolitical unit in Konda Dani society. It is divided into halves or subconfederacies, each a part of a different clan.[3] The confederacy takes its name from the clan names of its subconfederacies (e.g., Figure 2, lineages from Jukkwa clan are part of three confederacies in the mid-Konda: Jukkwa-Watnipmbo, Jukkwa-Wandik, and Jukkwa-Weja). Altogether the confederacy is composed of three to seven lineages from two different clans. Men belonging to lineages from the same clan occupy a limited number of contiguous hamlets and form the core of the subconfederacy's population. The confederacy is ideally endogamous, with men of one constituent subconfederacy exchanging women with men of the opposite subconfederacy. The actual population of the confederacy consists of the men of two subconfederacies plus their wives—some of whom are from clans and lineages outside the confederacy—and children, and a few other persons incorporated through common residence and nonagnatic kin links.[4] The preference for confederacy endogamy is followed in a significant number of cases (see discussion below and Table 9) and thus, because marriage is validated by transfers of wealth between the families of the bride and groom, multiple economic bonds are created between the constituent halves of a confederacy. Ideally war does not occur within a confederacy, which is the basic unit in a war alliance. The confederacy is, therefore, the most inclusive political unit among the Konda Dani, since interconfederacy alliances vary in membership from war to war. Leadership is achieved rather than ascribed and each confederacy has two or three men who are "Big Men" due to their wealth, bravery and success in war, skill at public speaking, and ceremonial knowledge.

The confederacies of the mid-Konda Valley are mapped in Figure 2. Residential mobility within a confederacy is fairly high. At any

---

[3] There are no moieties in the Konda, though they have been reported from neighboring Dani populations to the north and east (Wirz, 1924: 47, Ploeg, 1966: 264).

[4] Men may leave their natal lineages to live with affinal or uterine kin. Thus men who are members by birth of other clans, or other lineages within the same clan, can be incorporated either temporarily or permanently into a subconfederacy. Small scale forced migrations were often the fate of Dani defeated in war. Refugees usually fled into a neighboring valley; eventually they adopted the clan name of a subconfederacy and were regarded as agnatic members of that subconfederacy. Within a generation or two "adoption" was forgotten.

one time during 1962–63 the Jukkwa-Wandik confederacy had 9 or 10 occupied hamlets and a total population of approximately 160.[5]

MARRIAGE "RULES"

The Konda Dani have several sets of cultural norms relating to marriage which I discuss in decreasing order of generality. Few of these could be called rules: they are preferential rather than prescriptive; only those relating to incest and divorce are reinforced by specific sanctions.

Table 1. MARITAL EXPERIENCE OF LIVING KONDA DANI: MARRIAGES TERMINATED BY DEATH

| | *Men* | | *Women* | | |
	Over 45	*All*	*Over 45*	*All*	*Totals*
Number of Wedded Persons	16	40	12	81	121
Number of Marriages Ended by Spouse's Death:					
None	7	28	6	53	81
One	2	5	4	22	27
Two	2	2	2	6	8
Three	1	1			1
Four	1	1			1
Five	2	2			2
Six	0	0			0
Seven	1	1			1
Mean Number of Spouse's Deaths Per Head of Population	1.88	.83	.67	.42	.55
Number of Persons Widowed at Least Once	9	12	6	28	40
Percentage of Wedded Population Widowed at Least Once	56.3%	30.0%	50.0%	34.6%	33.0%

1. Everyone should marry.

Celibacy is rare among the Konda Dani, particularly for women. I

---

[5] Residential mobility, traditionally high within the confederacy, increased as a result of contact. The significance and function of the confederacy declined with the abolition of warfare in 1961, and the abandonment of intergroup mariage, death, and indemnity payments in 1962. In 1963 many Dani from the ridges of the valley began moving to the lower slopes and plateau area, to be closer to the mission. The census figure of 160 for Jukkwa-Wandik confederacy refers to the traditional inhabitants only and ignores the 1963 immigrants.

recorded only two instances of adult unmarried women, one a woman about fifty-five who died in 1962. She had no apparent physical or mental abnormalities and her relatives had no explanation for her failure to marry. The other unmarried woman was an albino about twenty-two. Other women with physical infirmities including goiter, deafness, and dumbness have all married. From genealogies involving over 1,000 persons there are three cases of men who never married and were past forty at the time of death. In only one of these cases, a deaf mute, was the failure to marry attributed to any specific cause. I observed three mature men who never married and had no intention of doing so. In only one case was a specific infirmity—deafness—given as a cause. More important is the general standing of these bachelors in the community. All are poor, two are short (height is a desirable physical attribute), and none has a good war record.

The valuation of marriage as normal and desirable leads to remarriage among widowed and divorced persons. Remarriage after divorce is discussed below; here I treat widowing. Tables 1 and 2

Table 2. MARITAL EXPERIENCE OF DECEASED KONDA DANI: MARRIAGES TERMINATED BY DEATH

	Men	*Women*	*Totals*
Number of Wedded Persons	16	57	73
Number of Marriages Ended by Spouse's Death:			
None	4	28	32
One	7	22	29
Two	4	7	11
Three	1	0	1
Mean Number of Spouse's Deaths Per Person	1.13	.63	.74
Number of Persons Widowed at Least Once	12	29	41
Percentage of Wedded Population Widowed at Least Once	75.0%	50.9%	56.2%

show the range of experience of marriages terminated by death.[6] Two specific norms affect the remarriages of widowed persons.

[6] I wish to be explicit regarding the samples from which the tables are drawn. About 65 per cent of the informants whose marital histories are summarized come from one political community, Jukkwa-Wandik confederacy. The remaining informants come from five of the other six confederacies in Figure 2. Among male informants from outside Jukkwa-Wandik there is a slight bias toward Big Men since they are the most willing and knowledgeable. Data on deceased persons were drawn from accounts of informants regarding their fathers, fathers' wives, and

a. Widows should be allowed a mourning period before being urged to marry. This mourning period usually lasts from three to six months. Younger widows are often compelled to remarry by their kin or their husband's agnates, since remarriage economically benefits these groups. If a man dies before completing his marriage payments, his widow is a valuable asset for her kin; if the husband has made substantial payments, his lineage has a direct interest in his widow who represents a group investment. Older women who do not wish to remarry may live with married children or return to their natal subconfederacies. Table 3 shows the tendency for widow remarriage.

b. It is good if a man marries his "brother's" widow. (In this context "brother" applies to any man of ego's clan.) The preference for the levirate is understandable in light of the patrilineal ideology and in economic terms since a man's agnates contribute about one-third

Table 3. REMARRIAGE OF KONDA DANI WIDOWS

	Living		Dead	
Number of Widows	28		29	
Number of Times Widowed	34		36	
	Widows			
	Number	Per Cent	Number	Per Cent
Remarriages:				
None	2	6.9%	9	28.1%
One	22	75.8	19	59.4
Two	5	17.3	4	12.5

of his total marriage payments. Another way of indicating the effect of the levirate is to examine its influence on men's marriages. Out of

_____

former spouses. As for actual marriage ceremonies and payments, I witnessed twelve "skirtings" (i.e., "weddings") and saw the bride's father's payment made in ten of these. I saw no betrothal payments, which are made secretly at night, but witnessed sixteen groom's payments and two sexual indemnity (*ka*) payments. Cases analyzed in Tables 10–17 include only payments for which I obtained specific data on each participant's name, clan, kin relationship to bride or groom, and share in the payment. Further partial data are available for each type of payment. My analysis of the raw data owes much to statistical analyses of marriage and divorce by Barnes (1949) and Meggitt (1965).

a sample of thirty-six men, twelve married a total of twenty-three widows; the levirate was followed in 60.9 per cent of the cases. As would be expected in a patrilineal society, the presence of children affects the degree to which the levirate is followed. Of the 32 widow remarriages tabulated above, data are available in 28 cases on the presence or absence of children, as well as their sex and number.

Table 4. ADHERENCE TO THE LEVIRATE BY KONDA DANI WIDOWS

	Living		Dead		Totals	
Number of Women	81		57		138	
Number of Women Widowed	28		29		57	
	Number	Per Cent	Number	Per Cent	Number	Per Cent
Levirate Followed	13	40.6%	12	44.4%	25	42.4%
Levirate Not Followed	19	59.4	15	55.6	34	57.6
Total Remarriages	32	100	27	100	59	100

However the data was analyzed, they indicate that adherence to the levirate is more likely if children are present. Neither the number nor sex of the children is significant. Children whose mothers' remarriages ignore the levirate ideally and usually remain with them until they are ten or twelve years old and then return to their natal lineages.

2. One should reach a certain level of maturity before marrying. a. Females should not marry until their breasts are developed. b. Males should not marry until they are "tall, broad-shouldered, and bearded."

Readiness for marriage is defined in physical terms for both males and females, though additional economic factors influence the time of a man's initial marriage. Since physical maturation varies among individuals and Dani ages can only be estimated, the age at first marriage cannot be precisely determined. Generally, however, girls are considered marriageable at twelve and men at twenty. Menarche is not significant in determining a girl's readiness for marriage, which often occurs first. Konda Dani youths put on a genital covering, the penis gourd, at age fifteen but this is not synonymous with readiness for marriage; they are not thought to achieve full physical growth

Table 5. EFFECT OF CHILDREN ON THE LEVIRATE AMONG KONDA DANI

| | Remarriages | | | | | |
| | With Children | | Childless | | Totals | |
	Num- ber	Per Cent	Num- ber	Per Cent	Num- ber	Per Cent
Levirate Followed	8	53.3%	4	30.8%	12	42.9%
Levirate Ignored	7	46.7	9	69.2	16	57.1
Total	15	100	13	100	28	100

	Remarriages					
	Levirate					
	Followed		Ignored		Totals	
	Num- ber	Per Cent	Num- ber	Per Cent	Num- ber	Per Cent
Children Present	8	67%	7	44%	15	53%
Number of Children	4	33	9	56	13	46
Totals	12	100	16	100	28	100

for several years.[7] In any case, a man cannot marry until he can contribute at least 50 per cent of his marriage payments.

3. Polygyny is prestigious.

Dani men are enthusiastic about polygyny. Some men extol its sexual advantages, saying that with only one wife opportunities for intercourse are limited when she is pregnant or nursing a child. Others note that with more wives one can expect to have more children. An often cited economic advantage is that with more wives one can have more gardens and hence more pigs. Above all, a second or third wife is a status symbol, tangible proof of virility and the ability to lay out the wealth necessary for several marriages. Women have a more ambivalent attitude toward polygyny. While they seldom

[7] Statements about Konda male initiation rites are contradictory, but it seems clear that initiation did occur and was marked by the donning of penis gourds.

hesitate to enter into polygynous unions, wives nearly always protest a husband's acquisition of another spouse. Despite practices intended to promote harmony among cowives, such as separate houses and addressing each other as "sister," cowife hostility is frequent and can lead to divorce.

Table 6. POLYGYNY AMONG CURRENTLY MARRIED LIVING MEN OF KONDA DANI

Wives Per Husband	Number of Men	Per Cent
One	83	74.8%
Two	23	20.7
Three	3	2.7
Four	1	.9
Five	1	.9
Total Men	111	100
Monogamous Men	83	74.8%
Polygynous Men	28	25.2
Total	111	100
Wives in monogamous unions	83	56.4%
Wives in polygynous unions	64	43.6
Total	147	100

Note: Mean number of wives per husband: 1.32.

4. One should marry outside one's clan.

The preference for clan exogamy decreases with genealogical distance. It is strongest within the subconfederacy whose linked lineages —all from the same clan—are said to have the same "original grandfathers" (three or four generations removed from the oldest men) and to be "from the same penis," though no single founder is recognized. Actual intraclan marriages are excused by saying that the spouses are not "related," meaning that they are from geographically distant lineages of the same clan or that one spouse formerly belonged to another clan. In a sample of 454 marriages, about 30 per cent occurring prior to 1930, there are ten intraclan marriages (representing 2.2 per cent of the total). Informants explained five of these marriages by saying one spouse, or the spouse's father, had migrated into the Konda from another valley where he or she had belonged to a different clan. There were no specific explanations for the other five cases, though two could have been affected by mission preaching which has created confusion over clan exogamy and incest taboos. Thus, several informants said, "We are all members of the Jesus clan now; we can throw away the old taboos."

5. It is taboo to have sexual intercourse with, and therefore to marry, certain classes of kin.

The incest taboos are supported by supernatural sanctions which predict sickness or death for infractions, as well as by social sanctions which predict strong kin and community disapproval and active intervention to prevent violations.

a. The primary taboo is directed against intercourse with parents and siblings. Informants stated that this taboo is the basis for clan exogamy. Although such incest is regarded with abhorrence, one informant reported a brother-sister marriage; the man and woman, the informant's FFB and FFZ, had the same father, but he was not sure whether they shared the same mother. Despite the strong incest prohibition the couple married, lived together for a long time, and had at least one child; he could not explain how they survived the social and supernatural sanctions against such a marriage. No other cases of primary incest were encountered.

b. Intercourse is allowed with some but not all individuals in kin classes which include cross-cousins, maternal parallel cousins, and sister's children (from a man's viewpoint).[8]

Interpretation of data concerning intercourse or marriage within these kin classes is difficult; informants tend to phrase the taboos to make them fit their conception of "Christianity" which varies widely from person to person and changes over time. Whatever the exact nature of traditional incest taboos I recorded no instances of marriage with an *actual* MBD, MZD, ZD, or FZD even though marriage preferences encourage men to marry into these categories.

6. One should marry into one's mother's clan and into the opposite half of one's confederacy.[9]

Neither preference is given explicit priority; ideally, they should coincide and apply equally to both sexes. Actual cases show, how-

---

[8] The relevant kin classes and their primary denotata for a male ego are: "sister's child": ZS/D, FZS/D, FBDS/D, FZDS/D, MBDS/D, MZDS/D, MZSS/D; "maternal aunt": MZ, MBD, MBSD; "cousin": MZS/D, MFZS/D, MMZS/D.

[9] Genealogies revealed a secondary tendency to marry into one's FM clan but the Dani do not recognize this.

ever, that confederacy preference outweighs mother's clan preference
and that women follow both preferences more often. For any individual the probability of congruence between both preferences is low.
In a sample of forty-five living men who have contracted 116 marriages,
in only six (13.3 per cent) did the mother and at least one wife come
from within the confederacy. Table 7 compares the preferences in 342
marriages for which data on both preferences are available (eight
intraclan marriages are listed as ignoring either preference).

Table 7. COMPARISON OF KONDA DANI PREFERENCES FOR MARRIAGE
WITH THE MOTHER'S CLAN AND WITHIN THE CONFEDERACY

	Marriages							
	Males				*Females*			
	Mother's Clan		*Intra-Con-federacy*		*Mother's Clan*		*Intra-Con-federacy*	
	Num-ber	*Per Cent*	*Num-ber*	*Per Cent*	*Num-ber*	*Per Cent*	*Num-ber*	*Per Cent*
Follow Preference	23	10%	54	23%	18	17%	30	29%
Ignore Preference	215	90	184	77	86	83	74	71
Total	238	100	238	100	104	100	104	100

	Total			
	Mother's Clan		*Intra-Con-federacy*	
	Num-ber	*Per Cent*	*Num-ber*	*Per Cent*
Follow preference	41	12%	84	25%
Ignore preference	301	88	258	75
Total	342	100	342	100

The greater tendency for females to contract marriages following
both preferences is partially due to polygyny. There is a positive
correlation between number of wives and a man's political power.

An ambitious man consolidates his position by taking a second wife who is a member of the same subconfederacy as his first wife, or he extends his affinal ties to other confederacies by taking wives from several clans. Affines and uterine kin are useful allies in war and should provide economic support when an individual makes marriage, death, or indemnity payments, so a Big Man or any man attempting to increase his prestige strives to have brothers-in-law and sister's sons in several confederacies.[10] Analysis of marriages of current polygynists,

Table 8. JUKKWA-WANDIK CONFEDERACY: DISTRIBUTION OF MARRIAGES BY CLANS[a]

Clan Name	Number of Clans	Jukkwa Subconfederacy		Number of Clans	Wandik Subconfederacy	
		Number	Per Cent		Number	Per Cent
Wandik		25	21%		0	—%
Jukkwa		5	4		26	30
Kwogoja		14	12		14	16
Welenga		16	12		1	1
Watnipmbo		11	9		3	3
Wonda		11	9		2	2
Mabu		0	—		7	8
Bogom		2	2		7	8
Janenga		2	2		5	6
Subtotals	9	86	71	8	65	74
Other clans	12	31	29	11	22	26
Totals	21	117	100	19	87	100

[a] Note that Table 8 shows the distribution of marriages by clans and does not differentiate among lineages of the same clan which are part of two different confederacies.

and of all marriages, shows that very few men contract more than two marriages with women from the same clan.

The 342 marriages in Table 7 concern individuals in seven of the

[10] In their sexual attitudes and behavior the Konda Dani correspond to the "Kuma type" described by Meggitt (1964: 220-21) for the Australian highlands in which men are lechers, male initiation is unimportant, and "affine" is not synonymous with "enemy."

fourteen subconfederacies in Figure 2. The percentage of marriages contracted with the confederacy partner in these seven subconfederacies ranges from 11 per cent to 49 per cent, the mean being 28 per cent. In any subconfederacy marriages which do not follow confederacy endogamy are not randomly distributed among neighboring confederacies but show definite patterns. Table 8 demonstrates that, aside from a propensity to marry into Kwogoja clan (one of the two largest clans in the Konda), both halves of this confederacy tend not to marry members of the same clan. The major factor influencing this differential distribution appears to be contemporary and historical propinquity.

Examination of wars involving Jukkwa-Wandik confederacy from 1920 to 1960 indicates that affinally related confederacies tend to become allies. This is illustrated in Table 9, which also shows that although such confederacies usually become allies *rather* than enemies, they can fight. However, most affinally linked confederacies remain neutral.

Table 9. JUKKWA-WANDIK CONFEDERACY: AFFINES AND ALLIES

	Confederacies Affinally Linked to Jukkwa-Wandik									
	Wad-Wel		*Juk-Wat*		*Bom-Kwo*		*Won-Kwo*		*Jan-Kwo*	
	Num-ber	*Per Cent*	*Num-ber*	*Per Cent*	*Num-ber*	*Per Cent*	*Num-ber*	*Per Cent*	*Num-ber*	*Per Cent*
Ally	10	33%	5	16%	5	16%	3	9%	2	6%
Enemy	1	3	2	6	2	6	1	3	6	18
Uninvolved	22	64	26	78	26	78	29	88	25	76
Totals	33	100	33	100	33	100	33	100	33	100

In addition to providing a framework for understanding Dani marriage, I have demonstrated the *political* significance of marriage for groups and individuals. The preference for confederacy endogamy over marriage with the mother's clan (Table 7: 25 per cent to 12 per cent) indicates that political considerations outweigh kinship in contracting marriages. On the group level marriage integrates the basic political community—the confederacy—and reduces hostility between contiguous political communities. On the individual level marriage enables a man to acquire and demonstrate prestige and to accumulate useful ties outside his political community.

CONTRACTING A MARRIAGE

Dani say that marriage choices are made primarily by the bride and her mother, and clearly young girls and mature women do have considerable freedom in rejecting husbands (see Table 23: Declared Causes of Specific Divorce Cases).

Courting parties similiar to those in the Australian highlands (Reay, 1959: 22, Read 1965: 192–93) traditionally occurred after a funeral or other public event, and sometimes spontaneously.[11] Marriage negotiations grow out of such encounters or are initiated by kinsmen of a prospective bride or groom. Konda Dani apply explicit standards of physical beauty to potential spouses and to sexual partners. These preferences may not affect initial marriages but do influence divorces, remarriages, and polygynous marriages.

Marriage to a spinster entails wealth exchange among the kinsmen of the bride and groom: a betrothal payment by the groom to the bride's parents, a bride's father's payment to the bride's mother's brothers, and a groom's payment to the bride's father. The most important components of any payment are pigs, exchange stones, and bands of cowrie shells. Exchange stones are of two kinds, male (narrow and rounded) and female (broad and flat). In marriage payments the stones are laid out in pairs to represent sexual intercourse and to provide an example for the bride and groom. Items of lesser value (e.g., salt, single shells, nets, stone tools) also occur in marriage payments. It is impossible to establish a single standard of value for these diverse items, especially after the changes wrought by contact, but some idea of the relative value of traditional goods is seen in the ideal price for pigs in 1962, ranging from ten individual cowries for a small piglet to four cowrie shell bands, one male exchange stone, and salt for the largest boar or sow.

The groom makes the betrothal payment to the bride's parents before or immediately after initial cohabitation. The most important action symbolically and legally is the transfer of cooked pork, especially a tongue, from the groom to the bride's mother. After the bride's mother accepts the tongue from an agnatic kinsman of the groom, the marriage is formally sealed. The remainder of the payment accom-

[11] I attended courting parties in 1962 but, due to the mission influence, the institution had vanished by 1963.

panies the tongue or follows it within a few days. The payment is not publicly displayed and the groom receives nothing in return. Tables 10 and 11 show the size of the betrothal payment and the range of kinsmen who are donors and recipients.[12]

Presentation of the bride's father's payment is the only ceremony which could be called a "wedding," even though the groom is absent. The festivities last two or three days, during which the bride's father solicits contributions to the payment, primarily from his agnates. During the second day, pigs are killed and eaten, the bride is rubbed with pig grease in order to ensure her health and fertility, and toward the same ends, she wears armbands of testicles and penes from these pigs. She is then publicly dressed in a married woman's skirt. Traditionally another ceremony called "cutting the girl's skirt" (as distinguished from the "married woman's skirt") occurred after the bride dressed as a married woman. Her female kin chanted songs telling her to be a good wife and gardener while dancing and rubbing male exchange stones.[13] The bride also receives nets and braid from her female lineage mates, the wives of her lineage mates, and from women and wives of her mother's lineage. The nets and braid become her property but she may give some to her new affines, the women and wives of the groom's lineage. Ideally the bride's father's payment and the bride's skirting occur before initial cohabitation, when the betrothal payment has been accepted, and the festivities end when the bride is escorted to her husband's hamlet. Tables 12 and 13 show the size of the bride's father's payment and kin relationships of participants.

The groom collects the final payment from his paternal and maternal kin and gives it to the bride's father, who distributes it to his relatives who contributed to his payment to the bride's mother's lineage. Formerly the groom's payment was publicly paid and re-

[12] In all tabulations relating to the kin status of participants in marriage payments the kin categories derive from kin terms and hence are classificatory. The most important kin types in the various categories are: "father": F, FB, FFBS; "siblings": B, Z, FBS/D; "mother's brother": MB, MBS, MFBS; "child"; *groom*: S, D, BS/D, FZSS/D, FBSS/D; *bride*: S, D, ZS/D, BS/D, HS/D, HBS/D; "sister's child"; *groom*: ZS/D, FZS/D, FZDS/D, MBDS/D, etc.; *bride*: FZS/D, FZDS/D; "cousin": MZS/D, MBDS/D. *NB*: "Child" is placed under "Other Consanguines" rather than "Agnates" because, although the category includes agnates such as S, BS, it also includes many nonagnatic participants.

[13] Ploeg (personal communication) reports that at Bokondini this portion of the marriage cycle included a mock spear fight between the bride's and groom's female kin and a simulated abduction of the bride by the groom's kin. The "cutting the girl's skirt" ceremonies vanished quickly in the Konda at the instigation of the mission, and by 1961 were no longer practiced.

Table 10. Konda Dani Donors to Betrothal Payment: Analysis of Twelve Cases

Donor Classification	Donors		Pigs		Stones		Shell Bands		Other Items		Total Items	
	Number	Per Cent	Number	Per Cent	Number	Per Cent	Number	Per Cent	Number	Per Cent	Number	Per Cent
Total Donors	99	100%	47	100%	53	100%	136	100%	29	100%	265	100%
Male	93	94	44	94	53	100	130	96	29	100	256	97
Female	6	6	3	6	0	0	6	4	0	0	9	3
Clan Membership:												
Groom's F's	78	79	47	100	46	87	122	90	29	100	244	92
Groom's M's	6	6	0	0	0	0	6	4	0	0	6	2
Other	15	15	0	0	7	13	8	6	0	0	15	6
Groom	12	12	30	64	36	68	66	49	26	91	158	60
Groom's Agnates:	64	65	16	34	9	17	55	40	3	9	83	31
Father	7	7	1	2	0	0	9	6	0	0	10	4
Siblings	57	58	15	32	9	17	46	34	3	9	73	27
Father's Sister	0	0	0	0	0	0	0	0	0	0	0	0
Groom's Uterine Kin:	3	3	0	0	0	0	3	2	0	0	3	1
Mother	0	0	0	0	0	0	0	0	0	0	0	0
Mother's Brother	3	3	0	0	0	0	3	2	0	0	3	1
MM Clan	0	0	0	0	0	0	0	0	0	0	0	0
Groom's Other Consanguines:	15	15	1	2	4	8	11	8	0	0	16	6
Child	2	2	0	0	1	2	1	1	0	0	2	1
Sister's Child	11	11	1	2	2	4	9	6	0	0	12	4
Cousin	0	0	0	0	0	0	1	0	0	0	0	0
FM Clan	2	2	0	0	1	2	1	1	0	0	2	1
Groom's Affines	4	4	0	0	3	5	1	1	0	0	4	1
Non-Kin	1	1	0	0	1	2	0	0	0	0	1	1

Table 11. Konda Dani Recipients of Betrothal Payment: Analysis of Fourteen Cases

Recipient Classification	Recipients		Components									
			Pigs		Stones		Shell Bands		Other Items		Total Items	
	Number	Per Cent	Number	Per Cent	Number	Per Cen	Number	Per Cent	Number	Per Cent	Number	Per Cent
Total Recipients	132	100%	52	100%	38	100%	107	100%	29	100%	226	100%
Male	107	81	41	79	30	79	89	83	28	97	188	83
Female	25	19	11	21	8	21	18	17	1	3	38	17
Clan Membership:												
Bride's F's	94	71	42	81	22	58	86	80	27	93	177	78
Bride's M's	20	15	6	11	10	26	15	14	0	0	31	14
Other	18	14	4	8	6	16	6	6	2	7	18	8
Bride's Agnates:	100	75.8	42	81	26	68	88	82	27	93	183	80.5
Father	27	20	17	33	12	31	24	22	20	69	73	32
Siblings	72	55	25	48	14	37	63	59	7	24	109	48
Father's Sister	1	0.8	0	0	0	0	1	1	0	0	1	0.5
Bride's Uterine Kin:	16	12	7	13	9	24	11	10	0	0	27	12
Mother	11	8	6	11	6	16	10	9	0	0	22	10
Mother's Brother	5	4	1	2	3	8	1	1	0	0	5	2
MM Clan	0	0	0	0	0	0	0	0	0	0	0	0
Bride's Other Consanguines:	10	7.6	2	4	2	5	6	6	0	0	10	4.5
Child	0	0	0	0	0	0	0	0	0	0	0	0
Sister's Child	1	0.8	0	0	0	0	1	1	0	0	1	0.5
Cousin	9	6.8	2	4	2	5	5	5	0	0	9	3
FM Clan	0	0	0	0	0	0	0	0	0	0	0	0
Bride's Affines	1	0.8	0	0	0	0	1	1	0	0	1	0.5
Non-Kin	1	0.8	0	0	1	3	0	0	0	0	1	0.5
Status Unknown	4	3	1	2	0	0	1	1	2	7	4	2

Table 12. KONDA DANI DONORS TO BRIDE'S FATHER'S PAYMENT: ANALYSIS OF SIX CASES[b]

Donor Classification	Donors		Components Pigs		Stones		Shell Bands		Other Items		Total Items	
	Number	Per Cent	Number	Per Cent	Number	Per Cent	Number	Per Cent	Number	Per Cent	Number	Per Cent
Total Donors	187	100%	38	100%	10	100%	125	100%	142	100%	315	100%
Male	114	61	34	89	9	90	106	85	13	29	162	51
Female	73	39	4	11	1	10	19	15	129	71	153	49
Clan Membership:												
Bride's F's	108	58	32	84	9	90	89	71	43	39	173	55
Bride's M's	29	15	2	5	1	10	17	14	46	23.3	66	21
Other	50	27	4	11	0	0	19	15	53	37.7	76	24
Bride's Agnates:	110.5	59	33	87	10	100	89	71	51	44.7	183	58
Father	32	17	15	39	5	50	36	29	1	2.3	57	18
Siblings	66.5	36	18	48	4	40	51	40	27	29	100	32
Father's Sister	12	6	0	0	1	10	2	2	23	13.3	26	8
Bride's Uterine Kin:	20	11	0	0	0	0	11	9	32	17.3	43	14
Mother	13	7	0	0	0	0	5	4	31	15	36	11
Mother's Brother	6	3	0	0	0	0	6	5	0	0	6	2
MM Clan	1	1	0	0	0	0	0	0	1	2.3	1	1
Bride's Other Consanguines:	29	15	5	13	0	0	20	16	15	13	40	13
Child	3	1	0	0	0	0	2	2	1	2.2	3	1
Sister's Child	7	4	2	5	0	0	4	3	12	8.2	18	6
Cousin	15	8	3	8	0	0	11	9	1	.3	15	5
FM Clan	4	2	0	0	0	0	3	2	1	2.3	4	1
Bride's Affines	24.5	13	0	0	0	0	5	4	40	21.3	45	14
Non-Kin	3	2	0	0	0	0	0	0	4	3.7	4	1
Status Unknown	0	0	0	0	0	0	0	0	0	0	0	0

b The divided individual in the donor's column is a woman who donated items in two different kin roles. As a consanguine she gave...

Table 13. Konda Dani Recipients of Bride's Father's Payment: Analysis of Four Cases

Recipient Classification	Recipients		Pigs		Stones		Shell Bands		Other Items		Total Items	
	Number	Per Cent	Number	Per Cent	Number	Per Cent	Number	Per Cent	Number	Per Cent	Number	Per Cent
Total Recipients	108	100%	22	100%	11	100%	82	100%	15	100%	130	100%
Male	72	67	14	64	11	100	59	72	2	14.5	86	66
Female	36	33	8	36	0	0	23	28	13	85.5	44	34
Clan Membership:												
Bride's F's	21	19	2	9	2	18	17	21	6	37.5	27	21
Bride's M's	73	68	17	77	9	82	56	68	7	50	89	68
Other	14	13	3	14	0	0	9	11	2	12.5	14	11
Bride's Agnates:	7	6	0	0	0	0	3	4	6	37.5	9	7
Father	0	0	0	0	0	0	0	0	0	0	0	0
Siblings	5	4	0	0	0	0	3	4	4	50	7	5
Father's Sister	2	2	0	0	0	0	0	0	2	12.5	2	2
Bride's Uterine Kin:	83	77	17	77	7	64	71	87	7	50	102	78
Mother	21	19	6	27	0	0	15	19	5	35.5	26	20
Mother's Brother	59	55	10	45	7	64	54	66	2	14.5	73	56
MM Clan	3	3	1	5	0	0	2	2	0	0	3	2
Bride's Other Consanguines:	10	9	4	18	4	36	2	2	0	0	10	8
Child	0	0	0	0	0	0	0	0	0	0	0	0
Sister's Child	0	0	0	0	0	0	0	0	0	0	0	0
Cousin	9	8	3	13	4	36	2	2	0	0	9	7
FM Clan	1	1	1	5	0	0	0	0	0	0	1	1
Bride's Affines	4	4	0	0	0	0	4	5	1	6.25	5	3
Non-Kin	2	2	1	5	0	0	0	0	1	6.25	2	2
Status Unknown	2	2	0	0	0	0	2	2	0	0	2	2

Table 14. Konda Dani Donors to Groom's Payment: Analysis of Twenty-Seven Cases

| Donor Classification | Donors | | Components | | | | | | | | | |
| | | | Pigs | | Stones | | Shell Bands | | Other Items | | Total Items | |
	Number	Per Cent	Number	Per Cent	Number	Per Cent	Number	Per Cent	Number	Per Cent	Number	Per Cent
Total Donors	385	100%	190	100%	42	100%	438	100%	89	100%	759	100%
Male	332	86	177	93	37	88	408	93	78	88	700	92
Female	53	14	13	7	5	12	30	7	11	12	59	8
Clan Membership:												
Groom's F's	254	66	171	90	28	67	360	82	41	46	600	79
Groom's M's	28	7	2	1	2	5	19	4	7	8	30	4
Other	103	27	17	9	12	28	59	14	41	46	129	17
Groom	27	7	121	64	18	43	205	47	18	20	362	48
Groom's Agnates:	216	56	45	24	11	26	149	34	24	27	229	30
Father	27	7	6	3.5	1	2.5	16	4	3	3	26	3.4
Siblings	187	48.5	38	20	9	21	133	30	21	24	201	26.6
Father's Sister	2	0.5	1	0.5	1	2.5	0	0	0	0	2	0.2
Groom's Uterine Kin:	30	8	5	3	0	0	17	4	10	11	32	4
Mother	7	2	2	1.25	0	0	3	1	2	2	7	1
Mother's Brother	15	4	1	0.5	0	0	10	2	5	6	16	2
MM Clan	8	2	2	1.25	0	0	4	1	3	3	9	1
Groom's Other Consanguines:	62	16	16	8	8	19	41	9	16	18	81	11
Child	10	3	2	1	0	0	7	1.5	10	11	19	3
Sister's Child	38	10	9	4.5	7	17	24	5	6	7	46	6
Cousin	5	1	1	0.5	1	2	3	1	0	0	5	1
FM Clan	9	2	4	2	0	0	7	1.5	0	0	11	1
Groom's Affines	23	6	1	0.5	1	2	22	5	1	1	25	3
Non-Kin	14	4	1	0.5	2	5	2	0.5	12	14	17	2
Status Unknown	13	3	1	0.5	2	5	2	0.5	8	9	13	2

TABLE ... : RECIPIENTS AND COMPONENTS OF GROOM'S PATRILINY PAYMENTS OF SIXTEEN CASES

Recipient Classification	Recipients		Components									
			Pigs		Stones		Shell Bands		Other Items		Total Items	
	Number	Per Cent	Number	Per Cent	Number	Per Cent	Number	Per Cent	Number	Per Cent	Number	Per Cent
Total Recipients	346	100%	95	100%	22	100%	254	100%	35	100%	406	100%
Males	285	82	81	85	17	77	215	85	26	74	339	83.5
Females	61	18	14	15	5	23	39	15	9	26	67	16.5
Clan Membership:												
Bride's F's	208	60	69	73	10	45	159	63	18	51	256	63
Bride's M's	46	13	12	12	3	14	30	12	3	9	48	12
Other	92	27	14	15	9	41	65	25	14	40	102	25
Bride's Agnates:	211	61	66	70	11	50	163	64	20	57	260	64
Father	48	14	19	20	3	14	38	15	8	23	68	17
Siblings	154	44	43	46	8	36	121	47	11	31	183	45
Father's Sister	9	3	4	4	0	0	4	2	1	3	9	2
Bride's Uterine Kin:	34	10	6	6	4	18	24	10	2	6	36	9
Mother	10	3	2	2	2	9	5	2	2	6	11	3
Mother's Brother	24	7	4	4	2	9	19	8	0	0	25	6
MM Clan	0	0	0	0	0	0	0	0	0	0	0	0
Bride's Other Consanguines:	56	16	16	17	4	18	36	14	6	17	62	15
Child	17	4.9	6	6	2	9	7	2.7	5	14	20	5
Sister's Child	24	6.9	9	10	2	9	15	5.9	0	0	26	6
Cousin	14	4	1	1	0	0	13	5	1	3	15	3.7
FM Clan	1	0.2	0	0	0	0	1	0.4	0	0	1	0.3
Bride's Affines	10	3	5	5	1	5	6	2	0	0	12	3
Non-Kin	11	3	1	1	0	0	4	2	6	17	11	3
Status Unknown	24	7	1	1	2	9	21	8	1	3	25	6

distributed in installments several years apart, the first being delayed until the bride bears one or two children. Since contact most of the groom's payment is usually paid within a few weeks of the bride's father's payment, and small installments follow the birth of one or two children. Informants stated that the post-contact increase in the supply of cowries allows larger and earlier groom's payments. Tables 14 and 15 show the size of the groom's payment and kin relationships of participants.

Comparative statements can be made about the three types of marriage payments (see Tables 10 to 17). First (Table 16) the betrothal

Table 16. KONDA DANI SIZE AND COMPOSITION OF MARRIAGE PAYMENTS

Payments	Components						Totals	Cases
	Pigs	Stones	Shell Bands	Other Items	Nets	Braid		
Bethrothal:								
Number	61	64	152	41	0	0	318	
Mean	3.6	3.8	8.9	2.4	—	—	18.7	17
Percentage	19%	20	48	13	—	—	100	
Bride's Father's:								
Number	57	16	132	15	86	49	355	
Mean	8.1	2.3	18.9	2.1	12.3	7.0	50.7	7
Percentage	16%	5	37	4	24	14	100	
Groom's:								
Number	200	43	479	89	0	0	811	
Mean	6.7	1.4	16.0	3.0	—	—	27.0	30
Percentage	25%	5	59	11	—	—	100	
All:								
Number	318	123	763	145	86	49	1484	
Mean	5.9	2.3	14.1	2.7	1.6	0.9	27.5	54
Percentage	21.5%	8	51.5	10	6	3	100	

payment is much smaller than either of the other payments. Discounting the nets and braid in the bride's father's payment, which are not redistributed, the total mean size of that payment is 31.4 items and the mean size of the groom's payment is 27.0. It is functionally important that the two payments be roughly equal in value (see below). Second (Table 16), shell bands are the biggest component of all payments; their preponderance is partly due to the post-contact increase in cowries. A third factor is the sex of the participants (see Table 17).

Table 17. SEX AND NUMBER OF PARTICIPANTS IN KONDA DANI PAYMENTS

Payments	Participants							
	Male		Female		Totals		Cases	Mean
	Num-ber	Per Cent	Num-ber	Per Cent	Num-ber	Per Cent		
Betrothal:								
Donors	93	94%	6	6%	99	100%	12	8
Recipients	107	81	25	19	132	100	14	9
Bride's Father's:								
Donors	114	61	73	39	187	100	6	31
Recipients	72	67	36	33	108	100	4	27
Groom's:								
Donors	332	86	53	14	385	100	27	14
Recipients	285	82	61	18	346	100	16	22

Dani men control more wealth than do women and greatly out-number them in marriage payments. Women are most important in the bride's father's payment; they constitute 39 per cent of the donors and give 49 per cent of the total wealth. But if nets and small items are discounted, they donate only 14 per cent of the major items—pigs, stones, and shell bands. Women are more significant as recipients than as donors in the other payments, strikingly so in the betrothal payment where the bride's mother receives a large share. Finally, the kin status of participants in the three payments should be noted (Tables 10 to 15). Dani say that the man who makes a marriage payment, whether groom or bride's father, expects most help from his own lineage. His "mother's brothers" (MB, MFBS, MBS, etc.) and "sister's sons" (including children of all females in his lineage) should also help him. Quantitatively this expectation is borne out for agnates and "sister's sons" but not for "mother's brothers." In the betrothal payment the groom and his agnates constitute 77 per cent of the donors and give 91 per cent of the wealth; in the groom's payment this same group forms 63 per cent of the donors and gives 78 per cent of the wealth. Taking the bride's father's payment as a whole, the father and his agnates form 59 per cent of the donors and give 58 per cent of the total wealth; but of this they donate 87 per cent of the pigs, 100 per cent of the stones, and 71 per cent of the shell bands. Comparing recipients, the bride's agnates, who should receive most of the betrothal and groom's payments, in fact comprise 75.8 per cent of the recipients in the betrothal payment and receive 80 per cent of the wealth. Corresponding figures for the groom's payment are 61 per cent and 64 per cent. The bride's mother's kin should share most of the bride's father's payment; in fact they constitute 77 per cent of the recipients and receive 78 per cent of the wealth.

The Dani state that the betrothal payment should impress the bride's family with the groom's wealth and generosity, and so persuade them that he will make an adequate groom's payment. If the betrothal payment is small or delayed, the girl's family may urge her to leave her stingy husband for a generous one. In the ethnographer's view the betrothal payment is the prime legal marker of marriage. A man protects himself by giving a girl's parents more than the legal minimum for formalizing a marriage; then if his wife elopes, he is entitled to compensation from her family or her next husband. Also, if marriage negotiations are completed when a girl is too immature for cohabitation, the betrothal payment formally defines her married status.

Dani see the bride's father's payment and the groom's payment as linked but not reciprocal. The bride's father's payment repays those people (or their heirs) who, fifteen or more years before, contributed to the skirting payment made for the bride's mother by *her* father. In turn, the groom's payment repays persons who donated to the bride's father's payment. Ideally, the groom's payment should match the bride's father's payment in value though not necessarily in composition.

Men say that the groom's payment, in addition to repaying the bride's lineage for their donations to her skirting payment, enables a man to demonstrate his prestige. The size of the groom's payment depends not so much on an estimation of the bride herself, as on the ability and desire of the groom and his lineage to display wealth. The status of the bride's father also affects the size of the groom's payment. A Big Man makes a larger payment to his wife's lineage at his daughter's skirting; only a Big Man or his son can make a matching groom's payment.

A man must pay his wife's lineage at the skirting of each daughter.[14]

[14] Male initiation in other Dani groups (Bromley, 1965; Larson, 1962) includes payment by the boy's agnates to his mother's agnates, thus paralleling the payment made by a bride's father at her skirting. Possibly a similar payment for males was made in the Konda. Informants recognized terms used for initiation and payment at Ilaga but were unwilling to discuss them in detail.

Contributors to a bride's father's payment (or their heirs) are guaranteed one repayment, at the groom's payment, and they may be reimbursed again if the bride's daughters reach adolescence, at the bride's father's payments made for them. Contributors to a groom's payment are not guaranteed repayment, although the Dani recognize the "double" reimbursement of donors to a bride's father's payment. Actually, the relationship between these two payments is eventually balanced. For any man who initiates a marriage, his lineage, within three generations, acts as a donor twice and as a recipient twice. In the first generation his lineage helps make his groom's payment. In the second his lineage contributes to the bride's father's payment for his daughter and receives most of the wealth from her groom's payment. In the third generation his lineage receives the bride's father's payment made for his daughter's daughter by his daughter's husband. For this balanced, though delayed, reciprocity to occur, a marriage need only produce a daughter who survives to marry and has a daughter who marries. Such equilibrium is not affected by divorce or by adherence to the preference for marriage with the mother's clan or within the confederacy.

Clearly, Dani marriage payments give a man sexual rights to a woman and validate his claim to her children. Like all economic transactions, they also allow a man to demonstrate and acquire prestige. For society at large, marriage payments, combined with preference for confederacy endogamy, help to unify the confederacy. The bride's father's payment, apparently an anomalous exchange solely within the bride's kindred, is in fact:

1. A man's final payment to his wife's lineage for sexual rights to her.
2. Part of a mechanism that regulates wealth exchange within the confederacy, through confederacy endogamy.
   a. Considered lineally within a female line, wealth exchange is duplicated in alternate generations.
   b. Considered within any one generation, the total payments between the two halves of a confederacy are balanced.

Figure 3 represents an ideal model, not a statistically derived model, although on the average 25 per cent of all marriages adhere to the model. The model assumes persistence of confederacy endogamy over time or a congruent adherence to preference for marriage with the mother's clan. There is little probability of such congruence for any one male or female line. But, considering only agnates of the bride and groom and their roles in the two larger payments, confederacy endogamy helps maintain confederacy unity within any generation by ensuring balanced reciprocity in marriage payments.

From a woman's viewpoint the series of marriage payments is a constant; it is always made for her if she survives and bears children. A man, however, usually makes the complete series only if he marries a spinster, the marriage endures and, in the case of the bride's father's payment, produces a daughter who survives to adolescence. If a man marries a divorcée or widow, he *may* make a full series of payments

		Payment	Donor	Recipient
G^{+1}	Ego's M = bride = Y	Betrothal	X ——>— Y	
		Bride's Father's	Y ——>— X	
	Groom = X	Groom's	X + Y ——>— Y	
G^0	Ego = bride = X	Betrothal	Y ——>— X	
		Bride's Father's	X ——>— Y	
	Groom = Y	Groom's	Y + X ——>— X	
G^{-1}	Ego's d = bride = Y	Betrothal	X ——>— Y	
		Bride's Father's	Y ——>— X	
	Groom = X	Groom's	X + Y ——>— Y	

Given: 1) X, Y = clan membership of participants.
2) Adherence to marriage preference by which one's spouse is a member of one's confederacy.
3) Marriage payments are listed in order of occurrence for each generation.
4) Arrow represents wealth and indicates direction of its transfer.

Figure 3. WEALTH EXCHANGE IN KONDA DANI MARRIAGE

but, of the two payments for which he is responsible as groom, he usually makes only a groom's payment. Payments in the case of divorce and remarriage are discussed below. Payments in a widow marriage vary with the size and number of previous payments, and adherence to the levirate (which, in turn, depend on the presence of children); but the governing principles are that the woman's agnates must be fully repaid for their payment at her skirting and that the deceased husband's investment must be recognized, either through the levirate or through repayment to his agnates. Thus, a man who marries a young widow reimburses her deceased husband's brother for the betrothal payment and then makes his own groom's payment; an older man who marries his deceased brother's mature wife makes no payments at all.

The description of marriage payments has shown how Dani marriages are contracted. I have stressed the legal significance of the payments in the validation of marriage and the incorporation of children into their father's lineage, and the importance of the payments as political instruments serving individuals and groups. The marriage payment system also supports the patrilineal descent ideology and stabilizes marriage, a point illustrated in the section on divorce. Finally, two unusual and interrelated features of the Konda Dani marriage payment system deserve emphasis. First, unlike the marriage payments reported for many other highland societies (e.g., Berndt, 1962: 121–24; Bromley, 1965: 33–34; Meggitt, 1965: 110ff.; Reay, 1959: 98–99; Salisbury, 1962: 95), there is no immediate "return gift" from the bride's agnates to the groom's agnates. In any marriage, a reciprocal wealth exchange between the lineages of bride and groom is never absolutely guaranteed. Balanced reciprocity may occur on a deferred basis (a minimum of thirty years) if a man's marriage results in both a daughter and the marriage of a daughter's daughter, and it occurs more immediately (within five to ten years) if the preference for confederacy endogamy is followed. A related element, apparently unique to the Dani system of marriage payments, is the bride's father's payment. No other example of a marriage payment entirely within the bride's kindred has been reported outside the Western Dani.[15]

DIVORCE

The Dani describe the termination of a marriage in which both spouses survive by saying, "he sent her away," "she just ran away," or "he stole her from her husband." No single Dani concept expresses "divorce," but men distinguish between women with whom they have sexual relations "freely, informally" and those women they call

[15] An identical tripartite marriage payment system has been reported for Dani adjacent to the Konda, at Bokondini to the east (Ploeg, personal communication) and by a missionary at Kangime to the west (Dekker personal communication) as well as among the more distant Dani at Ilaga (Larson, 1962:34). The only marriage payment system reported in detail for Grand Valley Dani (Bromley, 1965) has some similar elements but lacks the bride's father's payment and guarantees more immediate and balanced reciprocity between agnates of the bride and groom. There are systems reported from southeast Africa in which a daughter's bride wealth is "used to make her mother's marriage 'legal' " (Pearsall, 1947: 21), i.e., the bride wealth is transferred by the bride's father to his wife's agnates, and from Assam where the bride's MB is the main recipient of a payment made for his sister's daughter (Leach, 1961: 117), but in both these instances the primary collector and donor of the wealth is the groom, rather than the bride's father.

"wife" and cohabit with permanently.[16] I define divorce for the Dani as the permanent termination of a legal marriage, marked behaviorally by the noninitiation or abandonment of cohabitation and, almost always, the woman's remarriage. Permanent separation, as distinct from divorce, is rare; I observed only one case.

Tables 18 and 19 illustrate the incidence of divorce among living

Table 18. MARITAL EXPERIENCE OF LIVING KONDA DANI: MARRIAGES TERMINATED BY DIVORCE

	Men		*Women*		*Totals*
	Over 45	*All*	*Over 45*	*All*	
Number of Wedded Persons	16	40	12	81	121
Number of Divorces Experienced:					
None	4	12	6	45	57
One	7	18	5	30	48
Two	4	8	1	5	13
Three	0	0	0	1	1
Four	0	1	0	0	1
Five	1	1	0	0	1
Mean Number of Divorces Per Head of Population	1.25	1.075	.58	.53	.71
Number of Persons Divorced at Least Once	12	28	6	36	64
Percentage of Wedded Population Divorced Once or More	75.0%	70.0	50.0	44.4	52.9

and deceased Dani. The lower number of divorces reported for deceased persons does not, I think, indicate that divorce has increased within the last generation or since contact. The eighty-six divorces in Table 18 represent, due to the overlap between husband and wives, sixty-seven cases dating from 1920 to 1963.[17] Aside from six cases which cannot be dated, this sample is almost evenly divided between pre-contact (29) and post-contact (32) cases. Many divorces occur early

[16] A man uses the kin term "wife" for three kin types: W, YBW, and YFBSW. A man may copulate occasionally with his "younger brother's" wife but cohabits permanently only with his own wife or wives. Due to the men's house, cohabitation must be understood here to mean residence in the same hamlet and regular sexual intercourse.

[17] All divorce tables are compiled from this sample of sixty-seven cases, but the number of cases analyzed in each table varies according to the sufficiency of data on the factors used to construct the table.

Table 19. MARITAL EXPERIENCE OF DECEASED KONDA DANI: MARRIAGES
TERMINATED BY DIVORCE

	Men	Women	Totals
Number of Wedded Persons	16	57	73
Number of Divorces Experienced:			
None	12	47	59
One	2	10	12
Two	2	0	2
Mean Number of Divorces Per Head of Population	.38	.18	.22
Number of Persons Divorced at Least Once	4	10	14
Percentage of Wedded Population Divorced Once or More	25.0%	17.5	19.2

in marriage, and informants for Table 19 remembered only those of their parents' divorces which they actually witnessed.

Another measure of divorce is provided in Table 20, dealing with the living population from Table 18 (who also appear in Tables 1 and

Table 20. KONDA DANI DIVORCE RATES

Marriages Terminated:	
By Divorce	67
By Separation	1
By Death of Spouse	67
Extant Marriages	82
Total Marriages	217

Type of Marriage Termination	Ratio to All Marriages		Ratio to All Completed Marriages		Ratio to All Marriages Less Deaths	
Divorces	67/217	30.9%	67/134	50.0%	67/150	44.7%
Separations	1/217	.5	1/134	.7	1/150	.7

2). Tables 18 and 20 indicate that divorce is "common" and that "marriage is brittle"; but without refining they give an inaccurate picture of the stability of Dani marriage. In fact, marriage is most unstable in its early months, and divorce is less common after the presentation of any portion of the groom's payment or the birth of children. Table 21 shows that over 90 per cent of Konda divorces occur before the major payment by the husband and his lineage to

Table 21. RELATIONSHIP BETWEEN MARRIAGE PAYMENTS AND MARRIAGE STABILITY AMONG KONDA DANI

	Number	*Per Cent*
Divorces Occurring After:		
No Payment	4	8.5%
Transfer of Pork Only	9	19.2
Betrothal Payment	30	63.8
Groom's Payment	4	8.5

the wife's kin. Table 22 indicates that childless marriages are much more likely to end in divorce than marriages with children. In fifty-eight cases no divorces occur in a marriage with more than two children. Children whose parents divorce invariably remain with the

Table 22. EFFECT OF CHILDREN ON KONDA DANI DIVORCE

	Divorces			
	Number		*Per Cent*	
Marriages with No Children:		51		88%
None Born	48		83	
None Surviving	3		5	
Marriages with Children:		7		12
One child	5		8.6	
Two children	2		3.4	
Total		58		100

Note: Sex of children: seven males, two females.

mother until age ten or twelve, then return to the father's subconfederacy, where the girls soon marry.

Informants' explanations of specific divorces provide insight into the nature of Dani divorce and are summarized in Table 23. "Incompatibility" may cover other more specific causes and is my gloss for the explanation commonly given by both men and women who left their spouses, "I didn't like him"; "I didn't want her." This is the usual reason given for a breakup occurring soon after marriage.

The twenty-four cases in which wives acted on their dislike illustrate the relative freedom of Dani women to manage their own lives. In only two cases did the woman's subsequent husband actively influence her divorce, although nineteen of the twenty-four remarried (data on

Table 23. DECLARED CAUSES OF SPECIFIC KONDA DANI DIVORCE CASES

Causes	Pre-contact Cases (1920–1956)		Post-contact Cases (1957–1963)		Total Cases	
	Number	Per Cent	Number	Per Cent	Number	Per Cent
Incompatibility:	11	33.3%	17	46.0%	28	40.0%
Action initiated by wife	11		13		24	
Action initiated by husband	0		4		4	
Inducement or Abduction of Wife by Another Man	11	33.3	7	18.9	18	25.8
Dissatisfaction over marriage:						
Payments	3	9.1	5	13.5	8	11.4
By wife and her kin	2		4		6	
By husband	1		1		2	
Physical:	4	12.1	4	10.8	8	11.4
Illness or Disability of Wife	0		3		3	
Illness or Disability of Husband	3		0		3	
Sterility of Wife	0		1		1	
Husband Too Young	1		0		1	
Cowife Hostility	3	9.1	3	8.1	6	8.6
Sorcery by Wife's Mother	—	—	1	2.7	1	1.4
Unspecified Objection by Wife's Kin	1	3.1	—	—	1	1.4
Total	33*	100.1	37*	100.0	70*	100.0

* In each period two causes were given for five cases, thus total pre-contact cases = 28, total post-contact cases = 32, total cases = 60.

remarriage are not available in the other five cases). Data on marriage payments are available for twenty-one of these twenty-four cases and show that even after payments have been made, a woman can successfully initiate a divorce. Predictably enough, most such divorces occur before the large groom's payment—two after only a pork payment, eighteen after a full betrothal payment, and only one after a groom's payment. In only two of the twenty-four cases did the women bear children to the husbands they left.

Since contact "wife-stealing" has declined due to mission preaching and the concomitant disappearance of warfare.

Most divorcées remarry within a year. The two in Table 24 who

Table 24. SUBSEQUENT STATUS OF DIVORCED WOMEN AMONG KONDA DANI

	Number	Per Cent
Women Who Remarry:	51	96%
Second Husband Influenced Divorce	18	34
Divorce Due to Other Causes	33	62
Women Who Remain Single (for a Year or More)	2	4
Total	53	100

did not remarry were "sent away" by their husbands, and because of physiological factors (albinism and age) failed to remarry. Both women went to live with agnates.

In about one-third of marriages and remarriages of divorcées the first and second husbands are kinsmen (Table 25). The practice may be an attempt to salvage a kin-sponsored investment. Data

Table 25. KIN RELATIONSHIP BETWEEN SUCCESSIVE HUSBANDS OF DIVORCED KONDA DANI WOMEN

Relationship		Second Husband Influenced Divorce	Divorce Due to Other Causes	Totals
First Husband	*Second Husband*			
"Father"	"Son"	1	0	1
"Son"	"Father"	0	1	1
	"Brothers"	3	3	6
	Same Clan	3	3	6
"Mother's Brother"	"Sister's Son"	0	2	2
Subtotals		7	9	16
	None	12	21	33
Totals		19	30	49

on marriage payments are available for twelve cases of related husbands, and in ten divorce occurred after a betrothal or groom's payment had been made. The second husband was probably a donor to all the payments and therefore already had an economic stake in the marriage. These ten cases exemplify a "secondary" effect of marriage payments on marriage stability. The presence of children does not ensure that their divorced mother's next husband will be a kinsman of their father. In the seven divorces involving children, six of the women remarried, but only two to kinsmen of their first husband. Divorce is unmarked by ceremony, but a divorced man expects compensation for any major economic investment in the marriage made by him and his kin. If a woman's divorce is influenced by a man who then marries her, he must make a *ka* payment to her previous husband. *Ka,* or "sexual indemnity" payments, are also required in cases of rape or adultery and are sometimes made to the deceased husband's kin in widow marriages.[18] Traditionally, failure to pay *ka* led to war. When a woman's divorce is not influenced by a subsequent husband, her divorced husband must seek other means of compensation. He asks his former wife's agnates to return part of any payment he has made or to find him another wife. When this man's former wife remarries, he and her kin expect the new husband, despite his noninvolvement in the divorce, to compensate him, but this is not an enforceable obligation. If a husband initiates divorce his chances for obtaining compensation diminish. Tables 26 and 27 show the relevance of a second husband's role to the incidence and size of compensation payments, and Table 27 indicates the small size of *ka* payments compared to marriage payments (cf. Table 16). Marriage payments made by nine men who were later divorced and received compensation show that *ka* payments do not always equal a husband's investment. Five of the men lost wealth, three received compensation equal to their payments, and one gained wealth in the transaction.

Considering only the twenty-six cases from Table 26 with full information on compensation, payments were made in 50 per cent of the cases. However, in the ten cases where the second husband provoked the divorce, he compensated the first husband in 80 per cent

---

[18] Adultery is normatively prohibited for married women, though it was never mentioned as a reason for divorce unless it culminated in desertion by the adulterous wife. Adulterous wives are beaten by their husbands but are not mutilated as in some highland cultures. Ideally a cuckold should demand compensation from his wife's lover but not all husbands display the prescribed aggressiveness. Some are content to ignore adulterous wives, or simply to beat them and to ignore their lovers.

Table 26. INCIDENCE OF DIVORCE COMPENSATION BY SECOND HUSBANDS
AMONG KONDA DANI

Compensation	Divorce Cases					
	Second Husband Influenced Divorce		Divorce Due to Other Causes		Totals	
	Num-ber	Per Cent	Num-ber	Per Cent	Num-ber	Per Cent
Paid by Second Husband:						
To First Husband	8		4		12	
To Wife's M and B			1		1	
Subtotal	8	50.0%	5	14.3%	13	25.5%
Definitely Not Paid	2	12.5	11	31.4	13	25.5
Apparently Not Paid	6	37.5	19	54.3	25	49.0
Totals	16	100	35	100	51	100

of the cases, and Table 26 shows that *ka* paid in these circumstances
is larger than if the second husband was blameless.

Table 27. MEAN SIZE OF KONDA DANI DIVORCE PAYMENTS

	Pigs	Stones	Shell Bands	Number of Cases
Second Husband (Payer) Influenced Divorce	2.5	.38	4.1	8
Divorce Due to Other Causes, Payer Uninvolved	.8	0	.4	5

Table 28 analyzes divorces in which the first husband received no
compensation from his successor. None of the mitigating factors requires comment, except the witchcraft case which occurred in 1962.
The aggrieved husband was a Big Man who deeply resented the
failure of his former wife's agnates to return any of his betrothal
payment. Traditionally he would have resorted to war; instead he
hired a witch to kill his former father-in-law, who did in fact die.

One conclusion evident from the Dani data is that a "high" divorce
rate can coexist in a patrilineal society with a system of "large"

Table 28. DIVORCES UNRESOLVED BY COMPENSATION PAYMENTS FROM SECOND HUSBANDS

Mitigating Factors	No Compensation		No Apparent Compensation		Totals	
	Second Husband Influenced Divorce	Divorce Due to Other Causes	Second Husband Influenced Divorce	Divorce Due to Other Causes	Number	Per Cent
Lack of Payment by First Husband:						
No Payment	1	0	0	0	1	40.8%
Only Pork	0	5	2	1	8	(group = 11)
Very Small Betrothal	0	0	0	2	2	
Compensation by Wife's Agnates:						
Refund of Marriage Payment	0	2	0	0	2	18.5
Arrange Marriage with Another Woman of Their Clan	0	1	0	2	3	(group = 5)
Kin Tie Between Husbands	0	3	0	2	5	18.5
Second Husband Wages Successful War	1	0	1	0	2	7.4
Second Husband Flees	0	0	1	0	1	3.7
First Husband Initiates Divorce	0	0	0	2	2	7.4
First Husband Gains Revenge Through Witchcraft	0	1	0	0	1	3.7
Totals	2	12	4	9	27	100

marriage payments, simply because most divorces occur before the major groom's payment is made.

CONCLUSIONS

My primary aim has been to describe the range of Dani norms concerning marriage and divorce, and then to illustrate the degree to which they are substantiated quantitatively—or, in other words, to show the differences between ideal and real behavior. In many respects —celibacy, polygyny, and the levirate, for example—both ideology and actual behavior resemble those in other highland societies, but a unique element in Dani marriage is the practice of restricting payment to the bride's kindred.

Second, I have demonstrated the political importance of marriage and marriage payments. Further corroboration of the political significance of marriage payments and the existence of a relationship between war alliances and marriage alliances is found in post-contact events. The last major war in the Konda occurred in April, 1961. In August, 1962, people began to talk of "throwing away" marriage payments and the last payments were made in November, 1962. The abolition of both warfare and marriage payments was largely due to mission influence (O'Brien and Ploeg, 1964), but the diminishing need to maintain traditional political units also facilitated the abandonment of payments.

Finally, the data on Dani marriage and divorce provide more ethnographic ammunition in the continuing discussion over the nature of unilineal descent in general (e.g., Lewis, 1965) and highland New Guinea descent systems in particular (e.g., Barnes, 1962, Langness, 1964). Adequate consideration of the implications of these data for descent theory would require further discussion of the ties between a married woman and her natal patrilineage and of other interclan payments made at death and male initiation.[19] Suffice it to say that, although membership in social units is somewhat optative (cf. note 4) and thus the Dani social organization could "loosely" be called "flexible," the ideology of Dani social structure is strictly agnatic and any actual nonagnatic relationships within agnatically based units are redefined to fit the prevailing ideology.

[19] The death of any named individual (i.e., at least six months old) requires a payment from the individual's agnates to his or her mother's agnates. The major donors to a married woman's death payment are her husband and his agnates. (See note 16.)

BIBLIOGRAPHY

Barnes, J. A., "Measures of Divorce Frequency in Simple Societies," *Journal Royal Anthropological Institute*, LXXIX (1949), 37–62.

———, "African Models in the New Guinea Highlands," *Man*, LXII (1962), 5–9.

———, "Agnation Among the Enga: A Review Article," *Oceania*, XXXVIII (1967), 33–43.

———, "The Frequency of Divorce," in *The Craft of Social Anthropology*, ed. A. L. Epstein. London: Tavistock Press, 1967, pp. 47–99.

Berndt, Catherine H., "Socio-Cultural Change in the East Central Highlands of New Guinea," *Southwestern Journal of Anthropology*, IX (1953), 112–38.

———, "Social and Cultural Change in New Guinea," *Sociologus*, VII (1957), 38–56.

———, "The Ghost Husband: Society and Individual in New Guinea Myth," *Journal of American Folklore*, LXXIX (1966), 244–77.

Berndt, R. M., "A Cargo Movement in the Eastern Central Highlands of New Guinea," *Oceania*, XXIII (1952–53), 40–65, 137–58, 202–34.

———, "Reaction to Contact in the Eastern Highlands of New Guinea," *Oceania*, XXIV (1954), 190–228, 255–74.

———, "Kamano, Jate, Usurufa, and Fore Kinship of the Eastern Highlands of New Guinea: A Preliminary Account," *Oceania*, XXV (1955), 23–53, 156–87.

———, "A Devastating Disease Syndrome: Kuru Sorcery in the Eastern Highlands of New Guinea," *Sociologus*, VIII (1958), 4–28.

———, *Excess and Restraint*. Chicago: University of Chicago Press, 1962.

———, "Warfare in the New Guinea Highlands," in *New Guinea: The Central Highlands*, ed. J. B. Watson. *American Anthropologist* Special Publication, LXVI (1964), 183–203.

———, "The Kamano, Usurufa, Jate, and Fore in the Eastern Highlands," in *Gods, Ghosts and Men in Melanesia*, ed. P. Lawrence and M. J. Meggitt. Melbourne: Oxford University Press, 1965, pp. 78–104.

Bijlmer, H. J. T., "Anthropological Results of the Dutch Scientific Central New Guinea Expedition A⁰ 1920, Followed by an Essay on the Anthropology of the Papuans," *Nova Guinea*, VII (1923), 355–448.

Bowers, Nancy, "Permanent Bachelorhood in the Upper Kaugel Valley of Highland New Guinea," *Oceania*, XXXVI (1965), 27–37.

Brockhuijse, J., *De Willigman-Dani: een Cultureel-Anthropologische Studie*

over Religie en Oorlogvoering in de Baliem-Vallei. Tilburg: H. Gianotten
N. V., 1967.

Bromley, H. M., *The Phonology of Lower Grand Valley Dani.* Verhandelingen
van het Koninklijk Instituut voor Taal-, Land, en Volkenkunde, XXXIV
(1961).

————, *The Even and the Odd: Basic Economic Concepts of the Grand
Valley Dani of Irian Barat. Manuscript,* 1965.

————, "The Linguistic Relationships of Grand Valley Dani: a Lexico-Statis-
tical Classification," *Oceania,* XXXVII (1967), 286–308.

Brookfield, H. C., "The Ecology of Highland Settlement: Some Suggestions,"
in *New Guinea: The Central Highlands,* ed. J. B. Watson. *American
Anthropologist* Special Publication, LXVI (1964), 20–38.

Brookfield, H. C., and Paula Brown, *Struggle for Land: Agriculture and
Group Territories among the Chimbu of the New Guinea Highlands.*
Melbourne: Oxford University Press, 1963.

Brown, Paula, "Chimbu Tribes," *Southwestern Journal of Anthropology,*
XVI (1960), 22–35.

————, "Chimbu Death Payments," *Journal Royal Anthropological Institute,*
XCI (1961), 77–96.

————, "Non-Agnates among the Patrilineal Chimbu," *Journal of the Polynesian Society,* LXXI (1962), 57–69.

————, "From Anarchy to Satrapy," *American Anthropologist,* LXVI (1963),
1–15.

————, "Enemies and Affines," *Ethnology,* III (1964), 335–56.

————, "Goodbye to all That?" in *An Integrated Approach to Nutrition and
Society: The Chimbu Case,* ed. E. Hipsley. New Guinea Research Unit
Bulletin 10 (1966), pp. 31–44.

————, "The Chimbu Political System," *Anthropological Forum,* II (1967),
36–52.

————, "Kondom," *Journal of the Papua and New Guinea Society* (in press
1968).

Brown, Paula, and H. C. Brookfield, "Chimbu Land and Society," *Oceania.*
XXX (1959), 1–75.

————, "Chimbu Settlement and Residence: A Study of Patterns, Trends, and
Idiosyncracy," *Pacific Viewpoint* (in press 1967).

Brown, Paula, and Gillian Winefield, "Some Demographic Measures Applied
to Chimbu Census and Field Data," *Oceania,* XXXV (1965), 175–90.

Bulmer, R. N. H., "Political Aspects of the Moka Ceremonial Exchange
System among the Kyaka People of the Western Highlands of New
Guinea," *Oceania,* XXXI (1960), 1–13.

————, "Why is the Cassowary not a Bird? A Problem of Zoological Tax-
onomy among the Karam of the New Guinea Highlands," *Man,* n.s., II
(1967), 5–25.

Bulmer, Susan, and R. N. H. Bulmer, "The Prehistory of the Australian New
Guinea Highlands," in *New Guinea: The Central Highlands,* ed. J. B.

Watson. *American Anthropologist* Special Publication, LXVI (1964), 39–76.

Bunn, G., and G. Scott, *Languages of the Mount Hagen Sub-district.* New Guinea: Summer Institute of Linguistics, 1962, mimeo.

Commonwealth Scientific and Industrial Research Organization, *Lands of the Goroka-Mount Hagen Area.* Canberra: Division of Land Research and Regional Survey Report 58/1, 1958.

Conklin, H. C., "The Lexicographical Treatment of Folk Taxonomies," *International Journal of American Linguistics,* XXVIII (1962), 119–41.

Cook, E. A., "Kinship and Genealogy in Manga Social Organization," paper presented, 65th American Anthropological Association Meeting, November 1966, Pittsburgh.

———, *Manga Social Organization.* Ph.D. Dissertation, Yale University, New Haven, 1967.

———, "Narak: Language or Dialect," *Journal of the Polynesian Society* (in press).

Craig, B., "Art of the Telefolmin Area, New Guinea," *Australian National History,* XV (1966), 218–24.

———, "The Houseboards of the Telefolmin Sub-district, New Guinea," *Man,* n.s., II (1967), 260–73.

de Lepervanche, Marie, "Descent, Residence, and Leadership in the New Guinea Highlands," *Oceania,* XXXVIII (1967–68), 134–58, 163–89.

Dubbeldam, L. F. B., "The Devaluation of the Kapauku Cowrie as a Factor of Social Disintegration," in *New Guinea: The Central Highlands,* ed. J. B. Watson. *American Anthropologist* Special Publication, LXVI (1964), 293–303.

Elkin, A. P., "Delayed Exchange in Wabag Sub-District, Central Highlands of New Guinea," *Oceania,* XXIII (1953), 161–201.

Fortune, R. F., "The Rules of Relationship Behavior in One Variety of Primitive Warfare," *Man,* XLVII (1947), 108–10.

Fox, R., *Kinship and Marriage.* Harmondsworth: Penguin Books, Ltd., 1967.

Gajdusek, D. C., "Kuru," *Transactions of the Royal Society of Tropical Medicine and Hygiene,* LVII [No. 3] (1963), 151–69.

Glasse, R. M., "Revenge and Redress among the Huli," *Mankind,* V (1959), 273–79.

———, "Leprosy at Karamui," *Papua and New Guinea Medical Journal,* VIII (1965), 95–98.

———, "Cannibalism in the Kuru Region of New Guinea," *Transactions of the New York Academy of Science,* Series II, XXIX (1967), 748–54.

———, *Huli of Papua.* Paris: Mouton, 1968.

Glasse (Lindenbaum), Shirley, "The Social Effects of Kuru," *Papua and New Guinea Medical Journal,* VII (1964), 36–47.

Glick, L. B., "The Role of Choice in Gimi Kinship," *Southwestern Journal of Anthropology,* XXIII (1967), 371–82.

Gluckman, M., "Kinship and Marriage Among the Lozi of Northern Rhodesia and the Zulu of Natal," in *African Systems of Kinship and Marriage*, ed. A. R. Radcliffe-Brown and D. Forde. London: Oxford University Press, 1950, pp. 166–206.

Goody, Esther, "Separation and Divorce among the Gonja," in *Marriage in Tribal Societies*, ed. M. Fortes. Cambridge: Cambridge University Press, 1962.

Goody, J., and Esther Goody, "Cross-cousin Marriage in Northern Ghana," *Man*, n.s., I (1966), 343–55.

———, "The Circulation of Women and Children in Northern Ghana," *Man*, n.s., II (1967), 226–48.

Heider, K. G., *The Dugum Dani: A Papuan Culture in the West New Guinea Highlands*. Ph.D. Dissertation, Harvard University, Cambridge, 1965.

Herskovits, M. J., "The Cattle Complex in East Africa," *American Anthropologist*, XXVIII (1926), 230–72, 361–88, 494–528, 633–64.

Koch, K-F., "Marriage in Jalemo," *Oceania* (forthcoming).

Langness, L. L., "Notes on the Bena Council, Eastern Highlands," *Oceania*, XXXIII (1963), 152–70.

———, "Some Problems of Conceptualization of Highlands Social Structure," in *New Guinea: The Central Highlands*, ed. J. B. Watson. *American Anthropologist* Special Publication, LXVI (1964), 162–82.

———, "Hysterical Psychosis in the New Guinea Highlands: A Bena-Bena Example," *Psychiatry*, XXVIII (1965), 258–77.

———, "Sexual Antagonism in the New Guinea Highlands: A Bena-Bena Example," *Oceania*, XXXVII (1967), 161–77.

———, "Political Organization," in *The Encyclopaedia of Papua and New Guinea*. Melbourne: Melbourne University Press (forthcoming).

Larsen, G. F., "Report on Linguistic Research in Western Dani and Migani (East Central Mountains)," *International Committee on Urgent Anthropological Research in New Guinea Bulletin* I (n.d.), Amsterdam.

———, "Warfare and Feuding in the Ilaga Valley," *Working Papers in Dani Ethnology*, I (1962), Holland: Bureau of Native Affairs.

Lawrence, P., and M. J. Meggitt, eds., *Gods, Ghosts and Men in Melanesia*. Melbourne: Oxford University Press, 1965.

Leach, E. R., *Pul Eliya*. Cambridge: The University Press, 1961.

———, *Rethinking Anthropology*. London: Athlone Press, 1961.

Leahy, M. J., and M. Crain, *The Land that Time Forgot*. New York: Funk & Wagnalls, 1937.

LeRoux, C. C. F. M., *De Bergpapoeas van Nieuw-Guinea en hun Woongebied*. 3 volumes. Leiden: E. J. Brill, 1950.

Lévi-Strauss, C., "The Future of Kinship Studies," *Proceedings Royal Anthropological Institute* (1965), 13–22.

Lewis, I. M., "Problems in the Comparative Study of Unilineal Descent," in *The Relevance of Models for Social Anthropology*, ed. M. Banton. London: Tavistock Publications, 1965.

Livingstone, F. B., "Prescriptive Patrilateral Cross-cousin Marriage," *Man,* LXIV (1964), 56–57.

Lounsbury, F. G., "The Structural Analysis of Kinship Semantics," in *Proceedings 9th International Congress of Linguists,* ed. H. G. Lunt. The Hague: Mouton, 1964, 1073–93.

Maybury-Lewis, D. H. P., "Prescriptive Marriage Systems," *Southwestern Journal of Anthropology,* XXI (1965), 207–30.

Meggitt, M. J., "The Valleys of the Upper Wage and Lai Rivers, Western Highlands, New Guinea," *Oceania,* XXVII (1956), 90–135.

———, "The Ipili of the Porgera Valley, Western Highlands, New Guinea," *Oceania,* XXVIII (1957), 31–55.

———, "The Enga of the New Guinea Highlands," *Oceania,* XXVIII (1958), 253–330.

———, "The Growth and Decline of Agnatic Descent Groups Among the Mae Enga of the New Guinea Highlands," *Ethnology,* I (1962), 158–65.

———, "Male-Female Relationships in the Highlands of Australian New Guinea," in *New Guinea: The Central Highlands,* ed. J. B. Watson. *American Anthropologist* Special Publication, LXVI (1964), 204–24.

———, *The Lineage System of the Mae Enga of New Guinea.* New York: Barnes & Noble, Inc., 1965.

———, "Patterns of Leadership among the Mae Enga of New Guinea," *Anthropological Forum,* II (1967), 20–35.

———, "Some Reflections on Marriage, Bride Price, and Social Structure," paper presented to City University of New York Anthropology Colloquium, March, 1968.

Mihalic, F., *Grammar and Dictionary of Neo-Melanesian.* Techny: The Mission Press, S.V.D., 1957.

Needham, R., *Structure and Sentiment.* Chicago: University of Chicago Press, 1962.

Newman, P. L., *Knowing the Gururumba.* New York: Holt, Rinehart & Winston, Inc., 1965.

Nilles, J., "The Kuman of Chimbu," *Oceania,* XXI (1950), 25–65.

O'Brien, Denise, and A. Ploeg, "Acculturation Movements Among the Western Dani," in *New Guinea: The Central Highlands,* ed. J. B. Watson. *American Anthropologist* Special Publication, LXVI (1964), 281–92.

Oosterwal, G., "The Position of the Bachelor in the Upper Tor Territory," *American Anthropologist,* LXI (1959), 829–38.

Pearsall, M., "Distributional Variations of Bride Wealth in the East African Cattle Area," *Southwestern Journal of Anthropology,* III (1947), 15–31.

Peters, H. L., *Enkele Hoefdstukken uit het Sociaal-Religieuze Leven van een Dani-Groep.* Venlo: Dagblad voor Nord-Limburg N.V., 1965.

Ploeg, A., "Some Comparative Remarks about the Dani of the Baliem Valley and the Dani at Bokondini," *Bijdragen tot de Taal, Land en Volkekunde,* CXII (1966), 256–73.

Pospisil, L., "The Kapauku Papuans and Their Kinship Organization," *Oceania*, XXX (1960), 188–204.

———, *Kapauku Papuans and Their Law.* Yale University Publications in Anthropology 54. New Haven: Yale University Press, 1958.

———, *Kapauku Papuan Economy.* Yale University Publications in Anthropology 67. New Haven: Yale University Press, 1963.

———, *The Kapauku Papuans of West New Guinea.* New York: Holt, Rinehart & Winston, Inc., 1963.

Pouwer, J., "A Social System in the Star Mountains," in *New Guinea: The Central Highlands*, ed. J. B. Watson. *American Anthropologist* Special Publication, LXVI (1964), 133–61.

———, "Towards a Configurational Approach to Society and Culture in New Guinea," *Journal of the Polynesian Society*, LXXV (1966), 267–86.

Radcliffe-Brown, A. R., "Introduction," in *African Systems of Kinship and Marriage*, ed. A. R. Radcliffe-Brown and D. Forde. London: Oxford University Press, 1950.

Rappaport, R. A., "Ritual Regulation of Environmental Relations in New Guinea," *Ethnology*, VI (1967), 17–30.

———, *Pigs for the Ancestors: Ritual in the Ecology of a New Guinea People.* New Haven: Yale University Press, 1968.

Read, K. E., "Marriage Among the Gahuku-Gama of the Eastern Central Highlands, New Guinea," *South Pacific*, VII (1954), 864–70.

———, "Cultures of the Central Highlands, New Guinea," *Southwestern Journal of Anthropology*, X (1954), 1–43.

———, "Leadership and Consensus in a New Guinea Society," *American Anthropologist*, LXI (1959), 425–36.

———, *The High Valley.* New York: Charles Scribner's Sons, 1965.

Reay, Marie, *The Kuma.* Melbourne: Australian National University Press, 1959.

———, "Structural Covariants of Land Shortage Among Patrilineal Peoples," *Anthropological Forum*, II (1967), 4–19.

———, "Bilateral Cross-cousin Marriage Among the Kuma," manuscript, n.d.

Romney, A. K., "Social Organization," in *Biennial Review of Anthropology*, ed. B. J. Siegel. Stanford: Stanford University Press, 1962.

Ryan, D'A. J., "Clan Formation in the Mendi Valley," *Oceania*, XXIX (1959), 257–89.

Sahlins, M. D., "Poor Man, Rich Man, Big-Man, Chief: Political Types in Melanesia and Polynesia," *Comparative Studies in Society and History*, V (1963), 285–303.

———, "On the Ideology and Composition of Descent Groups," *Man*, LXV (1965), 104–107.

Salisbury, R. F., "Asymmetrical Marriage Systems," *American Anthropologist*, LVIII (1956), 639–55.

———, *From Stone to Steel.* Melbourne: Melbourne University Press, 1962.

————, "New Guinea Highlands Models and Descent Theory," *Man*, LXIV (1964), 168–71.

————, "Despotism and Australian Administration in the New Guinea Highlands," in *New Guinea: The Central Highlands*, ed. J. B. Watson. *American Anthropologist* Special Publication, LXVI (1964), 225–39.

Scheffler, H. W., "Ancestor Worship in Anthropology: Observations on Descent Groups," *Current Anthropology*, VII (1966), 541–48.

Schneider, D. M., "Some Muddles in the Models: Or How the System Really Works," in *The Relevance of Models for Social Anthropology*, ed. M. Banton. London: Tavistock Publications, 1965.

Scott, G. K., "The Dialects of Fore," *Oceania*, XXXIII (1963), 280–86.

Souter, G., *New Guinea: The Last Unknown*. Sydney: Angus and Robertson, 1963.

Strathern, A. J., *Descent and Group Structure Among the Mbowamb*. Fellowship Dissertation, Trinity College, Cambridge, 1965.

————, "Despots and Directors in the New Guinea Highlands," *Man*, n.s., I (1966), 356–67.

Strauss, H., and H. Tischner, *Die Mi Kultur der Hagenberg Stämme im Ostlichen Zentral Neu Guinea*. Hamburg: Cram, de Gruyter, 1962.

Vayda, A. P., "The Pig Complex," in *Encyclopaedia of Papua and New Guinea*. Melbourne: Melbourne University Press (forthcoming).

Vayda, A. P., A. Leeds, and D. Smith, "The Place of Pigs in Melanesian Subsistence," in *Proceedings of the American Ethnological Society*, ed. Viola Garfield. Seattle: University of Washington Press, 1961, 69–77.

Vicedom, G. F., and H. Tischner, *Die Mbowamb*. 3 volumes. Hamburg: Cram, de Gruyter, 1943–48.

Wagner, R., *The Curse of Souw: Principles of Daribi Clan Definition and Alliance*. Chicago: University of Chicago Press, 1967.

Watson, J. B., "Anthropology in the New Guinea Highlands," in *New Guinea: The Central Highlands*, ed. J. B. Watson. *American Anthropologist* Special Publication, LXVI (1964), 1–19.

————, "Tairora: The Politics of Despotism in a Small Society," *Anthropological Forum*, II (1967), 53–104.

Williams, F. E., *Natives of Lake Kutubu*. Sydney: Oceania Monograph 6, 1940.

Wirz, P., "Anthropologische und Ethnologische Ergebnisse der Central Neu-Guinea Expedition 1921–22," *Nova Guinea*, XVI (1924).

Wurm, S. A., "The Linguistic Situation in the Highlands Districts of Papua and New Guinea," *Australian Territories*, I (no. 2), (1961), 14–23.

————, "The Languages of the Eastern, Western, and Southern Highlands, Territory of Papua and New Guinea," in *Linguistic Survey of the South-West Pacific*, ed. A. Capell. Noumea: South Pacific Commission, 1961.

————, "Australian New Guinea Highlands Languages and the Distribution of Their Typological Features," in *New Guinea: The Central Highlands*, ed. J. B. Watson. *American Anthropologist* Special Publication, LXVI (1964), 77–97.

Wynne-Edwards, V. C., *Animal Dispersion in Relation to Social Behavior.* Edinburgh: Oliver and Boyd, 1962.

INDEX